Company's Coming for Christmas

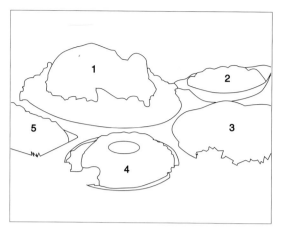

Cover:
1. Roast Turkey, page 138
   with Sausage Stuffing, page 141
2. Sauced Broccoli, page 168
3. Table Bread Wreath, page 58
4. Cranberry Mold, page 154
5. Christmas Cake, page 87

Second Printing October 1996

Canadian Cataloguing in Publication Data

Paré, Jean
    Company's Coming for Christmas

    Includes index.
    ISBN 1-895455-19-7

    1. Christmas cookery. I. Title.
TX739.2.C45P37 1996   641.5'66   C96-910244-5

Published also in French under title: Jean Paré Célèbre Noël
ISBN 1-895455-21-9

Published simultaneously in
Canada and the United States of America by
THE RECIPE FACTORY INC.
in conjunction with
COMPANY'S COMING PUBLISHING LIMITED
2311 - 96 Street
Edmonton, Alberta, Canada T6N 1G3
Tel: (403) 450-6223   Fax: (403) 450-1857

Company's Coming is a registered trademark owned by
Company's Coming Publishing Limited

Color separations, line drawings, printing and binding by Friesens, Altona, Manitoba, Canada
Printed in Canada

It is my most sincere wish that this book becomes part of your family's Christmas tradition as it has with mine.

Jean Paré

Company's Coming For Christmas was created thanks to the dedicated efforts of the people and organizations listed on this page.

COMPANY'S COMING PUBLISHING LIMITED

Author	Jean Paré
President	Grant Lovig
Research Assistant	Helen Urwin

Production Department:

Production Manager	Kathy Knowles
Design	Derrick Sorochan
Typesetting	Marlene Crosbie
Proofing	Hollie Heroux
Copy Writing	Cathie Bartlett

THE RECIPE FACTORY INC.

Managing Editor	Nora Prokop
Research Assistant	Lynda Elsenheimer

Test Kitchen Staff:

Mary Boratynec
Betty Boychuk
Ellen Bunjevac
Pam Klappstein
Audrey Thomas
Pat Yukes

Photo Studio:

Photographer	Stephe Tate Photo
Prop Stylist	Gabriele McEleney
Food Stylist	Nora Prokop

Our special thanks to the following businesses for providing extensive props for photography.

**The Bay
Chintz & Company
Eaton's
Enchanted Kitchen
Enchanted Forest**

Additional thanks to:

Call The Kettle Black
Dare Foods
Edmonton Wedding & Party Centre
IKEA
La Cache
Le Gnome
Libicz's kitchen essentials
Mystique
One Island Antik Ltd.
Sears
Sissy Walker's Country Interiors
Stokes
When Pigs Fly
Zellers
Zenari's

Table of Contents

Breads & Quick Breads
Easy Cinnamon Knots, page 66

Beverages   Traditional Eggnog, page 57

Cookies & Confections
Beer Nuts, page 99
Nutty Cherry Shortbread, page 91
Chocolate Drop Cookies, page 99

Main Courses
Cauliflower Ham Bake, page 142

Salads
Tomato Shrimp Aspic, page 155

Foreword

Of all the special occasions during the year, Christmas is truly the most wonderful—a time when young and old gather to celebrate the season in a spirit of joy and goodwill.

★

The cherished traditions that bind family and friends together are what make Christmas so special. It's reassuring and comforting to carry on the memorable traditions of your parents and grandparents and to teach your own children these beloved customs. Christmas is also a time to build on these traditions, so be open to change and new ideas.

★

Each family celebrates Christmas in its own way. When looking through old pictures and home movies or more recent photos and videos, you can't help but notice that much of Christmas celebration happens around the tree and the table.

★

The food that goes on that table is an important part of the holiday as well. Of all the meals you'll serve or consume throughout the year, Christmas dinner has to be the one that stands out the most.

Mealtime is an important part of any event over the Yuletide season. That holds true whether a meal is the focal point of the occasion—such as supper on Christmas Eve, dinner on Christmas Day or brunch on Boxing Day—or following an activity such as skating or carolling. Indeed, foods such as turkey and cranberry sauce, Christmas cake and pudding have become synonymous with the word "Christmas".

★

At Company's Coming we are believers in tradition and that is why we put this book together. Company's Coming for Christmas is an exciting new venture for us—a keepsake book that involves all aspects of the Christmas menu and all manner of Yuletide occasions.

★

No doubt you already have your own treasured Christmas recipes collected from family and friends or clipped from newspapers and magazines over the years. Company's Coming for Christmas is here not to intrude, but to supplement your repertoire and to offer old favorites with a different twist.

You'll find several kinds of Christmas cakes and puddings, salads that are pleasing to the eye and even better to eat, and favorite vegetables in rejuvenated form. There's new focus on breads and soups. Main dishes and desserts have their day with a range that will delight everyone.

★

To top it off, we help you to set a fine table with suggestions for centerpieces, decorations and settings for a truly memorable occasion.

★

We don't stop there! Experience the spirit of giving with Baskets Of Gifts. Enjoy social occasions through Exchanging With Friends.

As well, we want to help you tackle situations that may be new to you. Cooking for a crowd or holding a brunch may be a departure from the sorts of get-togethers you usually hold. Our tips, suggestions, sample menus and recipes will take the guesswork out of the preparations and make these holiday gatherings the enjoyable events they should be.

★

More than 250 new recipes were created especially for this book. Every recipe is pictured and all have been painstakingly tested in our own kitchen. The result is quick and easy recipes from everyday ingredients—and the results will make you proud.

★

More than anything else, we at Company's Coming want this book to become a part of your family's Christmas tradition for years to come. From everyone at Company's Coming, we wish you all the best this festive season. May all your Christmas dreams come true.

Jean Paré

Baskets Of Gifts

A gift basket is a wonderful thing— especially when it's filled with something special and topped off with a holiday bow or two.

★

A gift basket shows you care because of the time and thought you put into selecting the appropriate contents. Gift baskets are perfect because they are so easy to personalize. Food makes an excellent gift because it is appreciated and enjoyed by everyone.

★

Best of all, the scope is endless—from one item in a tiny basket to a much larger basket overflowing with a potpourri of goodies. Your "basket" can be a bowl, a colander, a sleigh or any other suitable container.

★

Theme baskets are particularly effective, letting you build around a favorite food group. Pasta noodles and special utensils make a good start toward a pasta basket. For the citrus fan, a few jars of jam or marmalade nestled inside colorful napkins would be nice. Consider yourself blessed if there is a "sweet tooth" on your list!

A Christmas tin full of cookies or confections is quick, easy and oh-so appreciated.

★

These recipes are included because the results look good and keep well—two prerequisites for gift baskets. Feel free to call on other sections of this book for more recipes to round out your special selections.

★

Have fun creating your holiday masterpieces!

Seasoned Tomato Sauce

Adjust the spices to personal preference. Seal in decorative jars for gift-giving.

Canned tomatoes, chopped	4 × 28 oz.	4 × 796 mL
Worcestershire sauce	1 tbsp.	15 mL
Salt	2 tsp.	10 mL
Whole oregano	1½ tsp.	7 mL
Onion powder	1 tsp.	5 mL
Seasoned salt	½ tsp.	2 mL
Garlic powder	¼ tsp.	1 mL
Celery salt	¼ tsp.	1 mL
Sweet basil	¼ tsp.	1 mL
Cayenne pepper	¼ tsp.	1 mL
Brown sugar	2 tbsp.	30 mL

Put tomatoes and remaining ingredients in large pot. Heat, stirring often, until mixture boils. Boil, stirring often, for about 25 minutes until thick. For a smooth sauce, cool a bit and run through blender. Return purée to pot. Return to boil. Pour boiling sauce into hot sterilized pint jars to within ½ inch (1 cm) of top. Place sterilized metal lids on jars and screw metal bands on securely. For added assurance against spoilage, you may choose to process in a boiling water bath for 10 minutes. This may also be cooled and frozen. Makes 6 pints sauce.

Pictured on page 8.

Meaty Tomato Sauce

Before serving, add about ½ to ¾ pound (250 to 375 g) scramble-fried lean ground beef to 1 pint Tomato Spaghetti Sauce.

Pictured on page 8.

1. Meaty Tomato Sauce, page 9
2. Seasoned Tomato Sauce, page 9

Freezer Zucchini Marmalade

Pretty light yellow. Use decorative jars.

Peeled and grated zucchini	8 cups	2 L
Oranges, quartered and seeded	6	6
Lemons, quartered and seeded	2	2
Crushed pineapple, well-drained	19 oz.	540 mL
Granulated sugar	5 cups	1.25 L
Orange-flavored gelatin (jelly powder)	2 × 3 oz.	2 × 85 g
Lemon-flavored gelatin (jelly powder)	1 × 3 oz.	1 × 85 g

Put zucchini into large pot. Grind oranges and lemons including rind. Add to pot. Add pineapple and sugar. Heat, stirring often, until mixture boils. Boil 15 minutes.

Add gelatin powders. Stir to dissolve. Cool. Pour into containers, leaving 1 inch (2.5 cm) headroom. Freeze. Makes 12 cups (3 L) or 6 pints marmalade.

Pictured on page 11.

Freezer Strawberry Jam

Make in the fall, well in advance of holiday company.

Crushed strawberries, fresh or frozen whole	3 cups	750 mL
Granulated sugar	5 cups	1.25 L
Water	1 cup	250 mL
Pectin crystals	1 × 2 oz.	1 × 55 g

Stir strawberries and sugar together in bowl. Let stand for 10 minutes.

Combine water and pectin crystals in saucepan. Heat and stir until mixture reaches a boil. Boil for 1 minute, stirring continually. Remove from heat. Pour over strawberries. Stir for 2 minutes. Fill freezer containers, leaving 1 inch (2.5 cm) headroom. Let stand on counter for 24 hours to set. Freeze. Makes 7 cups (1.75 L) jam.

Pictured on page 11.

1. Orange Marmalade, page 12
2. Peach Zucchini Jam, page 12
3. Freezer Strawberry Jam, page 12
4. Freezer Zucchini Marmalade, page 12

Orange Marmalade

Always popular on toast or biscuits.

Oranges, quartered and seeded	2	2
Lemon, quartered and seeded	1	1
Grapefruit, cut in eights and seeded	1	1
Water, 3 times as much as fruit		
Granulated sugar, equal to amount of fruit mixture		

Grind first 3 fruits including rind. Measure then put into large saucepan.

Add water. Boil, stirring occasionally, for 20 minutes. Let stand at room temperature for 24 hours.

Measure fruit mixture and return to saucepan. Add sugar. Heat, stirring often, until mixture boils. Boil until it jells. This will take about 1¼ hours. Fill hot sterilized half pint jars to within ¼ inch (0.5 cm) of top. Place sterilized metal lids on jars and screw metal bands on securely. For added assurance against spoilage, you may choose to process in a boiling water bath for 10 minutes. Makes 8 half pints marmalade.

Pictured on page 10 and on page 76.

Peach Zucchini Jam

Wonderful yellow color with red specks of cherry.

Grated and peeled zucchini, 4 lbs. (1.8 kg)	11 cups	2.75 L
Granulated sugar	6 cups	1.5 L
Unsweetened crushed pineapple, well-drained	19 oz.	540 mL
Red maraschino cherries, quartered (add more if desired)	12	12
Peach-flavored gelatin (jelly powder)	3 × 3 oz.	3 × 85 g

Combine zucchini and sugar in large saucepan. Heat and stir until sugar dissolves and mixture comes to a boil. Boil for 15 minutes.

Stir in pineapple. Boil for 5 minutes. Remove from heat.

Add cherries. Stir. Cut off corners of gelatin packages so you can pour granules in slowly as you keep stirring to dissolve. Fill hot sterilized pint jars to within ½ inch (1 cm) of top. Place sterilized metal lids on jars and screw metal bands on securely. For added assurance against spoilage, you may choose to process in a boiling water bath for 10 minutes. Makes 5 pints jam.

Pictured on page 10.

Irish Cream

So rich and creamy!

Rye whiskey	1½ cups	375 mL
Sweetened condensed milk	11 oz.	300 mL
Light cream (half and half)	1 cup	250 mL
Large eggs	2	2
Instant coffee granules	1 tsp.	5 mL
Dry chocolate drink mix (such as QUIK)	1 tsp.	5 mL
Vanilla	1 tsp.	5 mL

Measure all ingredients into blender. Process until smooth. Pour into bottle or jar to store in refrigerator. If using as a gift, be sure it's fresh with a label stating to keep refrigerated and to use within 2 weeks. Makes 4½ cups (1 L) liqueur.

Pictured below.

Mock Crème De Menthe

Just like the real thing!

Granulated sugar	1½ cups	375 mL
Boiling water	2 cups	500 mL
Peppermint flavoring	½ tsp.	2 mL
Vodka	2 cups	500 mL
Green food coloring	⅛ tsp.	0.5 mL

Stir sugar into boiling water in bowl until sugar dissolves. Cool.

Add flavoring, vodka and food coloring. Pour into containers. Let stand in cool spot for 2 weeks. Ready for use or for gifts. Makes approximately 4¾ cups (1 L) liqueur.

Pictured below.

Irish Cream

Mock Crème De Menthe

Antipasto

Make this well in advance of the holiday season. Great to give as a hosting gift.

Pickled onions, drained and halved	1 cup	250 mL
Canned mushroom pieces, drained and chopped	2 × 10 oz.	2 × 284 mL
Red pepper, seeded and chopped	1	1
Green pepper, seeded and chopped	1	1
Green pimiento stuffed olives, chopped	1 cup	250 mL
Pitted ripe olives, chopped	1 cup	250 mL
Chopped dill pickles	1 cup	250 mL
Canned tuna, drained and flaked	2 × 6½ oz.	2 × 184 g
Ketchup	2½ cups	625 mL
White vinegar	¼ cup	60 mL
Olive oil or cooking oil	¼ cup	60 mL
Canned cut green beans, drained	14 oz.	398 mL

Place all ingredients in large saucepan. Heat, stirring often, until mixture comes to a boil. Simmer for 20 minutes, stirring often. Cool. Fill freezer containers, leaving 1 inch (2.5 cm) at the top to allow for expansion. Freeze. Makes 13 cups (3.2 L) antipasto.

Pictured on page 15.

1. Salsa, page 16
2. Antipasto, page 14
3. Hot Pepper Jelly, page 16

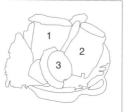

Salsa

Tangy and hot. Make it hotter by adding more cayenne.

Canned tomatoes	2 × 28 oz.	2 × 796 mL
Tomato sauce	2 × 7½ oz.	2 × 213 mL
Red pepper, seeded and chopped	1	1
Green peppers, seeded and chopped	2	2
Chopped onion	2 cups	500 mL
White vinegar	⅔ cup	150 mL
Granulated sugar	3 tbsp.	50 mL
Coarse (pickling) salt	2 tsp.	10 mL
Paprika	2 tsp.	10 mL
Garlic powder	½ tsp.	2 mL
Whole oregano	½ tsp.	2 mL
Cayenne pepper, to taste	¼-1 tsp.	1-5 mL

Measure all ingredients into large saucepan. Heat, stirring often, until mixture starts to boil. Boil slowly, uncovered, for about 1½ hours until thickened. Pour into hot sterilized half pint jars to within ¼ inch (0.5 cm) of top. Place sterilized metal lids on jars and screw metal bands on securely. For added assurance against spoilage, you may choose to process in a boiling water bath for 5 minutes. Makes 7 half pints salsa.

Pictured on page 15.

Hot Pepper Jelly

Great colors for Christmas. Serve over a block of softened cream cheese.

Medium red or green peppers, seeded and chopped	2	2
Cider vinegar	1½ cups	350 mL
Granulated sugar	6½ cups	1.45 L
Hot pepper sauce (add more, if desired)	1 tsp.	5 mL
Liquid pectin	6 oz.	175 mL
Drops of red or green food coloring, if desired	3-4	3-4

Put peppers and vinegar in blender. Process until smooth. Pour into large saucepan.

Add sugar and hot pepper sauce. Heat and stir until sugar dissolves and mixture starts to boil. Boil for 3 minutes.

Stir in pectin. Return to a full rolling boil on medium-high. Boil hard for 1 minute. Remove from heat. Skim off foam.

Add a bit of food coloring if desired. You can also add more hot pepper sauce. Pour into hot sterilized half pint jars to within ¼ inch (0.5 cm) of top. Place sterilized metal lids on jars and screw metal bands on securely. For added assurance against spoilage, you may choose to process in a boiling water bath for 5 minutes. Makes 6 half pints jelly.

Pictured on page 15.

No-Cook Cranberry Relish

Couldn't be easier. Quite tangy.

Cranberries	2 cups	500 mL
Apple, peeled and cored	1	1
Orange, quartered and seeded	1	1
Part of lemon, seeds removed	½	½
Granulated sugar	1¼ cups	300 mL

Put first 4 ingredients, including orange and lemon rind, through coarse blade of food chopper.

Add sugar. Stir well. Chill overnight. Makes 3 cups (750 mL) relish.

Pictured below.

Cranberry Relish

Superb color for the Christmas dinner table.

Cranberries, fresh or frozen	2 cups	500 mL
Sultana raisins	1 cup	250 mL
Apple, peeled, cored and diced	1	1
Orange, peeled and diced	1	1
Prepared orange juice	¼ cup	60 mL
Granulated sugar	1 cup	250 mL
Cinnamon stick, 4 inch (10 cm)	1	1
Whole cloves	6	6
Whole allspice	6	6
Rum flavoring	1 tsp.	5 mL

Measure first 6 ingredients into large saucepan.

Tie cinnamon stick, cloves and allspice in double layer cheesecloth. Add to saucepan. Bring to a boil, stirring often. Boil slowly for about 15 minutes until thickened. Discard spice bag.

Stir in rum flavoring. Pour into hot sterilized pint jars to within ½ inch (1 cm) of top. Place sterilized metal lids on jars and screw metal bands on securely. For added assurance against spoilage, you may choose to process in a boiling water bath for 10 minutes. May also be frozen. Makes 1 pint relish.

Pictured below.

No-Cook
Cranberry Relish

Cranberry Relish

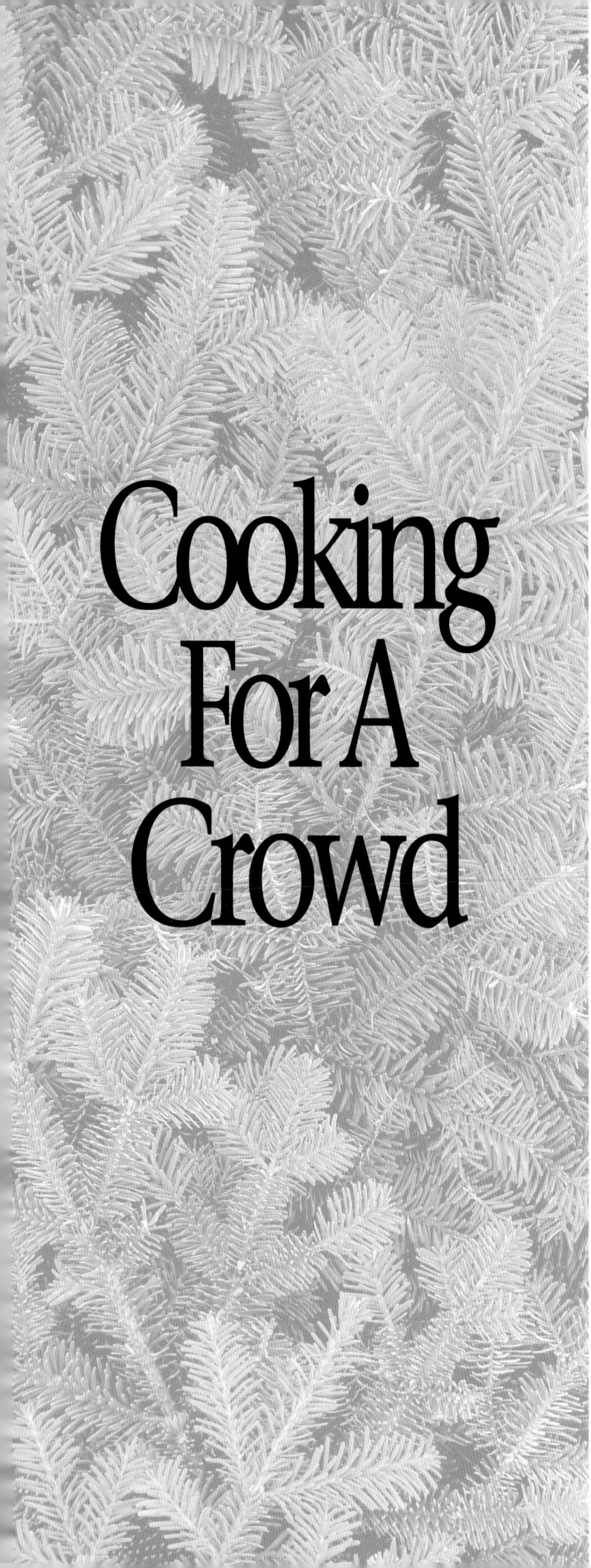

Cooking For A Crowd

Holiday gatherings are so much fun for everyone.

★

But feeding a crowd can be daunting. Most recipes are intended to serve four to six, or maybe six to eight. Suddenly you're having twelve for dinner, or a holiday buffet for even more—what to do?

★

Start planning, that's what! With a bit of advance work you can put on a repast that memories are made of and still enjoy the festivities.

★

Handling a crowd calls for different considerations in planning the menu, preparing and serving the food. When choosing recipes keep in mind that you want to offer a choice of colors and textures as well as tastes.

★

When deciding the menu, keep in mind several factors:

1. How many guests will there be?

2. What ages are the guests—any teens or young children?

3. How many people can I seat at the table?

4. Can I split my guests up between the dining room and kitchen tables? Do I want to?

5. Can my guests sit down and use a fork and knife,or will most be standing requiring fork-only food?

6. How many serving dishes, plates and utensils do I have or need? Can I increase my settings by borrowing, renting or using disposable products?

★

When choosing the recipes, remember that some of your favorite recipes may not double or triple well. A smorgasbord of several dishes is one option. Set out two or three meat dishes, complemented with a side selection of lighter dishes.

★

A second option is to double, or even triple one recipe and serve with two or three salads, rolls and a choice of two desserts. Either make the recipe in a larger dish that will accommodate the large quantity (foil roasting pan works well) or divide it into two or three smaller dishes.

★

Recipes that are particularly well-suited to cooking and serving in large quantities, especially buffet style are:

Cauliflower Ham Bake, page 142
Lazy Ravioli, page 138
Gourmet Burgers, page 70
Sausage Rice Casserole, page 145
Seafood Deluxe, page 144
Seafood Lasagne, page 145
Tamale Casserole, page 135
Triple Seafood Noodles, page 144
Turkey Au Gratin, page 132
Turkey Wizard, page 140

★

Now get out your pad and pencil, draw up your checklist and come the big day, the compliments from happy guests around the table will be music to your ears.

★

Exchanging With Friends

Sharing the bounty of the kitchen with friends and neighbors is as old as time. So it's only logical that exchanging food has become part of Christmas.

★

An exchange lets you add variety to your stock of Christmas goodies. Most cookie recipes yield four to six dozen, making it cumbersome to bake more than two or three kinds. An exchange provides the opportunity to make just one recipe (doubled or tripled) and end up with the same amount but in a variety of six to twelve different kinds.

★

You can ask participants to attach the recipe to each individually wrapped dozen or to give recipe cards to each participant. Remind your guests to pack their items for safe travel home to prevent breaking or squashing.

★

You can give a little or a lot of direction as to what is to be exchanged. Do you simply want cookies, or narrow it down to shortbread or Christmas cake? Do you want a specific kind from each person or go potluck-style and make it a surprise?

★

Plan to have no less than six and no more than twelve participants (including yourself). How many dozen each person provides can be determined in several ways:

1) If there are ten people, each person brings ten times one dozen; for six people each person brings six times one dozen and so on;

or

2) If there are ten people, each person brings a predetermined number (say eight dozen) and a large empty container. Everyone walks around and around the table taking an agreed number of each kind until everything has been divided up.

★

Traditionally cookies have been exchanged but in recent years appetizers and squares have joined the scene. Squares make an excellent exchange. Lining the pan with foil makes removal and cutting much easier.

★

Christmas cake is another possibility. Granted, the ingredients are expensive and making the cake can be time-consuming. But a tray of light and dark cakes in a variety of shapes is so attractive and appealing.

★

Generally recipes for Christmas cake make two or three large loaves. By baking them in 19 ounce (540 mL) cans or mini loaf pans, a single or double recipe could suffice for an exchange.

★

If exchanging appetizers, they should be made fresh and be suitable for storing in the freezer.

★

Get in on the holiday fun early and play host to an exchange. Circle a date on the calendar, cover the dining room table with a festive tablecloth, and make way for friends bearing boxes of luscious treats.

★

Recommended Cookies/Confections

Almond Roca, page 103
(approximately ½ lb., 225 g per participant)

Jolly Fruit Drops, page 89
(1 dozen per participant)

Breton Brittle, page 102
(approximately ½ lb., 225 g per participant)

Peanut Brittle, page 103
(approximately ½ lb., 225g per participant)

Cherry Surprise, page 101
(1 dozen per participant)

Rum Balls, page 101
(1 dozen per participant)

Christmas Fudge, page 96
(⅓ pan per participant)

Scotch Shortbread, page 98
(1 dozen squares per participant)

Christmas Trees, page 94
(1 dozen per participant)

Shortbread Squares, page 98
(1 dozen squares per participant)

Condensed Fudge, page 96
(⅓ pan per participant)

Special Chocolate Fudge,
page 96 (⅓ pan per participant)

Dipped Vanillas, page 105
(1 dozen per participant)

Spritz, page 91
(1 dozen per participant)

Divinity Drops, page 95
(1 dozen per participant)

Sugar Cookies, page 95
(1 dozen per participant)

Merry Fruit Cookies, page 90
(1 small unbaked roll or 1 dozen baked cookies per participant)

Whipped Shortbread, page 89
(1 dozen per participant)

Recommended Appetizers

Baked Cheese Balls, page 45
(1 dozen per participant)

Salty Caraway Sticks, page 44
(1 dozen per participant)

Curried Nuts, page 51
(2 cups, 500 mL per participant)

Snackies, page 51
(2 cups, 500 mL per participant)

Fun Party Mix, page 50
(2 cups, 500 mL per participant)

Spinach Squares, page 42
(¼ pan per participant)

Lazy Sausage Rolls, page 37
(1 dozen slices per participant)

Welsh Cakes, page 45
(1 dozen per participant)

Onion Tarts, page 44
(1 dozen mini tarts per participant)

Zucchini Squares, page 32
(¼ pan per participant)

Recommended Christmas Cakes & Puddings

Carrot Pudding, page 86
(1 can per participant) *

Steamed Fruit Pudding,
page 80
(1 can per participant) *

Orange Gumdrop Loaf,
page 83
(1 mini loaf per participant) *

White Fruitcake, page 81
(1 mini loaf per participant) *

Plum Pudding, page 81
(1 per participant) *

* See: For Gift Giving, page 86

1. Sugar Cookies, page 95
2. Chocolate Spritz, page 91
3. Baked Cheese Balls, page 45
4. White Fruitcake, page 81
5. Steamed Fruit Pudding, page 80

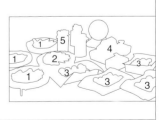

Make-ahead Recipe Ideas

★

You're looking at photographs or videos of Christmas

past when you realize that someone significant

is missing. Where is the cook?

★

Out in the kitchen, that's where. There's so much to

do to pull this special dinner together that he or she

can't join the others until the food is on the table.

★

Some aspects of Christmas dinner are part of the day

itself, such as the smell of the turkey as it roasts to

perfection. But much of the work can be done ahead,

reducing stress and clutter and allowing the cook

to enjoy conversation with family and guests.

★

★

Baking ahead clears the oven for the big bird and

means you're not cooking and cleaning up all day.

So go through the menu with a view to what can be done

ahead. Make sure dishes prepared well ahead of time

will freeze well. Clear the refrigerator for those

dishes you make the day before.

★

With some effort beforehand you'll be relaxed

and smiling on the big day and you'll even

make it into the Christmas video!

★

Appetizers

Appetizers can be made in November or early
December and put in the freezer. Broiling is best done
at the last minute, but do everything up to the
broiling step then freeze. Sauces and dips
are best left to the day before.

Remember that appetizers are much smaller in
individual size and will dry out somewhat in the freezer.
Wrap them well and remove as much air as
possible. To give you flexibility, spread individual
items like Oriental Meatballs, page 33, Sesame Wings,
page 36 or Sausage Balls, page 36, on a baking
sheet and freeze for three hours. Place in freezer
bag or container and refreeze. They will remain
separated so that you can take out as many as
you need for any one occasion.

Beverages

Most punches can be made the day before, but add carbonated or sparkling liquids just prior to serving. Any beverage containing eggs should be made close to serving time. Liqueur recipes can be made two weeks to two months in advance.

Breads And Quick Breads

All the recipes in this section, with the exception of Lemon Spread, page 66, can be made in advance and frozen. If you won't need large quantities at any one time, cut loaves in half and wrap each half individually. All loaves should be cooled completely before freezing, wrapped airtight in plastic wrap and wrapped a second time in foil.

Brunches

The Baked Omelet, page 71, Lobster Fantans, page 75, Eggs Lyonnaise, page 77 and Oven Apple Pancake, page 77 must be made on the day of serving. However, Make-Ahead Eggs Benedict, page 68, Quick Fruit Bowl, page 69, Orange Fruit Dip, page 73, Overnight Oven French Toast, page 76 and Sausage Strata, page 77 can all be made or partially made the day before. The rest of the recipes in this section can be frozen well in advance.

Christmas Cakes And Puddings

With the exception of the sauces, all these recipes can be frozen. As with breads and quick breads, they should be wrapped airtight in plastic wrap and wrapped again in foil. All the sauces can be made several days ahead of time then reheated quickly in the microwave just before serving.

Christmas Cookies And Confections

Absolutely every recipe in this section can be made in November, or even October! Most can be frozen (without icing), others can be stored in airtight containers at room temperature or in the refrigerator. Make squares in foil-lined pans. To freeze, remove from pan, fold foil over top edges and wrap with a second layer of foil.

Desserts

The recipes in this category are all make-aheads with the exception of Sherry Trifle, page 114 and Fluffy Frosting, page 122. Most of the recipes can be frozen; the rest are best if made the day before serving. Cool squares completely and then either cut and freeze, or freeze first then cut when ready to use. Some squares cut better when partially frozen. Remember, this is the season to serve a tray of mixed goodies, so cut pieces a bit smaller than you might when serving only one or two choices.

Main Courses

This may be the one section you concentrate on the day of entertaining. But just in case you'd rather visit, most can be frozen several weeks in advance or assembled the day before and heated just before serving. You may choose to do Beef Roast In Gravy, page 135, Roast Goose, page 140, Golden Glazed Ham, page 132 and Roast Turkey, page 138 one week ahead. Remove the meat, slice it and freeze. Be sure to wrap it airtight.

Pies And Tarts

These are fancy desserts that can be frozen ahead for the most part. Add any whipped topping the day of serving, but only after pie has completely thawed. Some pies will slice better when still partially frozen.

Salads

Molded (or jellied) salads can easily be made the day before. Keep chilled in mold and cover exposed area with plastic wrap to prevent drying. Unmold up to one hour before serving but keep chilled. To help with the tossed or creamy salads, make dressings a day or two in advance. Wash and tear lettuce or spinach several days ahead and store airtight, wrapped in paper towel in plastic bag. Drain or cut fruit the day before but add bananas and apples at the last minute.

Soups

Freeze all the soups if you wish. When reheating, do so over low to medium heat, stirring fairly often.

Vegetables

Most of these dishes are best done a few days before serving. Vegetables can be washed and cut and kept in cold water. Some of these recipes can be assembled the day before and cooked the day of, and some can be cooked two to three days in advance and reheated just before serving.

Menus

More often than not "menu" means you're
dining out. But home cooking is just as worthy
of a menu, especially during the holiday season
when you want to put your best foot forward.
So before you start cooking, take the time to draw
up your own list from the kitchen.

★

Make your menu suit the occasion. An afternoon
of toboganning or skating calls for something hot and
substantial, while nibblies are fine to munch on as
you and your guests sit around the fireplace
for an evening of carols.

★

Take into account how many you are serving and
the age range. Don't forget that looks are important,
so consider color in addition to texture and flavor, and
hot versus cold. Remember to add a festive touch
wherever possible—turning out a cranberry jellied
salad, or decorating chocolate cupcakes with
miniature candy canes and so on.

★

These sample menus span a range of occasions.
Try the menus as is, adjust them a little or a lot, or
take out pen and paper and start from square
one. Planning is the key to success and in
the kitchen the menu is the plan.

Cookie Decorating Party

Gingerbread Figures, page 100

Sugar Cookies, page 95

Cocoa Cookies, page 91

Quick Fruit Punch, page 56

Cookie Exchange Brunch

Perked Wassail, page 54

Shrimp Dip, page 49 (served with veggies and crackers)

Cottage Salad, page 156

Sausage Strata, page 77

Chocolate Truffle, page 109

Tree-Trimming

Perked Wassail, page 54

Creamy Cranberry Punch, page 53

Crab Ball, page 42 (served with crackers)

Last Minute Appetizer, page 46

Creamy Stuffed Mushrooms, page 40

Artichoke Strudel, page 37

Tray of assorted cookies and squares

Neighborhood Carolling

Christmas Punch, page 56

French Silk Chocolate, page 54

Stuffed Edam, page 48 (served with crackers)

Mushroom Nappies, page 38

Sausage Rice Casserole, page 145

Creamy Chilled Dessert, page 116

Celebrate The Snowman (Kids)

French Silk Chocolate, page 54

Cinnamon Crisps, page 50

Banana Pancakes, page 76

Cookies 'N Cake, page 114

Christmas Eve Gathering

Traditional Eggnog, page 57

Christmas Punch, page 56

Lobster Chowder Feed, page 164

Potato Rolls, page 59

Lazy Ravioli, page 138

Just For The Elves

Quick Fruit Punch, page 56

Fancy Macaroni, page 136

Drop Cheese Biscuits, page 61

Frozen Peanut Butter Pie, page 148

Christmas Morning Brunch

French Silk Chocolate, page 54

Rhubarb Cocktail, page 56

Orange Fruit Dip, page 73 (served with fresh fruit)

Make-Ahead Eggs Benedict, page 68

Overnight Oven French Toast, page 76

Holiday Brunch Cake, page 60

Cranberry Orange Muffins, page 67

Christmas Day Dinner

Shrimp Cocktail, page 43

Roast Turkey, page 138, with Gravy, page 133

(served with mashed potatoes)

Sausage Stuffing, page 141

Sweet Potato Bake, page 170

Sauced Broccoli, page 168

Cranberry Mold, page 154

Table Bread Wreath, page 58

Plum Pudding, page 81

Rum Sauce, page 87

Boxing Day Brunch

Rhubarb Cocktail, page 56

Coffee Nog, page 57

Ham Quiche, page 75

Turkey Wizard, page 140

Pastry Biscuits, page 70

Breakfast Pull-Aparts, page 73

Cranberry Pear Pie, page 148

Open House

Easy Eggnog, page 57

Christmas Punch, page 56

Punch Ice Ring, page 56

Date Nut Log, page 48

Welsh Cakes, page 45

Onion Tarts, page 44

Oriental Meatballs, page 33

Cinnamon Crisps, page 50

Breton Brittle, page 102

Seafood Lasagne, page 145

Cauliflower Ham Bake, page 142

Easy Overnight Buns, page 60

Tray of assorted Christmas cakes,
cookies and squares

Fork-Food Buffet

Lazy Sausage Rolls, page 37

Salmon Canapés, page 41

All-Season Dip, page 49 (served with veggies)

Sauerkraut Salad, page 158

Fruit Salad Mold, page 154

Coquilles St. Jacques Casserole, page 143

Showy Meatloaf, page 139

Turkey Au Gratin, page 132

Broccoli Casserole, page 170

Stewed Tomato Casserole, page 166

Mince Tarts, page 152

Black Russian Pie, page 151

Après Ski

Coffee Nog, page 57

Mulled Wine, page 52

Spinach Dip, page 48 (served with veggies)

Turkey Fajitas, page 133

Tamale Casserole, page 135

Colorful Tossed Salad, page 158

Bread Pudding, page 112

Skating/Tobogganing Party

Mulled Apple Drink, page 54

Snackies, page 51

Sesame Wings, page 36

Ripe Olive Canapés, page 41

Corn Chowder, page 160

Gourmet Burgers, page 70

Luscious Chocolate Cake, page 110

Mistletoe Magic

Scallop Attraction, page 43

Citrus Salad, page 156

Chicken Breasts Florentine, page 142

Carrot Medley, page 171

(served with oven-roasted potatoes)

Chocolate Crêpes, page 111

Irish Cream, page 13

Mock Kahlua, page 53

Wine & Nibblies

Mulled Wine, page 52

Perked Wassail, page 54

Baked Cheese Balls, page 45

Nutty Cheese Ball, page 46 (served with crackers)

Dilled Carrot Sticks, page 44

Antipasto, page 14

Sausage Balls, page 36

Shrimp Stuffed Mushrooms, page 40

Almond Roca, page 103

Dipped Vanillas, page 105

Cherry Pound Cake, page 64

New Year's Eve

Champagne Punch, page 53

Shrimp Canapés, page 41

King Artichoke Dip, page 44 (served with veggies)

Beer Nuts, page 99

Cajun Spareribs, page 130

(served with rice)

Broccoli Casserole, page 170

Mock Black Bottom Pie, page 152

New Year's Day Casual

Mulled Cranberry Juice, page 54

Tomato Cabbage Soup, page 165

Green Pepper Salad, page 155

Lobster Fantans, page 75

Festive Savory Cheesecake, page 74

Golden Glazed Ham, page 132

Hasselback Potatoes, page 168

Dressed Peas, page 168

Glimmering Slice, page 119

Butter Tarts, page 149

Appetizers

The festive season sees many kinds of social occasions, and that makes appetizers especially appropriate at this time of the year. As part of a dinner menu they are an extra touch that adds to the special atmosphere. For a casual get-together a tray of appetizers is the perfect way to provide that little something to nibble on.

Appetizers are wonderfully easy to prepare and they look good, offering your guests a sampler of tastes and textures. Moreover, they're convenient. Make them ahead, refrigerate or freeze until needed, heat them up, arrange on a tray and voila—another happy holiday event is under way!

Top: Oriental Meatballs, page 33
Center: Sausage Balls, page 36
Bottom: Zucchini Squares, page 32

Bruschetta

A great blend of flavors. Make filling the day before and chill. Spread on bread just before baking.

Salad dressing (or mayonnaise)	½ cup	125 mL
Grated mozzarella cheese	1 cup	250 mL
Medium tomatoes, halved, seeded and finely diced	2	2
Chopped ripe pitted olives	¼ cup	60 mL
Grated fresh Parmesan cheese (or 2 tbsp., 30 mL dry)	¼ cup	60 mL
Whole oregano	1 tsp.	5 mL
Pepper	½ tsp.	2 mL
Sweet basil	¼ tsp.	1 mL
Baguette (must be fresh), about 2½ inches (6 cm) round, 24-27 inches (40-48 cm) long	1	1
Butter or hard margarine, softened	⅓ cup	75 mL

Mix first 8 ingredients in small bowl.

Cut baguette into 1 inch (2.5 cm) slices. Butter each slice on 1 side. Arrange, buttered side up, on ungreased baking sheet. Divide tomato mixture among slices and spread. Bake in 350°F (175°C) oven for 15 minutes until hot and cheese is melted. Serve warm. Makes 24 to 27 appetizers.

Pictured on page 33.

Zucchini Squares

Such a pretty light green. Freeze and cut when partially thawed.

Large eggs	4	4
Parsley flakes	1 tsp.	5 mL
Whole oregano	½ tsp.	2 mL
Seasoned salt	½ tsp.	2 mL
Garlic powder	½ tsp.	2 mL
Salt	¼ tsp.	1 mL
Cooking oil	½ cup	125 mL
Biscuit mix	1 cup	250 mL
Grated zucchini, with peel	3 cups	750 mL
Finely chopped onion	½ cup	125 mL
Grated medium Cheddar cheese	½ cup	125 mL
Grated Parmesan cheese	¼ cup	60 mL

Beat eggs in mixing bowl until smooth.

Add next 7 ingredients. Mix well.

Add remaining ingredients. Stir until mixed. Pour into greased 9 x 13 inch (22 x 33 cm) pan. Bake in 350°F (175°C) oven for 40 to 45 minutes until set and golden brown. Serve warm or cool. Cuts into 54 squares.

Pictured above.

Oriental Meatballs

The tangy flavor of the sauce will agree with everyone.
Make the meatballs ahead and freeze.

Meatballs:

Lean ground beef	1 lb.	454 g
Large egg	1	1
Worcestershire sauce	1 tsp.	5 mL
Finely chopped onion	¼ cup	60 mL
Sour cream	½ cup	125 mL
Fine bread crumbs	⅓ cup	75 mL
Salt	¾ tsp.	4 mL
Pepper	¼ tsp.	1 mL

Sweet And Sour Sauce:

Brown sugar, packed	⅔ cup	150 mL
Cornstarch	3 tbsp.	50 mL
Dry mustard powder	2 tsp.	10 mL
Pineapple juice	1 cup	250 mL
White vinegar	½ cup	125 mL
Ketchup	½ cup	125 mL
Water	½ cup	125 mL
Soy sauce	½ tsp.	2 mL

Meatballs: Measure all ingredients into bowl. Mix well. Shape into 1 inch (2.5 cm) balls. Arrange on baking sheet. Bake in 350°F (175°C) oven for 15 minutes.

Sweet And Sour Sauce: Stir brown sugar, cornstarch and mustard powder together in saucepan.

Stir in pineapple juice. Add vinegar, ketchup, water and soy sauce. Heat and stir until it boils and thickens. Sauce can be served separately for dipping or can be poured over meatballs to serve from chafing dish. Makes 64 meatballs and 2⅓ cups (575 mL) sauce.

Pictured on page 32.

Bruschetta, page 32

Bacon Cheddar Dip

Everybody raves over this. Easy to spread or dip.

Salad dressing (or mayonnaise)	1 cup	250 mL
Buttermilk	1 cup	250 mL
Grated medium Cheddar cheese	1 cup	250 mL
Onion flakes	¼ cup	60 mL
Bacon bits	⅓ cup	75 mL
Garlic salt	¾ tsp.	4 mL

Mix all 6 ingredients in bowl. Cover. Chill for 30 minutes. Serve with raw vegetables and assorted crackers. Makes 2⅓ cups (575 mL) dip.

Pictured below.

Simple Shrimp Dip   Bacon Cheddar Dip

Simple Shrimp Dip

Lots of flavor for dipping. Also delicious with
raw vegetables.

Sour cream	2 cups	450 mL
Chili sauce (or ketchup)	¼ cup	60 mL
Canned broken or small shrimp, drained and mashed	4 oz.	113 g
Lemon juice, fresh or bottled	½ tsp.	2 mL
Worcestershire sauce	½ tsp.	2 mL
Minced onion	1 tsp.	5 mL
Beef bouillon powder	½ tsp.	2 mL

Combine all 7 ingredients in bowl. Mash or beat together well. Serve chilled with chips and assorted crackers. Makes 2½ cups (575 mL) dip.

Pictured above.

Turkey Appetizers

Assemble these the day before. Chill then bake just before serving.

Butter or hard margarine	1 tbsp.	15 mL
Canned pineapple chunks, drained and patted dry	16	16
Prepared orange juice	1 cup	250 mL
Granulated sugar	⅓ cup	75 mL
Cranberries, fresh or frozen	32	32
Cooked turkey cubes	16	16
Savory Sauce:		
Ketchup	1 cup	250 mL
Mild molasses	¼ cup	60 mL
Cider vinegar	¼ cup	60 mL

Melt butter in frying pan. Add pineapple. Quickly brown both sides. Remove to plate.

Heat and stir orange juice and sugar in saucepan until mixture boils.

Add cranberries. Return just to a boil. Drain. Pour onto a separate plate.

To arrange on skewers, start with a cranberry, then a turkey cube, followed by a cranberry in center, then a pineapple chunk, another cranberry, another pineapple chunk, another turkey cube and ending with a cranberry.

Chill until ready to add sauce. Makes 8 appetizers.

Savory Sauce: Mix all 3 ingredients together. Lay chilled skewers on greased baking sheet. Brush or dab sauce on skewer contents. Heat in 425°F (220°C) oven for 5 to 10 minutes until hot. Use remaining sauce for dipping. Other dips could be orange marmalade or cranberry chutney. Makes 1½ cups (375 mL) sauce. Makes 8 skewers.

Pictured on page 36.

1. Sauced Crab Ball, page 42
2. Shrimp Canapés, page 41
3. Favorite Clam Dip, page 49
4. Crab Ball, page 42
5. Dilled Carrot Sticks, page 44
6. Shrimp Dip, page 49

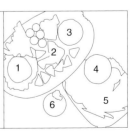

Bottom Left: Lazy Sausage Rolls, page 37
Bottom Center: Turkey Appetizers, page 35

Top Center: Sesame Wings, page 36
Bottom Right: Sauerkraut Balls, page 38

Sausage Balls

Serve with cocktail picks and a dipping sauce.
Try Sweet And Sour Sauce, page 33.

Sausage meat	½ lb.	225 g
Cayenne pepper	⅛ tsp.	0.5 mL
Grated sharp Cheddar cheese	2 cups	500 mL
Biscuit mix	1½ cups	375 mL

Scramble-fry sausage meat and cayenne pepper in frying pan. Drain off fat.

Add cheese. Stir until it melts.

Stir in biscuit mix. Remove from heat. Shape into 1 inch (2.5 cm) balls. Place about 1 inch (2.5 cm) apart on ungreased baking sheet. Bake in 400°F (205°C) oven for 10 to 12 minutes. To reheat frozen balls, heat in 325°F (160°C) oven for 10 minutes until hot. Makes 32 appetizers.

Pictured on page 32.

Sesame Wings

Always popular, these can be made ahead, frozen and reheated in oven.

Cornstarch	½ cup	125 mL
All-purpose flour	¼ cup	60 mL
Granulated sugar	¼ cup	60 mL
Soy sauce	⅓ cup	75 mL
Cooking oil	¼ cup	60 mL
Sesame seeds	2 tbsp.	30 mL
Salt	1½ tsp.	7 mL
Garlic powder	¼ tsp.	1 mL
Large eggs	2	2
Chicken drumettes, or whole wings	3 lbs.	1.3 kg

Measure first 9 ingredients into bowl that has a tight fitting lid. Mix well.

Add drumettes. (If using whole wings, discard tips. Cut owing apart at joint.) Add to marinade. Put lid on tightly. Rotate bowl to coat all pieces. Turn bowl often as wings marinate. Refrigerate at least 2 hours. Remove from marinade. Discard marinade. Arrange chicken on foil-lined baking sheet. Bake in 350°F (175°C) oven for about 30 minutes until tender. Makes about 3 dozen hot appetizers.

Pictured above.

Variation: Deep dry in hot oil for 8 minutes instead of baking in oven.

Lazy Sausage Rolls

These have an attractive pinwheel design. Try a combination of the basic recipe plus some of each of the variations. All freeze well.

Biscuit mix	2 cups	500 mL
Onion powder	1 tsp.	5 mL
Water	½ cup	125 mL
Pork sausage meat, mild or hot	1 lb.	454 g
Cayenne pepper	½-1 tsp.	2-5 mL

Stir biscuit mix and onion powder together. Add water. Mix until it forms a ball. Turn out onto lightly floured surface. Knead 6 to 8 times. Roll out into a rectangle about 15 x 18 inches (30 x 45 cm).

Mash sausage meat with fork to make it more pliable. Spread over dough. Roll up dough like a jelly roll, beginning at long end. Slice ⅜ inch (9 mm) thick. Arrange on greased baking sheet, cut side down, about 1 inch (2.5 cm) apart. Bake in 450°F (230°C) oven for about 15 minutes. Makes about 3 dozen appetizers.

Variation: Brush tops with beaten egg and sprinkle with poppy seeds, sesame seeds or parsley flakes. Bake as above.

Pictured on page 36.

Artichoke Strudel

Fussy but fantastic! Can be frozen.

Butter or hard margarine	¼ cup	60 mL
Finely chopped onion	1 cup	250 mL
Garlic powder	½ tsp.	2 mL
Cream cheese, softened	8 oz.	250 g
Creamed cottage cheese	1 cup	250 mL
Large eggs	3	3
Garlic salt	1 tsp.	5 mL
Parsley flakes	1 tsp.	5 mL
Tarragon	¾ tsp.	4 mL
Pepper	½ tsp.	2 mL
Jars of marinated artichokes, drained and chopped	3 x 6 oz.	3 x 175 mL
Grated fresh Parmesan cheese (or 2 tbsp., 30 mL dry)	¼ cup	60 mL
Cracker crumbs	½ cup	125 mL
Filo pastry dough sheets	15	15
Butter or hard margarine, melted	½ cup	125 mL

Melt first amount of butter in frying pan. Add onion. Sauté until soft. Do not brown.

Add garlic powder. Stir.

Beat cream cheese and cottage cheese in bowl until cheese is mixed in. Beat in eggs 1 at a time. Add garlic salt, parsley, tarragon and pepper. Beat to mix. Add onion with any leftover drippings.

Add artichokes, Parmesan cheese and cracker crumbs. Stir.

Lay out filo sheets. Brush with melted butter. Stack 5 sheets on top of each other, making 3 stacks. Spoon ⅓ artichoke mixture down one end of each stack. Roll up, tucking end edges of sheets around filling. Arrange rolls on greased baking sheet. Bake in 350°F (175°C) oven for 30 to 40 minutes until nicely browned. Cut each roll into 10 pieces. Serve warm or room temperature. Makes 30 appetizers.

Pictured below.

Artichoke Strudel

Mushroom Nappies

An incredible edible. Mixture can be made ahead and frozen.

Butter or hard margarine	3 tbsp.	50 mL
Chopped onion	1 cup	250 mL
Chopped fresh mushrooms	2 cups	500 mL
Grated mozzarella cheese	1 cup	250 mL
Grated Parmesan cheese	1/4 cup	60 mL
Parsley flakes	1 tsp.	5 mL
Large egg	1	1
Whole oregano	1/2 tsp.	2 mL
Salt	1/2 tsp.	2 mL
Pepper	1/4 tsp.	1 mL
Bread Nappies:		
White bread slices	12	12
Butter or hard margarine, softened	1/3 cup	75 mL
Yellow cheese slices	3	3

Melt butter in frying pan. Add onion and mushrooms. Sauté until soft.

Stir in next 7 ingredients. Stir for 1 minute. Remove from heat.

Bread Nappies: Cut off crusts from bread slices. Roll each slice lightly with rolling pin to flatten. Butter slices. Cut each slice into 4 squares. Press, buttered side up, into tiny muffin tins. Fill with mushroom mixture using about 1½ tsp. (7 mL) for each one.

Cut each cheese slice into 16 small squares. Put 1 square on top of each tart. Bake in 350°F (175°C) oven for 20 to 25 minutes. Makes 4 dozen appetizers.

Pictured above.

Sauerkraut Balls

Crunchy on the outside and creamy on the inside.

Pork sausage meat	1/2 lb.	225 g
Finely chopped onion	1/3 cup	75 mL
All-purpose flour	1 tbsp.	15 mL
Canned sauerkraut, well drained and finely chopped	14 oz.	398 mL
Cream cheese, softened, cut up	4 oz.	125 g
Prepared mustard	1 tsp.	5 mL
Parsley flakes	1 tsp.	5 mL
Salt	1/8 tsp.	0.5 mL
Garlic powder	1/4 tsp.	1 mL
Pepper	1/4 tsp.	1 mL
Coating:		
All-purpose flour	1/3 cup	75 mL
Large eggs	2	2
Water	2 tbsp.	30 mL
Fine dry bread crumbs	1 cup	250 mL
Fat, for deep-frying		

Scramble-fry sausage meat and onion in frying pan until no pink remains in meat and onion is soft.

Sprinkle flour over top. Mix. Add sauerkraut, cream cheese, mustard, parsley, salt, garlic powder and pepper. Stir until blended. Chill until it will hold its shape. Roll into 1 inch (2.5 cm) balls.

Coating: Measure flour into small bowl.

Beat eggs and water with a fork in another bowl.

Roll balls in flour to coat. Dip in egg mixture. Coat with bread crumbs.

Carefully drop 1 at a time until there are about 4 in hot 385°F to 400°F (195°C to 205°C) fat. Deep-fry until browned, about 3 minutes. Remove with slotted spoon to tray lined with paper towels to drain. These may be made ahead and heated in 400°F (205°C) oven for 8 minutes until hot. If frozen, heat in 350°F (175°C) oven for 12 minutes until hot. Makes about 30 appetizers.

Pictured on page 37.

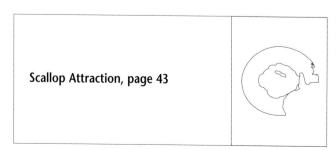

Scallop Attraction, page 43

Shrimp Stuffed Mushrooms

This is a stuffed mushroom that is served chilled rather than the usual broiled or baked type.

Large whole mushrooms	24	24
Lemon juice, fresh or bottled	1/4 cup	60 mL
Granulated sugar	2 tbsp.	30 mL
Cream cheese, softened	4 oz.	125 g
Sour cream	2 tbsp.	30 mL
Broken shrimp, drained and chopped (or use fresh cooked)	4 oz.	113 g
Green onions, finely chopped	4	4
Hot pepper sauce	1/4 tsp.	1 mL
Paprika, sprinkle		

Remove stems from mushrooms and save for another recipe. Mix lemon juice with sugar in bowl with tight-fitting cover. Add mushrooms. Cover and marinate 3 to 4 hours, shaking bowl often. Drain well.

Mix cream cheese and sour cream together well. Add shrimp, onions and pepper sauce. Stir together. Stuff mushroom caps. Garnish with additional tiny shrimp if desired.

Sprinkle with paprika. Serve chilled. Makes 24 cold appetizers.

Pictured on this page.

Creamy Stuffed Mushrooms

Always popular. The fresher the mushrooms the better.

Large mushrooms	24	24
Cream cheese, softened	4 oz.	125 g
Grated Parmesan cheese	1/4 cup	60 mL
Finely chopped green onion	2 tbsp.	30 mL
Reserved mushroom stems, chopped		
Salt	1/8 tsp.	0.5 mL
Dill weed	1/8 tsp.	0.5 mL
Garlic powder	1/16 tsp.	0.5 mL

Gently twist stems from mushrooms. Reserve stems.

Mash cream cheese and Parmesan cheese together using fork. Add onion, mushroom stems, salt, dill weed and garlic powder. Stuff mushroom caps. Arrange on ungreased baking sheet. Broil on second rack down from broiler until golden brown. Serve hot. Makes 24 appetizers.

When placing stuffed mushrooms on baking sheet, dab the bottoms in the filling to help "glue" onto the sheet. This helps keep them level while baking and keeps them from sliding around.

Pictured on this page.

Left: Salmon Canapés, page 41
Center: Shrimp Stuffed Mushrooms, page 40
Right: Creamy Stuffed Mushrooms, page 40

Shrimp Canapés

There is a nice nip to the flavor of these quick appetizers.

Jar of Old English cheese spread	⅓ cup	75 mL
Butter or hard margarine, softened	¼ cup	60 mL
Salad dressing (or mayonnaise)	2 tsp.	10 mL
Lemon juice, fresh or bottled	½ tsp.	2 mL
Cayenne pepper, just a pinch		
Onion powder, just a pinch		
Canned broken or tiny shrimp, rinsed and drained	4 oz.	113 g
English muffins, split	4	4

Put first 6 ingredients into small bowl. Beat until smooth.

Add shrimp. Beat on low just to mix.

Spread on 8 muffin halves. Broil until lightly browned. These may be frozen whole before broiling then broiled from the frozen state. Cut each muffin half into 8 pieces to serve. Makes 64 tiny appetizers.

Pictured on page 34.

Salmon Canapés

Serve these à la carte—let everyone make their own.

Canned salmon (red, such as Sockeye, is best for color)	2 × 7.5 oz.	2 × 213 g
Cream cheese, softened	8 oz.	250 g
Canned ham flakes	6½ oz.	184 g
Lemon juice, fresh or bottled	2 tsp.	10 mL
Horseradish	1 tsp.	5 mL
Liquid smoke	1 tsp.	5 mL
Onion powder	¼ tsp.	1 mL
Paprika (use with pink salmon)	2 tsp.	10 mL
Crackers or small bread rounds		

Drain salmon. Remove skin and round bones. Flake salmon in bowl.

Add next 7 ingredients. Mash and work together. Spread on crackers or bread rounds. Makes 3 cups (700 mL) spread.

Pictured on page 40.

Ripe Olive Canapés

Make the olive mixture the day before. Or spread on toasted bread slices and freeze. Broil when thawed.

Chopped ripe olives	14 oz.	398 mL
Grated medium Cheddar cheese	1 cup	250 mL
Salad dressing (or mayonnaise)	¼ cup	60 mL
Onion powder	¼ tsp.	1 mL
Curry powder	¼ tsp.	1 mL
Sandwich bread slices, crusts removed	8	8

Mix first 5 ingredients in small bowl.

Arrange bread slices on ungreased baking sheet. Toast 1 side under broiler. Spread olive mixture on untoasted side. Broil for about 2 or 3 minutes until bubbly. Cut each slice into 4 squares or 4 triangles. Makes 32 appetizers.

Pictured below.

Left: Ripe Olive Canapés, page 41
Center: Baked Cheese Balls, page 45
Right: Spinach Squares, page 42

Welsh Cakes, page 45   Date Nut Log, page 48

Spinach Squares

Make these well in advance and freeze. Cut when partially thawed.

Butter or hard margarine	2 tbsp.	30 mL
Chopped fresh mushrooms	2 cups	500 mL
Chopped onion	1 cup	250 mL
Large eggs	4	4
Dry bread crumbs	1/4 cup	60 mL
Grated Parmesan cheese	1/3 cup	75 mL
Salt	1/4 tsp.	1 mL
Pepper	1/8 tsp.	0.5 mL
Ground nutmeg	1/8 tsp.	0.5 mL
Ground oregano	1/8 tsp.	0.5 mL
Sweet basil	1/8 tsp.	0.5 mL
Frozen chopped spinach, thawed and squeezed dry	2 x 10 oz.	2 x 300 g
Condensed cream of mushroom soup	10 oz.	284 mL

Melt butter in frying pan. Add mushrooms and onion. Sauté until soft.

Beat eggs in bowl until frothy. Measure in remaining ingredients. Mix. Add mushroom mixture. Spoon into greased 9 x 13 inch (22 x 33 cm) pan. Bake in 350°F (175°C) oven for about 35 minutes until set and browned. Cool. To reheat frozen squares, arrange on ungreased baking sheet. Heat in 325°F (160°C) oven for about 12 minutes. Makes 54 appetizers.

Pictured on page 41.

Crab Ball

Covered in nuts and parsley, this has a nice sharp flavor. Serve with assorted crackers. Freezes well.

Cream cheese, softened	8 oz.	250 g
Hot pepper sauce	1/4 tsp.	1 mL
Salt	1/2 tsp.	2 mL
Pepper	1/4 tsp.	1 mL
Chopped green onion	2 tbsp.	30 mL
Crabmeat (or 1 can 4 oz., 113 g, drained, membrane removed)	1 cup	250 g
Finely chopped walnuts	1/4 cup	60 mL
Chopped fresh parsley (or 2 tsp., 10 mL, parsley flakes)	2 tbsp.	30 mL

Mash cheese with fork in bowl. Add pepper sauce, salt, pepper and onion. Mash well.

Add crabmeat. Mash to mix. Chill for 30 minutes or more before shaping into a ball. It will remain fairly soft.

Mix walnuts and parsley on large plate. Roll ball in mixture. Cover and chill. Makes 1 ball about 3½ inches (9 cm) in diameter.

Pictured on page 35.

Sauced Crab Ball

Recipe can be made several days ahead and can easily be doubled. Serve with assorted crackers.

Cream cheese, softened	4 oz.	125 g
Canned crabmeat, drained, membrane removed, flaked	4 oz.	113 g
Lemon juice, fresh or bottled	1 tsp.	5 mL
Onion powder	1/4 tsp.	1 mL
Hot pepper sauce, just a dash		
Seafood cocktail sauce	1/3 cup	75 mL

Beat cheese, crabmeat, lemon juice, onion powder and hot pepper sauce together well. Shape into ball. Cover and chill.

Just before serving, pour seafood sauce over crab ball. Add more seafood sauce as needed. Makes 1 small ball.

Pictured on page 34.

Scallop Attraction

Picture perfect and so easy!

Hard margarine (butter browns too fast)	2 tbsp.	30 mL
Thin slices of small zucchini, with peel	2	2
Medium tomatoes, halved, seeded and diced	3	3
Whole oregano	¼ tsp.	1 mL
Sweet basil	⅛ tsp.	0.5 mL
White wine	¼ cup	60 mL
Large scallops, cut in 3 slices each	1 lb.	454 g
Sauce:		
Butter or hard margarine	2 tbsp.	30 mL
All-purpose flour	2 tbsp.	30 mL
Evaporated skim milk (or light cream)	⅔ cup	150 mL
Reserved liquid from scallops	⅓ cup	75 mL
Red pepper or pimiento, for garnish		

Melt first amount of margarine in frying pan. Add zucchini. Sauté about 5 minutes until it looks lightly browned. Remove to warm plate.

Put tomatoes in frying pan. Sauté briefly until tomato skin wrinkles a bit. Sprinkle with oregano and basil. Stir. Remove to warm plate.

Add wine to frying pan. Poach scallop slices in wine until just done, stirring occasionally. Remove to warm plate. Reserve liquid.

Sauce: Melt butter in small saucepan over medium heat. Stir in flour. Whisk in reserved liquid. Add milk slowly. Whisk until smooth and thickened.

To assemble, overlap ¼ zucchini slices in a circle on individual salad plate. Spoon ¼ tomato pieces on top. Overlap ¼ scallop slices on tomatoes. Lay 1 scallop slice on top. Pour ¼ cup (60 mL) sauce on top. Garnish with red pepper or pimiento. Repeat for remaining 3 plates. Serves 4.

Pictured on page 39.

Shrimp Cocktail

Sauce is just right for this traditional dinner appetizer. So elegant in appearance. Set at each place before calling guests.

Seafood Sauce:		
Chili sauce	½ cup	125 mL
Ketchup	⅓ cup	75 mL
Sweet pickle relish	2 tbsp.	30 mL
Prepared horseradish	1 tsp.	5 mL
Worcestershire sauce	½ tsp.	2 mL
Lemon juice, fresh or bottled	½ tsp.	2 mL
Seasoned salt	¼ tsp.	1 mL
Torn lettuce, lightly packed	2 cups	500 mL
Jumbo shrimp, peeled, deveined, tail intact	40-48	40-48

Seafood Sauce: Stir first 7 ingredients in small bowl. Chill until ready to assemble. Makes ¾ cup (175 mL) sauce.

Divide lettuce among 8 sherbet dishes. Spoon about 2 tbsp. (30 mL) seafood sauce in center. Hook 5 or 6 shrimp around top outside edge of each sherbet with tails hanging downward. Serves 8.

Pictured below.

Shrimp Cocktail

Dilled Carrot Sticks

Pickled flavor with a crunchy texture.

Small carrots, peeled and quartered lengthwise	8	8
Dill pickle juice	1 cup	250 mL

Simmer carrots and pickle juice in covered saucepan for 20 to 25 minutes until you pierce them with tip of paring knife. Cool in juice. Chill in juice in refrigerator overnight. Makes 32 sticks.

Pictured on page 35.

Jean's Favorite

King Artichoke Dip

Yummy! Wonderful blend of cheese, bacon, spinach and artichoke. Looks pretty, too.

Bacon slices, diced	8	8
Finely chopped onion	1 cup	250 mL
Garlic cloves, minced	2	2
Canned artichoke hearts, drained and chopped	14 oz.	398 mL
Cream cheese, softened	8 oz.	250 g
Sour cream	½ cup	125 mL
Bunch of fresh spinach, finely chopped	1	1
Worcestershire sauce	¼ tsp.	1 mL
Milk, optional		
Baguette, sliced and quartered	1	1

Sauté bacon, onion and garlic in frying pan until bacon is done and onion is soft.

Add artichoke hearts. Sauté for 1 minute more.

Beat cream cheese and sour cream in bowl until smooth. Add bacon mixture. Stir.

Mix in spinach and Worcestershire. Thin with milk if desired.

Serve with bread chunks for dipping. Makes 3 cups (750 mL) dip.

Pictured on page 45.

Onion Tarts

These can be baked then frozen. Reheat in oven, not microwave, to keep pastry flaky.

Hard margarine (butter browns too fast)	¼ cup	60 mL
Medium onions, finely diced	4	4
All-purpose flour	2 tbsp.	30 mL
Large eggs	4	4
Milk	1 cup	250 mL
Seasoned salt	1 tsp.	5 mL
Pepper	⅛ tsp.	0.5 mL
Bacon slices, cooked crisp and crumbled	5	5
Grated Edam cheese	2 cups	500 mL
Pastry, your own, or a mix, enough for 3 shells		

Melt margarine in frying pan. Add onion. Sauté until onion is soft.

Sprinkle with flour. Mix. Remove from heat.

Beat eggs in mixing bowl. Add milk, seasoned salt and pepper. Stir in onion, bacon and cheese.

Roll out pastry. Cut and fit into ungreased mini muffin cups. Fill with onion mixture. Bake in 350°F (175°C) oven for 15 to 20 minutes. Makes about 4 dozen mini tarts.

Pictured on page 45.

Variation: Bake the filling in 9 inch (22 cm) unbaked pie shell and serve for a brunch or sit-down dinner.

Salty Caraway Sticks

A wonderful little breadstick appetizer. The caraway is a nice savory blend with other more zippy appetizers.

Packaged refrigerator biscuits (10 to a tube)	1	1
Crisp rice cereal, crushed	1¼ cups	300 mL
Caraway seed	1½ tbsp.	25 mL
Salt	1 tsp.	5 mL
Milk	½ cup	125 mL

Cut each biscuit in half. Roll each half into a pencil shape.

Mix cereal, caraway seed and salt in shallow bowl.

Dip each roll into milk, then roll in seed mixture. Arrange on greased baking sheet. Bake in 450°F (230°C) oven for 10 minutes. Makes 20 appetizers.

Pictured on page 45.

Welsh Cakes

A nice change from crackers. Serve with Date Nut Log, page 48.

All-purpose flour	2 cups	450 mL
Granulated sugar	1/3 cup	75 mL
Baking powder	2 tsp.	10 mL
Salt	1/2 tsp.	2 mL
Ground nutmeg	1/4 tsp.	1 mL
Ground cinnamon	1/4 tsp.	1 mL
Butter or hard margarine	1/2 cup	125 mL
Cut glazed mixed fruit (see Note)	3/4 cup	175 mL
Large egg	1	1
Milk	1/3 cup	75 mL

Measure first 6 ingredients into large bowl. Cut in butter until mixture is crumbly.

Add fruit. Stir.

Beat egg with fork in separate bowl. Stir in milk. Add egg and milk to flour mixture. Stir just until moistened. Roll out 1/4 inch (6 mm) thick on lightly floured surface. Cut into 2 inch (5 cm) rounds. Grease frying pan for first round of cakes. It shouldn't need greasing again. Fry on medium-low, browning both sides. Makes about 24 small cakes.

Note: Red and green glazed cherries can be used in place of the fruit.

Pictured on page 42.

Baked Cheese Balls

Shortbread-like texture. Freezes well.

Grated sharp Cheddar cheese	1 cup	250 mL
All-purpose flour	1 cup	250 mL
Butter or hard margarine, softened	1/2 cup	125 mL
Salt	1/2 tsp.	2 mL
Poppy seeds		
Toasted sesame seeds		

Mix cheese, flour, butter and salt in small bowl. Shape into 1/2 inch (12 mm) balls.

Roll in your choice of seeds. Arrange on greased baking sheets. Bake in 350°F (175°C) oven for about 20 to 25 minutes. Makes 36 appetizers.

Pictured on page 41 and on page 23.

1. Salty Caraway Sticks, page 44
2. Chestnuts In Jackets, page 48
3. All-Season Dip, page 49
4. Onion Tarts, page 44
5. King Artichoke Dip, page 44

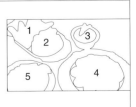

Nutty Cheese Ball

Serve with assorted fruit and crackers. Somewhat softer ball.
Make the day before.

Crushed pineapple, well-drained	14 oz.	398 mL
Cream cheese, softened	12 oz.	375 g
Salt	1 tsp.	5 mL
Onion powder	¼ tsp.	1 mL
Chopped pecans	¾ cup	175 mL
Chopped green pepper	2 tbsp.	30 mL

Combine pineapple, cream cheese, salt and onion powder in bowl. Beat slowly to mix well.

Mix in pecans and green pepper. Chill overnight. Shape into a ball. Serve with fruit and assorted crackers. Makes 1 medium cheese ball.

Pictured on page 47.

Round Cheese Spread

Nice strong curry flavor.

Cream cheese, softened	8 oz.	250 g
Salad dressing (or mayonnaise)	1 tbsp.	15 mL
Curry powder	1½ tsp.	7 mL
Worcestershire sauce	1 tsp.	5 mL
Seasoned salt	¼ tsp.	1 mL
Salt	¼ tsp.	1 mL
Paprika	¼ tsp.	1 mL
Chutney, your choice	½ cup	125 mL

Beat first 7 ingredients together on medium. Shape into a flattened ball. Chill.

When ready to use, place cheese round on serving plate. Spoon chutney over top allowing some to run down sides, using more chutney if desired. Makes 1 small ball.

Pictured on page 47.

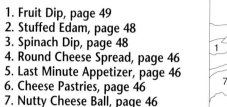

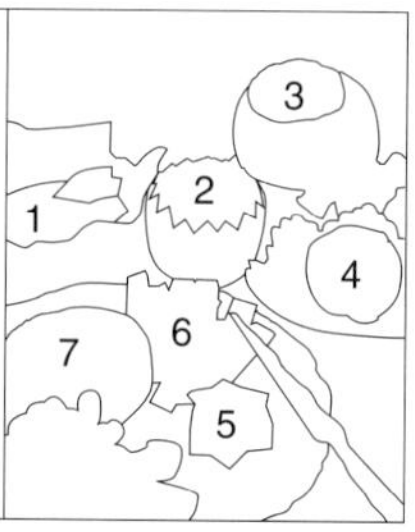

Cheese Pastries

Keep these in an open container to retain crispness.

All-purpose flour	1 cup	250 mL
Cornmeal	2 tbsp.	30 mL
Garlic powder	¼ tsp.	1 mL
Salt	⅛ tsp.	0.5 mL
Cayenne pepper	⅛ tsp.	0.5 mL
Butter or hard margarine	¼ cup	60 mL
Grated sharp Cheddar cheese	1 cup	250 mL
Grated Parmesan cheese	2 tbsp.	30 mL
Water	5 tbsp.	75 mL

Put first 5 ingredients into bowl. Cut in butter until crumbly.

Add both cheeses. Toss. Sprinkle with water. Mix into a ball. Roll out on lightly floured surface to 16 x 5 inch (40 x 12 cm) rectangle. Cut in ½ inch (12 mm) wide strips crosswise, making 32 strips. Place on greased baking sheet. Bake in 400°F (205°C) oven for about 10 minutes until golden. Cool on rack. Makes 32.

Pictured on page 47.

Last Minute Appetizer

Horseradish gives an unexpected tang.

Apple or crabapple jelly	½ cup	125 mL
Pineapple or apricot jam	½ cup	125 mL
Prepared horseradish	1 tbsp.	15 mL
Dry mustard powder, generous measure	¼ tsp.	1 mL
Cream cheese, softened	8 oz.	250 g

Put first 4 ingredients into small bowl. Stir well.

Place cheese on serving dish. Top with jam mixture, allowing it to run down sides. Serve with assorted crackers. Makes 1 cup (250 mL) sauce plus 1 block cream cheese.

Pictured on page 47.

Chestnuts In Jackets

A bit fussy to make but the outcome is like a Cheddar shortbread. Freeze uncooked in plastic container.

Canned whole water chestnuts	2 × 8 oz.	2 × 227 mL
Butter or hard margarine, softened	½ cup	125 mL
Grated sharp Cheddar cheese	2 cups	500 mL
Sesame seeds	2 tbsp.	30 mL
Garlic salt	½ tsp.	2 mL
Paprika	½ tsp.	2 mL
Cayenne pepper, just a pinch		
All-purpose flour	1½ cups	375 mL

Drain chestnuts. Dry with paper towels. Let stand to dry even more while making "jackets".

Beat butter and cheese in medium bowl. Add sesame seeds, salt, paprika and cayenne. Beat. Gradually work in flour until mixture holds together. Mold about 1 tbsp. (15 mL) dough around each chestnut. Cover and chill or freeze. Bake, chilled, in 425°F (220°C) oven for 15 to 20 minutes. If baking frozen, lower temperature to 400°F (205°C) and bake about 15 minutes longer. Makes 36 hot appetizers.

Pictured on page 45.

Stuffed Edam

Serve at room temperature but can be made the day before. Very tasty.

Edam cheese, with red wax coating (or Gouda)	1 lb.	454 g
Cream cheese, softened	8 oz.	250 g
Apricot jam	¼ cup	60 mL
Onion powder	½ tsp.	2 mL
Paprika	⅛ tsp.	0.5 mL
Milk	1-2 tbsp.	15-30 mL
Finely chopped red pepper	⅓ cup	75 mL
Chopped chives	1 tsp.	5 mL

Cut a thin slice from top of cheese. Use a sharp knife to cut a zig zag edge if you like. Use a spoon or melon baller to scoop out cheese, leaving shell intact. Dice cheese into fine pieces.

Beat cream cheese, jam, onion powder and paprika together in small bowl. Add diced cheese. Stir. Process in food processor 1 minute. Add milk. Process another 20 seconds. Remove to bowl.

Add green pepper and chives. Stir. Spoon into red shell. Serves 10.

Pictured on page 47.

Spinach Dip

This can be served in the bread loaf or as a separate heated dip with bread, crackers and fresh veggies.

Salad dressing (or mayonnaise)	½ cup	125 mL
Cream cheese softened	2 × 8 oz.	2 × 250 g
Grated medium or sharp Cheddar cheese	1 cup	250 mL
Frozen chopped spinach, thawed, squeezed dry	10 oz.	300 g
Chopped fried bacon, 6 slices	½ cup	125 mL
Finely chopped onion	¼ cup	60 mL
Dill weed	2 tsp.	10 mL
Garlic powder (or 1 clove, minced)	¼ tsp.	1 mL

Beat salad dressing and cream cheese together in small bowl until smooth. Stir in next 6 ingredients. Makes 3 cups (750 mL) dip.

Variation: Cut top off round bread loaf. Hollow out loaf leaving shell 1 inch (2.5 cm) thick. Reserve removed bread  for dipping. Pour spinach mixture into hollow. Wrap in foil. Heat in 325°F (160°C) oven for 2 hours. Remove from oven. Turn back foil. Serve with bread pieces taken from loaf to use as dippers. Slice baguette for extra dippers. As dip disappears, break off sides for dippers. Good warm and also good as it cools. Makes 1 loaf.

Pictured on page 47.

Date Nut Log

Good on Welsh Cakes, page 45, or serve with assorted crackers.

Cream cheese, softened	8 oz.	250 g
Corn syrup	2 tbsp.	30 mL
Maple flavoring	½ tsp.	2 mL
Chopped dates	¾ cup	175 mL
Chopped walnuts	½ cup	125 mL
Finely chopped walnuts	¾ cup	175 mL

Beat cheese, corn syrup and maple flavoring in small bowl until smooth.

Stir in dates and first amount of walnuts. Chill overnight. Shape into log.

Roll in remaining walnuts. Chill until ready to serve. May be frozen. Makes 1 log about 1½ inches (4 cm) in diameter.

Pictured on page 42.

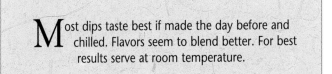

Most dips taste best if made the day before and chilled. Flavors seem to blend better. For best results serve at room temperature.

Favorite Clam Dip

The name says it all. It's mild but always popular.

Cream cheese, softened	8 oz.	250 g
Minced clams, drained, juice reserved	2 × 5 oz.	2 × 142 g
Lemon juice, fresh or bottled	1 tbsp.	15 mL
Worcestershire sauce	1 tsp.	5 mL
Onion salt	¼ tsp.	1 mL
Onion powder	¼ tsp.	1 mL
Reserved juice, as needed	5 tbsp.	75 mL

Beat first 6 ingredients together in small bowl.

Add a bit of reserved juice a small amount at a time until mixture is of dipping consistency. Makes 2½ cups (600 mL) dip.

Pictured on page 34.

All-Season Dip

This tangy dip will be a hit! Serve with assorted raw vegetables.

Salad dressing (or mayonnaise)	1 cup	250 mL
Chili sauce	1 cup	250 mL
Onion flakes	3 tbsp.	50 mL
Water	2 tbsp.	30 mL
Mustard seeds	2 tsp.	10 mL
Horseradish	2 tbsp.	30 mL

Put all 6 ingredients into small bowl. Stir together well. Chill at least 2 hours. Makes 2 cups (500 mL) dip.

Pictured on page 45.

Shrimp Dip

Very shrimpy tasting with the zip of cayenne. Serve with an assortment of crackers and veggies.

Canned broken shrimp, drained, mashed with fork	1 × 4 oz.	1 × 113 g
Salad dressing (or mayonnaise)	½ cup	125 mL
Onion powder	¼ tsp.	1 mL
Sherry (or alcohol-free sherry)	2 tbsp.	30 mL
Cayenne pepper	⅛ tsp.	0.5 mL
Salt	¼ tsp.	1 mL
Pepper	1/16 tsp.	0.5 mL
Milk	1 tbsp.	15 mL

Stir all 8 ingredients together in small bowl. Chill. Makes 1 cup (250 mL) dip.

Pictured on page 34.

Fruit Dip

Very quick. Dip can be prepared a day ahead. This has a nice hint of cinnamon.

Frozen whipped topping, thawed	2 cups	500 mL
Brown sugar, packed	¼ cup	60 mL
Ground cinnamon	¼ tsp.	1 mL
Apple slices, cored, with peel		
Pear slices		
Grapes		
Water	1 cup	250 mL
Lemon juice, fresh or bottled	2 tbsp.	30 mL

Stir whipped topping with brown sugar and cinnamon.

Combine fruit with water and lemon juice. Let stand about 30 minutes. Drain. Place dip in small dish. Arrange fruit around dip. Makes 2 cups (500 mL) dip.

Pictured on page 47.

Fun Party Mix

Double or triple this recipe and store in fridge or freezer for unexpected guests.

Crispix cereal	6 cups	1.35 L
Mini pretzels	1 cup	250 mL
Salted dry roasted peanuts	1 cup	250 mL
Butter or hard margarine	6 tbsp.	100 mL
Brown sugar, packed	¾ cup	175 mL
Honey	¼ cup	60 mL
Vanilla	1 tsp.	5 mL

Put cereal, pretzels and peanuts into large bowl. Stir gently.

Measure next 3 ingredients into saucepan. Heat on medium and stir until mixture boils. Boil gently on medium-low without stirring for 5 minutes.

Stir in vanilla. Remove from heat. Pour hot syrup over cereal mixture. Stir well to coat. Transfer to large greased roaster. Bake for 1 hour in 250°F (120°C) oven, removing every 15 minutes to stir. Cool. Store in airtight container. Freezes well. Makes 8 cups (2 L) snack mixture.

Pictured on page 51.

Cinnamon Crisps

A great snack or appetizer. Take in the car if you're traveling or to the skating rink.

Butter or hard margarine, melted	½ cup	125 mL
Flour tortillas, 10 inch (25 cm) diameter	10	10
Granulated sugar	½ cup	125 mL
Ground cinnamon	1 tbsp.	15 mL

Brush tops of tortillas with melted butter. Spread remaining butter over jelly roll pan. Cut tortillas into 13 wedges each for a total of 130 "chips". Fit as many chips as close together as you can.

Mix sugar and cinnamon in small bowl. Sprinkle over chips. Bake in 325°F (160°C) oven for about 10 to 12 minutes until golden. Cool. Store in covered container. Makes 130 small pieces.

Pictured above.

Variation: Substitute 1 package (16 oz., 454 g) of wonton wrappers for the tortillas. Cut each wrapper diagonally into 4 wedges. Proceed as above, baking for 8 minutes. Makes 288 small pieces.

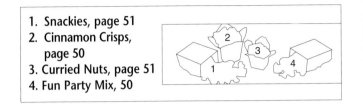

Snackies

Be prepared to refill the bowl often once guests get started on these.

Sultana raisins	1 cup	250 mL
Bite size shredded wheat cereal	2 cups	450 mL
Bite size shredded corn cereal	2 cups	450 mL
Oat squares cereal	2 cups	450 mL
Corn bran cereal	2 cups	450 mL
Pecan halves	1 cup	250 mL
Coating:		
Butter or hard margarine	½ cup	125 mL
Corn syrup	¼ cup	60 mL
Brown sugar, packed	1½ cups	375 mL
Ground cinnamon	1 tsp.	5 mL
Salt	¾ tsp.	4 mL
Vanilla	1 tsp.	5 mL

Combine raisins, cereals and pecan halves in large greased bowl.

Coating: Stir all ingredients in saucepan until mixture comes to a boil. Boil slowly for 3 minutes. Pour over cereal mixture. Stir well to coat all pieces. Spread on 2 greased baking sheets. Cool until firm. Break into pieces. Store in airtight container. Makes 2½ pounds (1.1 kg) or about 13 cups (3.2 L) snack mix.

Pictured on page 50.

Curried Nuts

The curry flavor is not too strong. Adjust curry powder as desired.

Butter or hard margarine	¼ cup	60 mL
Curry powder	1 tsp.	5 mL
Salt	1 tsp.	5 mL
Mixed nuts such as pecans, almonds, peanuts, walnuts, filberts	4 cups	1 L

Melt butter in large saucepan. Stir in curry powder and salt. Add nuts. Stir to coat. Turn into ungreased 10 x 15 inch (25 x 30 cm) jelly roll pan. Bake in 350°F (175°C) oven for 10 to 15 minutes. Stir occasionally while baking. Cool. Makes 4 cups (1 L) nut mixture.

Pictured on page 50.

Beverages

Certain foods have come to represent Christmas. Certain beverages play the same role. With their rich colors and inviting hues, these flavorful drinks are significant additions to any holiday occasion.

Hot and cold, traditional and contemporary selections are included for an extra special touch on your Yuletide table.

Mock Mint Julep

As green as green can be. Adjust mint flavoring as desired.

Lemon-lime drink mix (2 quart , 2 L size each, such as Kool-Aid)	2	2
Mint flavoring	¼ tsp.	1 mL
Lemon-lime soft drink	4 cups	1 L
Maraschino cherries, for garnish		

Make drink mix according to directions on envelope.

Stir in mint flavoring and soft drink. Pour over ice in glasses.

Garnish with cherries. Makes 64 ounces (2 L).

Pictured on this page.

Raspberry Liqueur

So smooth and sweet. Perfect color for Christmas.

Frozen raspberries, in syrup	15 oz.	425 g
Ground cinnamon	⅛ tsp.	0.5 mL
Brandy or kirsch	2 cups	500 mL
Vodka	2 cups	500 mL
Granulated sugar	½ cup	125 mL

Put all ingredients into jar. Put on lid. Let stand at room temperature for 6 weeks. Shake jar once a week. After 6 weeks, strain and bottle. Makes 5 cups (1.25 L) liqueur.

Pictured on page 53.

Mulled Wine

Full-bodied mulled flavor. Double the recipe for a larger crowd.

Cranberry cocktail juice	3 cups	750 mL
Whole cloves	10	10
Cinnamon sticks (about 2 inch, 5 cm length)	3	3
Ground nutmeg	¼ tsp.	1 mL
Honey	¼ cup	60 mL
Orange, sliced	1	1
Lemon slices	3	3
Dry red wine	3 cups	750 mL

Pour juice into large saucepan.

Add next 6 ingredients. Stir to dissolve honey. Simmer on low for about 1 hour.

Add wine. Heat and serve hot. Makes 8 cups (2 L).

Pictured on page 55.

Mock Mint Julep

Left: Mock Kahlua, page 53
Bottom Center: Raspberry Liqueur, page 52

Top Center: Champagne Punch, page 53
Right: Creamy Cranberry Punch, page 53

Mock Kahlua

Wow! It tastes very close to the real thing. Lasts in the fridge for several months.

Granulated sugar	4 cups	900 mL
Water	4 cups	900 mL
Instant coffee granules	²⁄₃ cup	150 mL
Rye whiskey	25 oz.	750 mL
Vanilla bean	1	1

Heat and stir sugar, water and coffee granules in saucepan until mixture boils. Boil 3 minutes without stirring. Cool. Pour into 2 quart (2 L) jar.

Add rye and vanilla bean. Cover. Let stand for 3 weeks. Remove vanilla bean. Makes 12 cups (3 L) liqueur.

Pictured above.

Creamy Cranberry Punch

Very refreshing and not too sweet. Different from traditional clear punches.

Cranberry cocktail, chilled	1¹⁄₃ cups	325 mL
Frozen whole strawberries, thawed	20 oz.	600 g
Small bananas, cut up	3	3
Plain yogurt	1¹⁄₃ cups	325 mL
Granulated sugar	¹⁄₂ cup	125 mL
Cranberry cocktail, chilled	5¹⁄₂ cups	1.4 L
Prepared orange juice	¹⁄₃ cup	75 mL

Put first 5 ingredients in blender. Process until smooth. Pour into punch bowl.

Add remaining cranberry cocktail and orange juice. Stir. Makes 10 cups (2.5 L) punch.

Pictured above.

Champagne Punch

Keep champagne chilled and add just before serving for most bubbly effect.

Champagne or sparkling white wine	25 oz.	750 mL
Cointreau	6 oz.	170 mL
Ginger ale	8 cups	2 L
Orange or lime slices, for garnish		

Pour champagne, cointreau and ginger ale into punch bowl. Garnish with fruit slices or add Ice Ring, below. Makes 96 ounces (3 L) punch.

Pictured above.

Ice Ring

Fill a 3 or 4 cup (750 or 1 L) ring mold with sugar free ginger ale. Freeze. Do not use ginger ale with sugar as it melts quickly.

Perked Wassail

Very nice—warming! Great for a crowd after skiing or skating.
Or serve while you decorate the Christmas tree.

Oranges	2	2
Lemons	2	2
Water	2 cups	500 mL
Apple cider	4 qts.	4 L
Whole allspice	1 tbsp.	15 mL
Cinnamon sticks, 4 inch (10 cm)	3	3
Whole cloves	1 tsp.	5 mL
Reserved sliced oranges		
Reserved sliced lemons		
Granulated sugar	1 cup	250 mL
Boiling water	2 cups	500 mL

Squeeze oranges and lemons to get juice. Remove any seeds. Pour juices into percolator at least 24 cup (6 L) size. Slice remaining fruit and reserve. Add first amount of water and apple cider to percolator.

Put next 5 ingredients into coffee basket. Perk until hot.

Stir sugar in boiling water until dissolved. Pour into basket. Serve hot. Makes 25 cups (5.2 L).

Pictured on page 55.

Mulled Apple Drink

Nice amber color with a spicy taste.

Apple juice	4 cups	1 L
Brown sugar, packed	1/3 cup	75 mL
Salt	1/8 tsp.	0.5 mL
Whole cloves	6	6
Whole allspice	6	6
Cinnamon sticks, 4 inch (10 cm)	2	2

Measure all ingredients in large saucepan. Heat, stirring often until it comes to a boil. Simmer for 10 minutes. Strain into punch cups. Makes almost 4 cups (1 L).

Pictured on page 55.

Mulled Cranberry Juice

Double or triple this recipe. Beautiful red color.

Cranberry cocktail	4 cups	1 L
Lemon juice, fresh or bottled	2 tbsp.	30 mL
Granulated sugar	1/4 cup	60 mL
Whole allspice	10	10
Cinnamon stick, 4 inch (10 cm)	1	1

Combine all ingredients in saucepan. Bring to a boil. Boil 5 minutes. Pour through strainer into punch cups. Makes 4 cups (1 L).

Pictured on page 55.

French Silk Chocolate

Fluffy and light with a silky smooth texture.
Creamy chocolate flavor. Delicious.

Semisweet chocolate chips	3/4 cup	175 mL
White corn syrup	1/2 cup	125 mL
Water	1/3 cup	75 mL
Vanilla	1 tsp.	5 mL
Whipping cream	2 cups	500 mL
Milk	8 3/4 cups	2 L

Combine chocolate chips, syrup, water and vanilla in saucepan. Heat, stirring often, on low until smooth and all chocolate is melted. Refrigerate until cold.

Beat whipping cream until it is beginning to thicken just a little. Add chocolate mixture gradually while continuing to beat. Beat until mixture will mound. Chill.

Heat milk in heavy saucepan. Pour 6 ounces (175 mL) hot milk into mugs. Add chocolate mixture to taste. Stir well. An 8 oz. (250 mL) mug would take about 4 heaping tbsp. (60 mL). Makes 20 servings, 8 oz. (250 mL) each.

Pictured on page 55.

1. Mulled Cranberry Juice, page 54
2. Mulled Wine, page 52
3. Mulled Apple Drink, page 54
4. French Silk Chocolate, page 54
5. Perked Wassail, page 54

Left: Quick Fruit Punch with Punch Ice Ring   Right: Christmas Punch

Quick Fruit Punch

This recipe doubles easily. Nice and sweet for children and adults alike.

Canned cranberry jelly	14 oz.	398 mL
Granulated sugar	½ cup	125 mL
Boiling water	1 cup	250 mL
Prepared orange juice	½ cup	125 mL
Lemon juice, fresh or bottled	½ cup	125 mL
Cold water	2 cups	500 mL

Stir cranberry jelly, sugar and boiling water in bowl to dissolve sugar and melt jelly. Beat on medium if necessary.

Add remaining ingredients. Stir. Pour into punch bowl. Carefully add Punch Ice Ring, page 56. Makes 6½ cups (1.5 L).

Pictured above.

Rhubarb Cocktail

Lovely rosé color. Great and refreshing!

Finely chopped rhubarb, fresh or frozen	6 cups	1.5 L
Boiling water	6 cups	1.5 L
Frozen concentrated lemonade	12 oz.	355 mL
Lemonade cans of water	2	2
Granulated sugar	½ cup	125 mL
Ginger ale, chilled	9 cups	2.2 L

Measure rhubarb into large bowl. Pour boiling water over top. Cover. Let stand overnight. Strain through cheesecloth into pitcher. Store for a few hours or 5 to 6 days in the refrigerator or freeze until needed.

When ready to make punch, thaw rhubarb juice and pour into punch bowl. Stir in concentrated lemonade, cans of water and sugar. Stir until sugar dissolves. Chill.

To serve add ginger ale. Pour over ice in glasses. Makes 18 cups (4.5 L).

Pictured on page 69.

Christmas Punch

Beautiful Christmassy red. Double or triple this recipe.

Cranberry cocktail	8¾ cups	2 L
Frozen concentrated lemonade, thawed	12 oz.	340 mL
Lemon-lime soft drink	8¾ cups	2 L
Lime slices, orange slices, maraschino cherries, for garnish		

Stir cranberry cocktail, concentrated lemonade and lemon-lime soft drink together in punch bowl.

Float fruit slices or cherries on top. Makes 18 cups (4.5 L).

Pictured on this page.

Punch Ice Ring

Any assortment of fruit or glazed cherries can be used. Be creative.

Distilled water, 1 inch (2.5 cm) depth		
Strawberries, halved	4	4
Mandarin orange sections	8	8
Distilled water, ⅛ inch (3 mm) depth		
Distilled water, 1 inch (2.5 cm) depth		
Distilled water, 1 inch (2.5 cm) depth		

Pour first amount of water into ring pan using a salad mold or a bundt pan. Freeze.

Arrange strawberries, cut side down around top as well as orange sections and holly leaves. Pour just barely enough water to freeze them in place. If you add too much water at this stage, fruit will float. Freeze.

Pour third amount of water over fruit. Freeze.

Add final layer of water. Freeze. Unmold to use in punch. Makes 1 ring.

Pictured on this page.

Note: For less dilution of punch as ring thaws, use a sugar-free drink such as diet 7-UP or diet ginger ale. If you use a soft drink containing sugar, ice will thaw too fast.

Traditional Eggnog

Creamy, foamy layer on top. Just stir a bit if it lessens.

Egg whites, large	12	12
Granulated sugar	1 cup	250 mL
Egg yolks, large	12	12
Salt	1/2 tsp.	2 mL
Whipping cream	3 cups	750 mL
Granulated sugar	2 tbsp.	30 mL
Vanilla	1 tbsp.	15 mL
Milk	7 cups	1.75 L
Light rum	2 cups	500 mL
Whiskey (rye or scotch)	1 cup	250 mL

Nutmeg, sprinkle

Beat egg whites in large bowl until they start to thicken. Add first amount of sugar. Beat until thick.

In second large bowl beat egg yolks and salt until thick. Add egg whites. Beat until mixed and thick.

In third large bowl beat cream until it starts to thicken. Add remaining sugar and vanilla. Beat until thick. Add egg mixture slowly as you stir in.

Add milk, rum and whiskey, beating continually. Chill.

Serve in a punch bowl or a pitcher. Garnish with a sprinkle of nutmeg. Makes 20 cups (5 L).

Pictured below.

Traditional Eggnog

Coffee Nog

A wonderful combination of two favorite beverages.

Instant coffee granules	2 tbsp.	30 mL
Boiling water	2 tbsp.	30 mL
Eggnog	8 3/4 cups	2 L
Brown sugar, packed	1/3 cup	75 mL
Ground cinnamon	1/4 tsp.	1 mL
Kahlua or Tia Maria liqueur, (optional)	1 cup	250 mL
Topping:		
Whipping cream (or 1 envelope topping)	1 cup	250 mL
Granulated sugar	1 tbsp.	15 mL
Vanilla	1/2 tsp.	2 mL

Nutmeg, sprinkle

Stir coffee granules into boiling water in large bowl. Add eggnog, brown sugar and cinnamon. Beat to dissolve sugar. Stir in Kahlua. Pour into punch bowl.

Topping: Beat cream, sugar and vanilla until thick. Spoon over top.

Sprinkle whipped cream with nutmeg. Makes about 18 servings 5 oz. (140 mL) each or 10 cups (2.5 L).

Pictured on page 72.

Easy Eggnog

Very easy to prepare. Not quite as rich as the Traditional Eggnog on this page.

Large eggs	12	12
Granulated sugar	1 1/2 cups	375 mL
Salt	3/4 tsp.	4 mL
Homogenized milk (for richness)	12 cups	3 L
Vanilla	3 tbsp.	50 mL
Brandy (see Note)	2 cups	500 mL
Rum (see Note)	1/2 cup	125 mL

Ground nutmeg, sprinkle

Beat eggs in extra large bowl until light. Continue beating while adding sugar and salt gradually. Beat until sugar is dissolved.

Add milk and vanilla. Add brandy and rum. Adjust strength by increasing or decreasing liquor. Stir. May be refrigerated up to 24 hours before serving or stored, covered, in refrigerator for 6 days. To serve, run through blender to foam.

Garnish with a sprinkle of nutmeg. Makes 28 servings, 5 oz. (140 mL) each.

Note: Liquor may be left out and 5-6 tbsp. (75 to 100 mL) rum flavoring added instead.

Pictured on page 72.

Breads & Quick Breads

Bread is important all year. But at Christmas this staple becomes as special as the season itself.

A yeast bread woven into a wreath has a place of its own on a holiday brunch or supper table. Breads filled with cherries, raisins and other goodies are just as enticing to the eye as they are to the palate. Quick breads like tea loaves and muffins are easy to make and wonderfully convenient for drop-in guests.

So don't overlook the potential of the bread group and do make room for these special breads and quick breads.

Table Bread Wreath

Very attractive. Use for a buffet or brunch.

Warm water	1 cup	225 mL
Granulated sugar	2 tsp.	10 mL
Active dry yeast	2 × ¼ oz.	2 × 8 g
Butter or hard margarine, softened	¾ cup	175 mL
Granulated sugar	½ cup	125 mL
Large eggs	2	2
Salt	1 tsp.	5 mL
All-purpose flour	2 cups	450 mL
Cut glazed mixed fruit	1 cup	250 mL
Raisins	½ cup	125 mL
All-purpose flour, approximately	2¾ cups	625 mL
Large egg, fork-beaten	1	1
Glaze:		
Icing (confectioner's) sugar	1½ cups	375 mL
Water	2½ tbsp.	40 mL
Vanilla	½ tsp.	2 mL
Glazed red or green cherries, for garnish		
Chopped walnuts, for garnish		

Stir warm water and first amount of sugar in small bowl. Sprinkle yeast over top. Let stand 10 minutes. Stir.

Cream butter and second amount of sugar in large bowl. Beat in eggs 1 at a time. Add salt and yeast mixture. Add first amount of flour. Beat on medium about 2 minutes until smooth.

Mix in glazed fruit and raisins. Work in remaining flour with a spoon. Turn out onto lightly floured surface. Knead for 5 to 8 minutes until smooth and elastic. Put into large greased bowl, turning once to grease top. Cover with tea towel. Let stand in oven with light on and door closed for about 2 hours until doubled in bulk.

Punch dough down. Divide into 3 equal portions. Roll each portion on lightly floured surface until it reaches 2 feet (60 cm) in length. Pinch 3 ends together on greased baking sheet. Braid the 3 ropes. Shape into a wreath, joining ends and pinching together. Cover with tea towel. Let stand in oven with light on and door closed for about 1 hour until doubled in size. Brush with beaten egg. Bake in 375°F (190°C) oven for 40 to 45 minutes until browned. Cool on rack.

Glaze: Mix icing sugar, water and vanilla, adding more water if needed to make a barely pourable glaze. Brush over wreath.

Garnish with cherries or nuts. Makes 1 wreath.

Pictured on this page and on front cover.

Table Bread Wreath

Christmas Braid

Rich golden appearance. Not too sweet. Very showy.

Granulated sugar	1 tsp.	5 mL
Warm water	¼ cup	60 mL
Active dry yeast	1 x ¼ oz.	1 x 8 g
Milk, scalded and cooled to lukewarm	1½ cups	375 mL
Salt	1 tsp.	5 mL
Butter or hard margarine	¼ cup	60 mL
Granulated sugar	6 tbsp.	100 mL
Large egg, beaten	1	1
Cardamom	¼ tsp.	1 mL
All-purpose flour	3 cups	750 mL
All-purpose flour, approximately	2½ cups	625 mL
Large egg, beaten	1	1

Stir first amount of sugar into warm water in small bowl. Sprinkle yeast over top. Let stand for 10 minutes. Stir to dissolve yeast.

Measure next 6 ingredients into large bowl. Mix. Add yeast mixture. Stir well.

Mix in first amount of flour.

Work in enough remaining flour as needed to make a soft dough. Place in greased bowl, turning once to grease top. Cover with greased waxed paper and tea towel. Let stand in oven with light on and door closed for about 1½ hours until doubled in bulk. Punch dough down. Using about ½ the dough, roll into rectangle 10 x 15 inches (25 x 38 cm). Place on greased baking sheet.

Prepare Prune Filling, below. Spread ½ down center using ⅓ of space. Cut sides almost to filling in strips about 1 inch (2.5 cm) wide. Turn each side strip over filling alternately as though braiding. Seal ends. Repeat with remaining dough and filling. Cover with greased waxed paper and tea towel. Let stand in oven with light on and door closed for about 40 minutes until doubled in size. Brush with beaten egg. Bake in 350°F (175°C) oven for 30 to 40 minutes. Decorate with Glaze, page 58 and cherries.

Pictured on this page.

Prune Filling

Dry pitted prunes	3 cups	750 mL
Water	½ cup	125 mL
Chopped walnuts	¾ cup	175 mL
Ground cinnamon	½ tsp.	2 mL

Simmer prunes in water for 10 to 15 minutes. Drain. Mash slightly. Stir in walnuts and cinnamon. Cool completely. Makes 3 cups (750 mL), enough for 2 Christmas Braids.

Pictured on this page.

Christmas Braid with Prune Filling

Potato Rolls

Golden brown rolls. Good with any meat or casserole.

Butter or hard margarine	½ cup	125 mL
Granulated sugar	½ cup	125 mL
Salt	½ tsp.	2 mL
Hot potato water, drained from cooked potatoes	1 cup	250 mL
Granulated sugar	1 tsp.	5 mL
Warm water	¼ cup	60 mL
Envelope active dry yeast	1 x ¼ oz.	1 x 8 g
Large eggs, fork beaten	2	2
All-purpose flour	4 cups	1 L

Stir first 4 ingredients together in large bowl until butter is dissolved. Set aside to cool to lukewarm.

Stir second amount of sugar into warm water in small bowl. Sprinkle yeast over top. Let stand 10 minutes. Stir to dissolve yeast. Add to potato mixture.

Beat in eggs. Add flour. Mix. Knead on floured surface about 7 to 10 minutes until smooth and elastic. Place in greased bowl, turning once to grease top. Cover with tea towel. Let stand in oven with light on and door closed about 2 hours until doubled in bulk. Punch dough down. Shape into rolls the size of eggs. Arrange on greased baking sheet. Cover with tea towel. Let stand in oven with light on and door closed about 1 hour until doubled in size. Bake in 350°F (175°C) oven for 15 to 18 minutes. Makes 24 rolls.

Pictured on page 141.

Holiday Brunch Cake

A real winner! Make this ahead and freeze.
Glaze just before serving.

Frozen bread loaves, thawed	2	2
Butter or hard margarine, softened	2 tbsp.	30 mL
Granulated sugar	½ cup	125 mL
Ground cinnamon	1 tsp.	5 mL
Chopped red glazed cherries	⅔ cup	150 mL
Butter or hard margarine, softened	2 tbsp.	30 mL
Large egg, beaten	1	1
Sliced almonds	⅓ cup	75 mL
Icing Drizzle:		
Icing (confectioner's) sugar	1 cup	250 mL
Vanilla	¼ tsp.	1 mL
Water	1 tbsp.	15 mL

Combine the 2 loaves then divide into 3 equal portions. Roll out 1 portion to fit greased 12 inch (30 cm) deep dish pizza pan.

Spread with first amount of butter.

Mix sugar, cinnamon and cherries in small bowl. Sprinkle ½ over first dough layer in pan. Roll out second portion. Lay it over top.

Spread with second amount of butter. Scatter second ½ cherry mixture over top. Roll out third portion of dough. Place over top. Position a 2 to 2½ inch (5 to 6.5 cm) cookie cutter in center of top. Mark dough in quarters, then mark each quarter in 4 wedges. This makes a total of 16 wedges. Using a sharp knife cut through marks to the bottom, taking care not to cut past the cookie cutter. Twist each wedge 5 times and arc slightly, twisting all in the same direction. Cover with greased waxed paper and tea towel. Let stand in oven with light on and door closed about 1 hour until doubled in size.

Brush with egg. Sprinkle with almonds. Bake in 375°F (190°C) oven for about 30 minutes until golden brown.

Icing Drizzle: Mix all ingredients together, adding more water if needed to make a drizzle consistency. Drizzle over warm coffee cake. Serve warm or cold. Makes 1 coffee cake.

Pictured on page 69.

Easy Overnight Buns

Have lots of these in the freezer for holiday guests.

All-purpose flour	2 cups	500 mL
Butter or hard margarine, softened	½ cup	125 mL
Granulated sugar	½ cup	125 mL
Large egg	1	1
Cold water	2 cups	500 mL
Salt	½ tsp.	2 mL
Baking powder	½ tsp.	2 mL
Active dry yeast	1 × ¼ oz.	1 × 8 g
All-purpose flour, approximately	4 cups	1 L

Put first 5 ingredients into large bowl. Beat slowly to moisten.

Sprinkle with salt, baking powder and yeast. Let stand for 1 minute. Beat well.

Work in enough remaining flour to make a stiff dough. Place in greased bowl, turning once to grease top. Cover with greased waxed paper and tea towel. Let stand on counter overnight. In the morning punch down dough. Shape into buns, using greased palms if necessary. Arrange in greased pan. Let stand in oven with light on and door closed for 2 to 3 hours until doubled in size. Bake in 375°F (190°C) oven for about 35 to 40 minutes until golden brown. Yield: about 20 medium buns.

Pictured on page 137.

Christmas Tree Buns, page 61

Christmas Tree Buns

Pretty as a picture for Christmas buffet or brunch table.

Granulated sugar	1 tsp.	5 mL
Warm water	¼ cup	60 mL
Active dry yeast	1 × ¼ oz.	1 × 8 g
Milk, scalded and cooled to lukewarm	1½ cups	375 mL
Salt	1 tsp.	5 mL
Butter or hard margarine, melted	¼ cup	60 mL
Granulated sugar	6 tbsp.	100 mL
Large egg, beaten	1	1
Cardamom	¼ tsp.	1 mL
All-purpose flour	3 cups	750 mL
Currants or dark raisins	¼ cup	60 mL
Sultana raisins	½ cup	125 mL
Cut mixed glazed fruit	½ cup	125 mL
All-purpose flour, approximately	2½ cups	625 mL
Candied cherries, for garnish	¼ cup	60 mL

Stir first amount of sugar into water in small bowl. Sprinkle yeast over top. Let stand 10 minutes. Stir.

Mix next 6 ingredients in large bowl. Add yeast mixture. Stir.

Beat in first amount of flour.

Add currants, sultana raisins and fruit. Stir.

Work in enough flour as needed to make a soft dough. Knead until smooth and elastic. Place in greased bowl turning once to grease top. Cover with tea towel. Let stand in oven with light on and door closed for about 1½ hours until doubled in bulk. Punch dough down. Make into small buns. Arrange on greased baking sheet in shape of a Christmas tree. Set buns fairly close together allowing some room to rise. Let stand in oven with light on and door closed about 1 hour until doubled in size. Bake in 350°F (175°C) oven for 30 to 40 minutes until golden. Cool. Ice thinly or drizzle with Glaze, page 59.

Use candied cherries to garnish tree. Makes 2 large trees.

Pictured on page 60.

Drop Cheese Biscuits

Light and flaky texture. So easy and quick to make.

All-purpose flour	2 cups	500 mL
Baking powder	4 tsp.	20 mL
Salt	¾ tsp.	4 mL
Butter or hard margarine	½ cup	125 mL
Water	1 cup	250 mL
Grated sharp Cheddar cheese	1½ cups	375 mL

Measure flour, baking powder and salt into medium bowl. Cut in butter until crumbly.

Add water and cheese. Stir to moisten. Drop by rounded tablespoonfuls about 2 inches (5 cm) apart onto greased baking sheet. Bake in 425°F (220°C) oven for about 15 minutes. Makes 16 biscuits.

Pictured below.

Left: Raisin Biscuits, page 62   Right: Drop Cheese Biscuits, page 61
Top Center: Lemon Spread, page 66

Banana Bran Nut Loaf

Moist and delicious and so nutritious.

Butter or hard margarine, softened	¼ cup	60 mL
Granulated sugar	¼ cup	125 mL
Large egg	1	1
All-bran cereal (100%)	1 cup	250 mL
Mashed banana (3 large, or 4 medium)	1½ cups	375 mL
Chopped pecans or walnuts	½ cup	125 mL
Vanilla	1 tsp.	5 mL
All-purpose flour	1½ cups	375 mL
Baking powder	2 tsp.	10 mL
Baking soda	½ tsp.	2 mL
Salt	½ tsp.	2 mL

Cream butter and sugar in large bowl. Beat in egg.

Add cereal, banana, pecans and vanilla. Beat until smooth.

Stir flour, baking powder, baking soda and salt together in separate bowl. Add. Stir or beat on lowest speed just to moisten. Turn into greased 9 x 5 x 3 inch (22 x 12 x 7 cm) loaf pan. Bake in 350°F (175°C) oven for about 1 hour until an inserted wooden pick comes out clean. Let stand for 15 minutes. Turn out onto rack to cool. Makes 1 loaf.

Pictured on page 63.

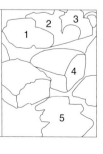

Eggnog Bread

Eggnog flavor comes through nicely.

Granulated sugar	1 cup	250 mL
Large egg	1	1
Butter or hard margarine, melted	¼ cup	60 mL
Egg nog	1½ cups	375 mL
All-purpose flour	3 cups	750 mL
Baking powder	1 tbsp.	15 mL
Salt	1 tsp.	5 mL
Cinnamon	½ tsp.	2 mL
Nutmeg	½ tsp.	2 mL
Chopped pecans or walnuts	⅔ cup	150 mL
Cut glazed mixed fruit	1 cup	250 mL

Beat sugar and egg in mixing bowl. Beat in melted butter. Add egg nog. Mix.

Sift flour, baking powder, salt, cinnamon and nutmeg over egg nog mixture. Stir until moistened.

Mix in pecans and fruit. Turn into greased 9 x 5 x 3 inch (22 x 12 x 7 cm) loaf pan. Bake in 350°F (175°C) oven for about 1 hour until an inserted wooden pick comes out clean. Let stand 20 minutes. Turn out onto rack to cool. Makes 1 loaf.

Pictured on page 63.

Raisin Biscuits

Nice flaky layer. Serve with cheese slices.

All-purpose flour	3 cups	750 mL
Granulated sugar	2 tbsp.	30 mL
Cream of tartar	2 tsp.	10 mL
Baking powder	1 tbsp.	15 mL
Baking soda	1 tsp.	5 mL
Salt	1 tsp.	5 mL
Ground cinnamon	½-1 tsp.	2-5 mL
Butter or hard margarine	½ cup	125 mL
Raisins or currants	1 cup	250 mL
Milk	1⅓ cups	325 mL

Measure first 7 ingredients into bowl. Stir well.

Cut butter into flour mixture until crumbly.

Add raisins and milk. Stir with a fork to form a soft ball. Knead on lightly floured surface 8 to 10 times. Roll or pat dough 1 inch (2.5 cm) thick. Cut into 2½ inch (6 cm) circles. Arrange about 2 inches (5 cm) apart on greased baking sheet. Bake in 425°F (220°C) oven for 20 to 30 minutes until risen and browned. Serve warm with butter, jam or Lemon Spread, page 66. Makes 18 biscuits.

Pictured on page 61.

Left: Lemon Cheese Loaf, page 64 Top Center: Raspberry Cream Muffins, page 67
Bottom Center: Holiday Banana Loaf, page 64 Right: Cherry Pound Cake, page 64

Lemon Cheese Loaf

Flavor is tangy. Texture is moist. Cream cheese cubes show evenly throughout.

Butter or hard margarine, softened	¹/₂ cup	125 mL
Granulated sugar	1¹/₄ cups	300 mL
Large eggs	2	2
Milk	³/₄ cup	175 mL
Grated rind of 1 lemon		
All-purpose flour	2 cups	450 mL
Baking powder	2 tsp.	10 mL
Salt	³/₄ tsp.	4 mL
Cream cheese, cut in ¹/₄ inch (6 mm) cubes	8 oz.	250 g
Chopped walnuts	¹/₂ cup	125 mL
Topping:		
Juice of 1 lemon		
Granulated sugar	¹/₄ cup	60 mL

Cream butter and sugar. Beat in eggs 1 at a time. Mix in milk and lemon rind.

Stir flour, baking powder and salt together in bowl. Add to batter. Stir just to moisten.

Fold in cream cheese and walnuts. Turn into greased 9 x 5 x 3 inch (22 x 12 x 7 cm) loaf pan. Bake in 350°F (175°C) oven for about 1 hour and 20 minutes, until an inserted wooden pick comes out clean.

Topping: Stir lemon juice and sugar in small saucepan. Heat and stir until sugar dissolves. Poke 8 or 10 holes in top of loaf with toothpick. Spoon syrup over hot loaf. Let stand for 10 minutes. Turn out onto rack to cool. Makes 1 loaf.

Pictured above.

Holiday Banana Loaf

Double this recipe to have enough for smaller gift loaves.

Butter or hard margarine, softened	¹/₂ cup	125 mL
Granulated sugar	1 cup	250 mL
Large eggs	2	2
Vanilla	1 tsp.	5 mL
All-purpose flour	1³/₄ cups	425 mL
Baking soda	1 tsp.	5 mL
Baking powder	1 tsp.	5 mL
Salt	¹/₂ tsp.	2 mL
Chopped walnuts	¹/₄ cup	60 mL
Fine coconut	¹/₂ cup	125 mL
Chopped cherries	¹/₂ cup	125 mL
All-purpose flour	¹/₄ cup	60 mL
Mashed banana (about 3)	1 cup	250 mL

Cream butter and sugar well. Beat in eggs, 1 at a time, beating well after each addition. Add vanilla. Stir.

Measure first amount of flour, baking soda, baking powder and salt into separate bowl. Stir.

Toss walnuts, coconut and cherries with second amount of flour in third bowl.

Add flour in 4 additions alternately with banana in 3 additions, beginning and ending with flour. Add fruit mixture. Mix only until blended. Do not over mix. Turn into greased 9 x 5 x 3 inch (22 x 12 x 7 cm) loaf pans. Bake in 350°F (175°C) oven for 50 to 60 minutes until an inserted wooden pick comes out clean. Let stand for 20 minutes. Turn out onto rack to cool. Makes 1 loaf.

Pictured on this page.

Cherry Pound Cake

Rich and buttery. Very colorful.

Butter or margarine, softened	1 cup	250 mL
Granulated sugar	1 cup	250 mL
Large eggs	3	3
All-purpose flour	2¹/₄ cups	550 mL
Glazed red and green cherries, halved	1 cup	250

Cream butter and sugar in large bowl until light and fluffy. Beat in eggs 1 at a time.

Mix flour and cherries in separate bowl to coat cherries. Stir into butter mixture until moistened. Turn into greased 9 x 5 x 3 inch (22 x 12 x 7 cm) loaf pan. Bake in 325°F (160°C) oven for 1 to 1¹/₄ hours until an inserted wooden pick comes out clean. Turn out onto rack to cool. Makes 1 loaf.

Pictured on this page.

Strawberry Bread

Light cake-like texture. Flecks of red jam throughout.

Butter or hard margarine	½ cup	125 mL
Granulated sugar	¾ cup	175 mL
Large eggs	2	2
Vanilla	¾ tsp.	4 mL
Lemon juice, fresh or bottled	¼ tsp.	1 mL
Strawberry jam, stirred	⅓ cup	75 mL
Sour cream	¼ cup	60 mL
All-purpose flour	1½ cups	350 mL
Cream of tartar	½ tsp.	2 mL
Baking soda	¼ tsp.	1 mL

Cream butter and sugar well in mixing bowl. Beat in eggs 1 at a time, beating well after each addition. Mix in vanilla and lemon juice.

Stir jam and sour cream together in small bowl .

Sift remaining 3 ingredients together. Add flour mixture in 3 parts alternately with jam mixture in 2 parts, beginning and ending with flour mixture. Stir only enough to moisten. Turn into greased 8 x 4 x 3 inch (20 x 10 x 7 cm) loaf pan. Bake in 350°F (175°C) oven for about 55 to 60 minutes until an inserted wooden pick comes out clean. Let stand for 20 minutes. Turn out onto rack to cool. Makes 1 loaf.

Pictured below.

Chocolate Zucchini Loaf

Make several in the fall when zucchini are more plentiful. Freeze and bring out for Christmas.

Butter or hard margarine, softened	6 tbsp.	100 mL
Granulated sugar	1 cup	225 mL
Large egg	1	1
Vanilla	1 tsp.	5 mL
Grated zucchini, with peel	1 cup	250 mL
All-purpose flour	1½ cups	375 mL
Cocoa	¼ cup	60 mL
Baking powder	1¼ tsp.	6 mL
Baking soda	¾ tsp.	4 mL
Salt	½ tsp.	2 mL
Ground cinnamon	½ tsp.	2 mL
Milk	¼ cup	60 mL
Chopped walnuts	½ cup	125 mL

Cream butter and sugar in mixing bowl. Beat in egg. Add vanilla and zucchini. Stir with spoon.

Add next 6 ingredients. Stir to moisten.

Add milk and walnuts. Stir slowly to mix in. Turn into greased 9 x 5 x 3 inch (20 x 12 x 7 cm) loaf pan. Bake in 350°F (175°C) oven for about 60 minutes. An inserted wooden pick should come out clean. Let stand for 10 minutes. Turn out onto rack to cool. Makes 1 loaf.

Pictured below.

Left: Strawberry Bread
Right: Chocolate Zucchini Loaf

Easy Cinnamon Knots

Experiment with different types of knots or twists.
These will be popular.

Water	2²/₃ cups	650 mL
Granulated sugar	²/₃ cup	150 mL
Cooking oil	²/₃ cup	150 mL
Salt	1¼ tsp.	6 mL
All-purpose flour	2 cups	250 mL
Instant yeast	2 tbsp.	30 mL
Large eggs	4	4
All-purpose flour, approximately	7½ cups	1.8 L
Coating:		
Ground cinnamon	3 tbsp.	50 mL
Granulated sugar	3 cups	750 mL
Butter or hard margarine, melted	1 cup	250 mL

Heat first 4 ingredients in large saucepan stirring until sugar is dissolved. It should be very warm but you should be able to hold your hand on side of pan.

Stir first amount of flour with yeast in medium bowl. Add to warm mixture. Stir.

Beat eggs in small bowl. Stir into batter in saucepan.

Add enough remaining flour until it pulls away from sides of bowl. Place in greased bowl, turning once to grease top. Cover with greased waxed paper and tea towel. Let stand in oven with light on and door closed for about 25 minutes until doubled in bulk. Punch dough down. Divide dough into 4 equal portions. Roll each into a rope. Mark off and cut each rope into 12 pieces. Roll each piece into a 10 inch (25 cm) rope.

Coating: Mix cinnamon and sugar. Brush working surface with butter. Roll each rope in butter to grease, then in cinnamon mixture. Tie each rope into a loose knot. Arrange on greased baking sheets. Cover with tea towel. Let stand in oven with light on and door closed about 30 minutes until doubled in size. Bake in 350°F (175°C) oven for 20 to 25 minutes. Makes 4 dozen buns.

Pictured below.

Easy Cinnamon Knots

Carrot Pineapple Muffins

Golden with flecks of carrot and pineapple showing.
Good all year round.

All-purpose flour	2 cups	500 mL
Granulated sugar	³/₄ cup	175 mL
Baking powder	1 tsp.	5 mL
Baking soda	1 tsp.	5 mL
Ground cinnamon	1 tsp.	5 mL
Salt	½ tsp.	2 mL
Large eggs, well-beaten	2	2
Cooking oil	½ cup	125 mL
Finely grated carrot	1 cup	250 mL
Crushed pineapple, with juice	½ cup	125 mL
Vanilla	1 tsp.	5 mL

Mix first 6 ingredients in large bowl.

Add eggs, cooking oil, carrot, pineapple, juice and vanilla. Beat on low until just moistened. Spoon into greased muffin cups, filling ²/₃ full. Bake in 350°F (175°C) oven for 20 to 25 minutes. Makes 12 muffins.

Pictured on page 63.

Bake muffins in pretty "Christmas theme" paper muffin cups. Do not grease muffin pans. Place 1 or 2 papers in each cup. Fill and bake according to recipe. Remove immediately from muffin pan to minimize moisture build-up on paper.

Lemon Spread

So refreshing. A nice change from butter and jam.

Hard margarine, softened	½ cup	125 mL
Granulated sugar	½ cup	125 mL
Finely grated rind of 1 orange		
Finely grated rind of 1 lemon		
Juice of 1 orange		
Juice of 1 lemon		

Beat margarine in small bowl until light-colored. Add sugar very gradually while beating. Add rinds and juices. Spread on raisin bread, Raisin Biscuits, page 62, or Welsh Cakes, page 45. Makes 1 cup (250 mL) spread.

Pictured on page 61.

Christmas Fruit Muffins

Fill a basket with these for Christmas morning breakfast. Very colorful.

All-purpose flour	1¾ cups	425 mL
Baking powder	1 tsp.	5 mL
Baking soda	1 tsp.	5 mL
Salt	½ tsp.	2 mL
Glazed red pineapple ring, diced	1	1
Glazed green pineapple ring, diced	1	1
Glazed yellow pineapple ring, diced	1	1
Chopped pecans	½ cup	125 mL
Butter or hard margarine, softened	½ cup	125 mL
Granulated sugar	1 cup	250 mL
Large eggs	2	2
Vanilla	1 tsp.	5 mL
Milk	⅔ cup	150 mL

Measure first 8 ingredients into large bowl. Stir. Make a well in center.

Cream butter and sugar in separate bowl. Beat in eggs 1 at a time. Add vanilla and milk. Stir. Pour into well. Stir just to moisten. Fill greased muffin cups almost full. Bake in 400°F (205°C) oven for 15 to 20 minutes until an inserted wooden pick comes out clean. Let stand 5 minutes before removing from pan. Makes 12 muffins.

Pictured on page 63.

Cranberry Orange Muffins

The melding of these flavors is wonderful.

Large egg	1	1
Cooking oil	¼ cup	60 mL
Granulated sugar	½ cup	125 mL
Chopped cranberries	1 cup	250 mL
Grated rind of 1 large orange		
Juice of 1 large orange, plus water to make	¾ cup	175 mL
All-purpose flour	2 cups	500 mL
Baking powder	2 tsp.	10 mL
Baking soda	½ tsp.	2 mL
Salt	½ tsp.	2 mL

Beat egg in large bowl. Add cooking oil and sugar. Beat to mix. Add cranberries, orange rind and juice. Stir.

Stir flour, baking powder, baking soda and salt together in separate bowl. Add to liquid ingredients. Stir just to moisten. Fill greased muffin cups almost full. Bake in 400°F (175°C) oven for 15 to 20 minutes. Let stand 5 minutes before removing from pan. Makes 12 muffins.

Pictured on page 63.

Raspberry Cream Muffins

Raspberry Cream Muffins

Strong raspberry flavor and red Christmas color. Serve at brunch, afternoon tea or as a late evening snack.

All-purpose flour	2 cups	500 mL
Baking powder	1 tsp.	5 mL
Baking soda	½ tsp.	2 mL
Salt	½ tsp.	2 mL
Ground cinnamon	¼ tsp.	1 mL
Butter or hard margarine, softened	½ cup	125 mL
Granulated sugar	⅔ cup	150 mL
Large eggs	2	2
Sour cream	½ cup	125 mL
Vanilla	1 tsp.	5 mL
Coarsely chopped frozen raspberries	1 cup	250 mL

Measure first 5 ingredients in bowl. Stir well.

Beat butter and sugar in medium bowl. Beat in eggs 1 at a time. Add sour cream and vanilla. Beat to mix. Add flour mixture. Stir just until moistened.

Fold in raspberries. Fill greased muffin cups almost full. Bake in 350°F (175°C) oven for 30 to 35 minutes until golden. An inserted wooden pick should come out clean. Let stand 10 minutes. Remove from pan to cool on rack. Makes 12 large muffins.

Pictured above and on page 64.

Brunches

Well-suited to hectic holiday schedules, the brunch bypasses those busy evenings, drawing on the late morning and early afternoon hours instead. It's a great way to bring family and friends together on Boxing Day and other special days over the Yuletide season.

Because it combines breakfast and lunch dishes, the brunch offers great scope. Hot and cold entrées, salads, breads and sweets are all welcome on the brunch table.

Call on the various sample menus we've included (page 28-31) to help you put your holiday brunch together, or explore the other sections of our book for more recipe suggestions.

Left: Make-Ahead Eggs Benedict, page 68
Bottom Center: Holiday Brunch Cake, page 60

Make-Ahead Eggs Benedict

Yes, the poached eggs are still slightly runny when served! This is a Christmas morning tradition!

English muffins, split	4	4
Bacon slices	16	16
Water		
Large eggs	8	8
Sauce:		
Butter or hard margarine	¼ cup	60 mL
All-purpose flour	¼ cup	60 mL
Paprika	1 tsp.	5 mL
Pepper	¼ tsp.	1 mL
Ground nutmeg	⅛ tsp.	0.5 mL
Milk	2 cups	450 mL
Grated Swiss cheese	2 cups	450 mL
White wine (or alcohol-free)	½ cup	125 mL
Topping:		
Butter or hard margarine	1 tbsp.	15 mL
Crushed corn flakes	½ cup	125 mL

Arrange muffin halves, cut side up, in greased 9 x 13 inch (22 x 33 cm) pan.

Fry bacon in frying pan until crisp. Blot on paper towel. Put 2 slices on each muffin half.

Heat water in large saucepan until it simmers. Carefully break in eggs to poach until just set. Transfer and center each egg on bacon using slotted spoon.

Sauce: Melt butter in saucepan. Mix in flour, paprika, pepper and nutmeg. Stir in milk until it boils and thickens.

Add cheese and wine. Stir until cheese melts. Spoon sauce over eggs.

Topping: Melt butter in small saucepan. Stir in corn flakes. Sprinkle over top of sauce. Cover and chill overnight. In the morning, remove cover. Bake in 375°F (190°C) oven for 20 to 25 minutes until heated through. Makes 8 servings.

Pictured above.

Top Center: Rhubarb Cocktail, page 56
Right: Quick Fruit Bowl, page 69

Quick Fruit Bowl

*This is a mix and match delight! Sauce adds just
the right sweetness.*

Canned sliced peaches or apricots, drained, juice reserved	14 oz.	398 mL
Canned pineapple chunks, drained, juice reserved	14 oz.	398 mL
Canned pears, drained, juice reserved	14 oz.	398 mL
Canned mandarin orange sections, drained, juice discarded	12 oz.	341 mL
Canned grapefruit sections, drained, juice discarded	14 oz.	398 mL
Maraschino cherries, halved or quartered	15	15
Reserved juices plus water, if needed, to make	2 cups	450 mL
Cornstarch	2 tbsp.	30 mL
Granulated sugar	1/4 cup	60 mL

Place sliced peaches into bowl. May be cut in half crosswise for smaller pieces. Add pineapple chunks. Slice pears, cutting in half crosswise for smaller pieces if desired. Add orange sections. Add grapefruit, cutting in half crosswise for smaller pieces, if desired. Add cherries. Toss.

Stir reserved juices, cornstarch and sugar in saucepan. Heat and stir until it boils and thickens. Cool. Stir into fruit. Add more drained fruit, if desired. Makes 5 cups (1.1 L).

Pictured above.

Gourmet Burgers

These are real winners! A nice change of flavor from ordinary hamburgers.

Lean ground beef	1 lb.	454 g
Finely chopped onion	⅔ cup	150 mL
Finely chopped celery	¾ cup	175 mL
Salted soda crackers, crushed	7	7
Hand-crushed corn flakes	1 cup	250 mL
Large egg	1	1
Plum sauce	1 tbsp.	15 mL
Hickory smoke sauce (liquid smoke)	2 tsp.	10 mL
Soy sauce	1 tsp.	5 mL
Whole oregano	½ tsp.	2 mL
Salt	½ tsp.	2 mL
Pepper	¼ tsp.	1 mL
All-purpose flour	1 tbsp.	15 mL
Hamburger buns, split and buttered	6	6
Condiments such as ketchup, relish, cheese, tomatoes, pickles		

Combine first 5 ingredients in bowl. Mix well.

Beat egg with fork in small bowl. Add next 7 ingredients. Beat well with fork. Add to beef and mix in. Shape into 6 patties. Let stand in refrigerator for at least 1 hour before cooking to allow flavors to mingle. Fry or grill about 3 minutes per side until no pink remains in meat.

Insert 1 patty in each bun. Let everyone help themselves to the condiments. Makes 6 burgers.

Pictured on page 75.

Blueberry Streusel Cake

Blueberry Streusel Cake

Wrap well and freeze ahead of time. Take out of freezer the night before your brunch. Heat just before serving.

Butter or hard margarine, softened	½ cup	125 mL
Granulated sugar	¾ cup	175 mL
Large eggs	3	3
Vanilla	1 tsp.	5 mL
Milk	1 cup	250 mL
All-purpose flour	3 cups	750 mL
Baking powder	1 tbsp.	15 mL
Ground cinnamon	1½ tsp.	7 mL
Ground nutmeg	1 tsp.	5 mL
Salt	1 tsp.	5 mL
Blueberries (thaw if using frozen)	3 cups	750 mL
Streusel Topping:		
All-purpose flour	¾ cup	175 mL
Quick cooking rolled oats	¾ cup	175 mL
Brown sugar, packed	¾ cup	175 mL
Butter or hard margarine	½ cup	125 mL

Cream butter and sugar in mixing bowl. Beat in eggs 1 at a time. Add vanilla and milk. Mix.

Add flour, baking powder, cinnamon, nutmeg and salt. Stir slowly to moisten. Continue to stir until smooth. Spread in greased 9 x 13 inch (22 x 33 cm) pan.

Sprinkle with blueberries.

Streusel Topping: Measure flour, rolled oats and brown sugar into bowl. Cut in butter until crumbly. Spread over blueberries. Bake in 350°F (175°C) oven for 40 to 50 minutes. Serves 15.

Pictured on this page.

Pastry Biscuits

These look like cookies but taste like biscuits. Serve with jam or jelly.

Butter or hard margarine, softened	½ cup	125 mL
Cream cheese, softened	4 oz.	125 g
All-purpose flour	1 cup	250 mL

Cream butter and cream cheese well. Mix in flour. Shape into 1 roll about 1½ inches (4 cm) in diameter and 7 inches (18 cm) long. Roll up in waxed paper. Chill all day or overnight in refrigerator. Cut into ¼ inch (6 mm) slices. Place on ungreased cookie sheet. Bake in 400°F (205°C) oven for about 10 minutes until browned. Makes 20 to 24 biscuits.

Pictured on page 72.

Cranberry Corn Bread

So quick to make. Savory corn bread flavor with the sweetness of cranberry. Freezes well.

Butter or hard margarine, melted	6 tbsp.	100 mL
Brown sugar, packed	½ cup	125 mL
Large egg	1	1
Buttermilk, fresh or reconstituted from powder	1 cup	250 mL
Coarsely chopped cranberries	1 cup	250 mL
Cornmeal (yellow)	1 cup	250 mL
All-purpose flour	1 cup	250 mL
Baking powder	1 tbsp.	15 mL
Salt	½ tsp.	2 mL
Chopped walnuts	⅔ cup	150 mL

Beat melted butter, brown sugar and egg together in mixing bowl. Mix in buttermilk. Add cranberries. Stir.

Add cornmeal, flour, baking powder and salt. Stir to moisten. Turn into greased 9 x 9 inch (22 x 22 cm) pan.

Sprinkle with walnuts. Bake in 400°F (205°C) oven for about 25 minutes until an inserted wooden pick comes out clean. Best served warm. Cuts into 16 pieces.

Pictured above.

Baked Omelet

Lovely golden brown on top. Serve with a tossed lettuce or spinach salad and rolls or toast.

Cream Sauce:		
Butter or hard margarine	6 tbsp.	100 mL
All-purpose flour	½ cup	125 mL
Salt	1½ tsp.	7 mL
Pepper	⅛ tsp.	0.5 mL
Milk	1½ cups	375 mL
Milk	1½ cups	375 mL
Large eggs	6	6
Diced cooked ham	1 cup	250 mL
Grated medium or sharp Cheddar cheese	1 cup	250 mL
Canned sliced mushrooms, drained	½ x 10 oz.	½ x 284 mL

Cream Sauce: Melt butter in large Dutch oven. Mix in flour, salt and pepper. Stir in first amount of milk until it boils and thickens.

Whisk in second amount of milk. Mixture can be refrigerated at this point until the next day.

Beat eggs in small bowl until smooth. Stir into cream sauce.

Add ham, cheese and mushrooms. Mix well. Pour into greased 8 x 8 inch (20 x 20 cm) pan. Bake in 350°F (175°C) oven for about 1½ hours. An inserted knife should come out clean. Let stand 10 minutes before cutting. Serves 9.

Pictured below.

Baked Omelet

Breakfast Pull-Aparts

Nice and gooey! Lots of cinnamon.

Butter or hard margarine	6 tbsp.	100 mL
Granulated sugar	½ cup	125 mL
Ground cinnamon	1 tbsp.	15 mL
Frozen bread dough buns	20	20
Sliced almonds	½ cup	125 mL
Halved glazed cherries	½ cup	125 mL
Corn syrup	⅓ cup	75 mL
Remaining butter		

Melt butter in small saucepan.

Stir sugar and cinnamon in small bowl.

Dip frozen dough buns in butter. Roll in sugar mixture. Put 10 in greased 12 cup (2.7 L) bundt pan.

Sprinkle with ½ almonds and ½ cherries. Repeat.

Mix corn syrup with remaining butter. Drizzle over top. Cover with damp tea towel. Let stand on counter for 6 to 8 hours or overnight. Bake in 350°F (175°C) oven for about 30 minutes. Let stand 5 minutes. Turn out onto plate. Makes 20 servings.

Pictured on page 72.

Orange Fruit Dip

Serve with a platter of assorted fresh fruits.

Sour cream	1 cup	250 mL
Brown sugar	1 tbsp.	15 mL
Grand Marnier liqueur (or other orange flavored liqueur)	1 tbsp.	15 mL

Stir all together. To make without liqueur, add more sugar to taste. Makes 1 cup (250 mL) dip.

Pictured on this page.

Jean's Favorite

Golden Cheesecake

Provide a small paté knife and serve with assorted breads and crackers.

Fine dry bread crumbs	3 tbsp.	50 mL
Grated cheese product (powdered Cheddar)	2 tbsp.	30 mL
Cottage cheese	1 cup	250 mL
Canned ham flakes, drained	6½ oz.	184 g
Cream cheese, softened, cut up	3 × 8 oz.	3 × 250 g
Grated sharp Cheddar cheese	3 cups	750 mL
Chopped green onion	¼ cup	60 mL
Large eggs	4	4
Onion powder	½ tsp.	2 mL
Garlic powder	¼ tsp.	1 mL
Hot pepper sauce	¼ tsp.	1 mL

Stir bread crumbs and dry cheese together in small bowl. Grease sides and bottom of 9 inch (22 cm) springform pan. Coat with crumb mixture, shaking out excess.

Run remaining ingredients through blender until smooth. This may need to be done in 2 parts. Pour into prepared pan. Bake in 325°F (160°C) oven for 1 to 1½ hours. Center will quiver slightly when you shake pan. Place on rack. Immediately run sharp knife around top edge so cheesecake can settle evenly. Cool, then chill for 3 to 4 hours or overnight. Serves 15 to 20.

Pictured below.

Golden Cheesecake

Festive Savory Cheesecake

For blue cheese lovers. Pleasant blend of cheese and bacon flavors with crunchy surprise from pecans.

Crust:		
Butter or hard margarine	½ cup	125 mL
Saltine cracker crumbs	1½ cups	375 mL
Grated Parmesan cheese	¼ cup	60 mL
Filling:		
Cream cheese, softened	3 × 8 oz.	3 × 250 g
Blue cheese, crumbled	4 oz.	125 g
Large eggs	4	4
Sour cream	¾ cup	175 mL
Hot pepper sauce	¼ tsp.	1 mL
Onion powder	½ tsp.	2 mL
Salt	¼ tsp.	1 mL
Pepper	⅛ tsp.	0.5 mL
Bacon slices, diced	8	8
Medium onion, finely chopped	1	1
Finely chopped pecans	½ cup	125 mL
Finely chopped green onion	½ cup	125 mL
Topping:		
Sour cream	1 cup	250 mL
Pimiento strips, for garnish		
Parsley sprigs, for garnish		

Crust: Melt butter in saucepan. Stir in crumbs and Parmesan cheese. Press firmly into bottom of ungreased 9 inch (22 cm) springform pan. Bake in 350°F (175°C) oven for 10 minutes. Cool.

Filling: Beat cream cheese, blue cheese and 1 egg in mixing bowl until light. Beat in remaining eggs, 1 at a time. Add sour cream, pepper sauce, onion powder, salt and pepper. Beat just to mix in.

Sauté bacon in frying pan for 4 to 5 minutes. Add onion, continuing to sauté until onion is soft. Drain off excess fat. Mix in pecans and green onion. Stir. Add to cream cheese mixture. Stir well. Pour over cooled crust in springform pan. Bake in 325°F (160°C) oven for 1 to 1½ hours. Center will quiver slightly when pan is shaken. Set on rack. Immediately run knife around top edge to allow it to settle evenly. Cool. Chill for 1 to 2 hours.

Topping: Spread top with sour cream. Decorate with pimiento strips and parsley sprigs. Serves 15 to 20.

Pictured on page 75.

Festive Savory Cheesecake, page 74   Lobster Fantans, page 75   Gourmet Burgers, page 70

Ham Quiche

Very tasty. Can be frozen and reheated just before serving.

Hard margarine (butter browns too fast)	1 tbsp.	15 mL
Finely chopped onion	½ cup	125 mL
Finely chopped cooked ham	1 cup	250 mL
Grated Swiss cheese	¾ cup	175 mL
Grated medium or sharp Cheddar cheese	¾ cup	175 mL
Unbaked 9 inch (22 cm) deep dish pie shell, your own or a mix	1	1
Large eggs	3	3
Evaporated skim milk (or light cream)	1½ cups	350 mL
Prepared mustard	1 tsp.	5 mL
Salt	½ tsp.	2 mL
Pepper	¼ tsp.	1 mL
Ground nutmeg	⅛ tsp.	0.5 mL

Melt margarine in frying pan. Add onion. Sauté until soft. Do not brown.

Spread ham and both cheeses in pie shell. Sprinkle onion over top.

Beat eggs in bowl until smooth. Mix in remaining ingredients. Pour into pie shell. Bake on bottom rack in 375°F (190°C) oven for 30 to 35 minutes until a knife inserted near center comes out clean. Makes 1 quiche. Serves 6 to 8.

Pictured on page 73.

Lobster Fantans

Make filling first thing in the morning then assemble before serving. Quite showy.

Canned lobster, drained, broken up	5 oz.	142 g
Grated Swiss cheese (or your favorite)	½ cup	125 mL
Chopped green pepper	3 tbsp.	50 mL
Minced onion	2 tbsp.	30 mL
Salt	½ tsp.	2 mL
Salad dressing (or mayonnaise)	¼ cup	60 mL
Lemon juice, fresh or bottled	1 tsp.	5 mL
Soft rolls, about 4 x 3 inch (10 x 7.5 cm) size	5	5
Butter or hard margarine, softened	2 tbsp.	30 mL

Place first 5 ingredients in bowl. Toss together.

Stir salad dressing and lemon juice together in cup. Pour over lobster mixture. Stir lightly.

Make 3 cuts from top to bottom in each roll, not cutting through bottom. Spread inside cuts with butter. Spread lobster mixture between cuts. Wrap each roll in foil. Heat in 350°F (175°C) oven for about 20 minutes until hot. Serves 4 to 5.

Pictured above.

Banana Pancakes

Definitely befitting a houseful of overnight guests. Serve hot with butter and maple syrup.

All-purpose flour	2 cups	500 mL
Granulated sugar	2 tsp.	10 mL
Baking powder	1 tbsp.	15 mL
Salt	½ tsp.	2 mL
Large eggs	2	2
Butter or hard margarine, melted	2 tbsp.	30 mL
Milk	1¾ cups	425 mL
Bananas, quartered lengthwise and thinly sliced (see note)	2	2

Measure flour, sugar, baking powder and salt into bowl. Stir. Make a well in center.

Beat eggs in separate bowl. Mix in butter and milk. Pour into well in flour mixture. Stir to moisten. Don't try to smooth out small lumps. Add more milk or flour to make thicker or thinner pancakes.

Fold in banana. Test pan for heat. Drops of water should bounce all over it. Drop batter by tablespoonfuls on lightly greased 380°F (190°C) pan. When bubbles appear and edges begin to dry, turn to brown other side. Pan should not need to be greased again. Makes about 40 pancakes, 4 inch (10 cm) size.

Pictured below.

Note: Bananas may turn dark as the pancakes cool. This is natural and will not affect the taste. Do not freeze.

Overnight Oven French Toast

A real time-saver when you have a houseful of guests. Serve with maple syrup.

Butter or hard margarine, melted	¼ cup	60 mL
Large eggs	7	7
Milk (see Note)	2 cups	450 mL
Granulated sugar	⅓ cup	75 mL
Ground nutmeg	¼ tsp.	1 mL
Ground cinnamon	¼ tsp.	1 mL
Salt	¼ tsp.	1 mL
Vanilla	1½ tsp.	7 mL
French bread loaf, cut into 1 inch (2.5 cm) slices	1	1
Icing (confectioner's) sugar, sprinkle		

Pour melted butter into bottom of baking sheet to coat.

Beat next 7 ingredients together well.

Dip both sides of each bread slice into egg mixture. Lay in baking sheet. Pour any remaining mixture over slices. Cover and refrigerate overnight. Can be frozen at this state. Uncover and bake in 450°F (230°C) oven on bottom rack for 20 to 25 minutes. Place on rack to cool.

Dust with icing sugar when warm. Serves 6 to 8.

Pictured below.

Note: Commercial eggnog can be substituted for milk for a richer flavor.

When bananas become too ripe to eat, peel and put them in a freezer bag. Or, peel and mash overripe bananas, then measure and freeze in 1 cup (250 mL) portions. Three medium bananas mashed equal approximately 1 cup (250 mL). Frozen bananas may darken when thawed but are not spoiled; in fact, their flavor is enhanced. Use in any recipe calling for mashed bananas.

Overnight Oven French Toast, page 76
Orange Marmalade, page 12
Banana Pancakes, page 76

Top: Oven Apple Pancake
Bottom Right: Sausage Strata
Left: Eggs Lyonnaise

Sausage Strata

A time-saver, as this is assembled the night before.

Bread slices, crusts removed	6	6
Grated sharp Cheddar cheese	2 cups	500 mL
Sausage meat	2 lbs.	900 g
Bread slices, crusts removed	6	6
Large eggs	8	8
Salt	1 tsp.	5 mL
Pepper	¼ tsp.	1 mL
Onion powder	½ tsp.	2 mL
Worcestershire sauce	1 tsp.	5 mL
Dry mustard powder	½ tsp.	2 mL
Milk	2⅔ cups	650 mL

Line bottom of greased 9 x 13 inch (22 x 13 cm) pan with first bread slices. Sprinkle with cheese.

Scramble-fry sausage meat. Drain off fat. Sprinkle meat over cheese.

Cover meat with remaining bread slices.

Beat eggs in bowl. Add remaining ingredients. Mix. Pour over bread. Cover. Refrigerate overnight. Bake, uncovered, in 350°F (175°C) oven for about 1 hour until set. Serves 10 to 12.

Pictured on this page.

Eggs Lyonnaise

An excellent quick breakfast. This is easily doubled or tripled.

Butter or hard margarine	2 tbsp.	30 mL
Chopped onion	3 tbsp.	50 mL
All-purpose flour	1 tbsp.	15 mL
Chopped parsley (or ½ tsp., 2 mL parsley flakes)	1 tbsp.	15 mL
Salt	¼ tsp.	1 mL
Pepper, sprinkle		
Milk	1 cup	250 mL
Hard-boiled eggs, sliced	4	4
Bread slices, toasted and buttered	4	4

Melt butter in saucepan. Add onion. Sauté until soft and golden.

Mix in flour, parsley, salt and pepper. Stir in milk until mixture boils and thickens.

Gently stir in egg slices.

Spoon over toast. Makes 4 servings.

Pictured above.

Oven Apple Pancake

Serve with maple syrup and sausages.

Butter or hard margarine	¼ cup	60 mL
Brown sugar, packed	⅓ cup	75 mL
Ground cinnamon, light sprinkle		
Apples, peeled, cored and sliced in wedges ¼ inch (6 mm) thick	2	2
Large eggs	3	3
Milk	¾ cup	175 mL
Salt	½ tsp.	2 mL
All-purpose flour	¾ cup	175 mL

Melt butter in 9 inch (22 cm) pie plate in 425°F (220°C) oven.

Stir brown sugar into melted butter. Sprinkle with cinnamon. Overlap apples in single layer. Cook in oven for 10 minutes.

Beat eggs with spoon in bowl. Add milk, salt and flour. Stir to moisten. Don't try to smooth out small lumps. Pour over apples. Return to oven. Bake for 20 to 25 minutes. Cut into wedges. Serves 4 to 6.

Pictured on this page.

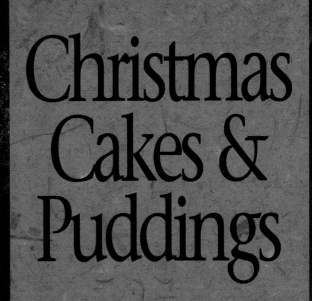

Christmas
Cakes &
Puddings

Christmas Cakes & Puddings

Chronicled in literature and steeped in tradition, Christmas cakes and puddings have been an honored part of the holiday menu for generations. Indeed if any single dish has come to represent Christmas, then surely it is the Christmas pudding, followed closely by Christmas cake.

Their esteemed status need not be intimidating. True, the ingredients for these special cakes and puddings are a step removed from the everyday but are readily available nonetheless.

Likewise, the preparation of Christmas cakes and puddings is simple enough and the result is well worth the time and effort.

1. **Plum Pudding,** page 81
2. **Pastel Hard Sauce,** page 86
3. **Steamed Chocolate Pudding,** page 83
4. **Light Fruitcake,** page 82

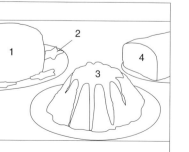

Steamed Fruit Pudding

An old-time suet pudding recipe for a light-colored and light-textured pudding. One of the best.

All-purpose flour	2 cups	500 mL
Brown sugar, packed	¾ cup	175 mL
Beef suet, ground	2 cups	500 mL
Ground cinnamon	2 tsp.	10 mL
Salt	1 tsp.	5 mL
Ground cloves	1 tsp.	5 mL
Baking soda	1 tsp.	5 mL
Cream of tartar	1 tsp.	5 mL
Large eggs, beaten	2	2
Milk	1¼ cups	300 mL
Sultana raisins	1 cup	250 mL
Golden raisins	½ cup	125 mL
Currants	1 cup	250 mL
Cut mixed peel, finely chopped or coarsely ground	¾ cup	175 mL

Mix first 10 ingredients in order given in large bowl.

Add next 4 ingredients. Mix in. Scrape into greased 8 cup (2 L) pudding container. Cover with double square greased foil, tying edges down with string. Place in steamer, with boiling water halfway up side. Steam, covered, for 4 hours adding more boiling water as needed to keep level up. Remove container from water. Let stand for ½ hour. Turn out of pan. Cool on rack. Remove from pan. Wrap in foil or plastic. Will keep in refrigerator for weeks. Freezes well. To reheat, steam about 1½ hours or until hot and serve with Rum Sauce, page 87. May also be reheated, covered with plastic wrap, in microwave. Makes 1 pudding.

Pictured below and on page 23.

Steamed Fruit Pudding, page 80, with Rum Sauce, page 87

Plum Pudding

The crowning touch for Christmas dinner.

Dark raisins	2 cups	450 mL
Currants	1 cup	225 mL
Ground almonds	7/8 cup	200 mL
Chopped glazed cherries	1/2 cup	125 mL
Cut mixed peel	1/2 cup	125 mL
Glazed pineapple rings, chopped	4	4
Medium coconut	1/2 cup	125 mL
All-purpose flour	1/2 cup	125 mL
Chopped beef suet	1 cup	225 mL
Dry bread crumbs	1 1/2 cups	350 mL
Baking powder	2 tsp.	10 mL
Baking soda	1/2 tsp.	2 mL
Salt	1 tsp.	5 mL
Ground cinnamon	1 tsp.	5 mL
Ground nutmeg	1 tsp.	5 mL
Ground ginger	1/2 tsp.	2 mL
All-purpose flour	3/4 cup	175 mL
Large eggs	3	3
Milk	3/4 cup	175 mL

Measure first 8 ingredients in large bowl. Stir well to coat fruit with flour.

Add next 9 ingredients. Mix well.

Beat eggs in small mixing bowl until frothy. Stir in milk. Pour over fruit mixture. Stir well until moistened. Turn into greased 2 quart (2 L) pudding pan. Cover with double square greased foil, tying sides down with string. Place in steamer with boiling water 2/3 way up pudding pan. Steam, covered, for 3 hours adding more boiling water as needed to keep level up. Serve with Rum Sauce, page 87, or Pastel Hard Sauce, page 86. Serves 12 to 15.

Pictured on page 78.

White Fruitcake

White Fruitcake

Wonderfully moist. Full of color.

Light raisins	3 cups	675 mL
Cut mixed glazed fruit	2 cups	450 mL
Candied pineapple slices, cut up	6	6
Chopped orange peel	1/3 cup	75 mL
Chopped lemon peel	1/3 cup	75 mL
Green glazed cherries	1 cup	225 mL
Red glazed cherries	1 cup	225 mL
Whole blanched almonds	1 1/2 cups	350 mL
Pecan halves	1 1/2 cups	350 mL
All-purpose flour	1 cup	225 mL
Butter or hard margarine, softened	1 lb.	454 g
Granulated sugar	2 cups	450 mL
Large eggs	10	10
Grated rind of 1 lemon		
Juice of 1 lemon		
Almond flavoring	2 tsp.	10 mL
Vanilla flavoring	1 tsp.	5 mL
All-purpose flour	3 cups	675 mL
Salt	1 tsp.	5 mL
Baking powder	1 tsp.	5 mL

Line 3 greased 9 x 5 x 3 inch (22 x 12 x 7 cm) loaf pans with brown paper. Grease paper. Measure first 10 ingredients into large bowl. Stir to coat fruit with flour.

Cream butter and sugar in large mixing bowl. Beat in eggs, 1 at a time. Add remaining ingredients. Stir. Add fruit mixture. Stir. Divide among prepared pans. Bake in 275°F (140°C) oven for 2 to 2 1/2 hours until an inserted wooden pick comes out clean. Cool on rack. Remove from pans. Wrap in plastic to store for 2 to 3 weeks before freezing. Makes 3 cakes or 8 pounds (3.6 kg) total.

Pictured above and on page 23.

Light Fruitcake

A traditional Christmas cake with a little something for everyone.

Glazed cherries, halved	1 cup	250 mL
Glazed pineapple rings, chopped	6	6
Cut citron	1/2 cup	125 mL
Cut mixed peel	1/2 cup	125 mL
Light raisins	1 cup	250 mL
Slivered almonds	1 1/2 cups	375 mL
Fine coconut	2 1/2 cups	575 mL
Butter or hard margarine, softened	1 cup	250 mL
Granulated sugar	1 1/2 cups	375 mL
Large eggs	6	6
Lemon juice, fresh or bottled	1 1/2 tbsp.	25 mL
Rum flavoring	1 tbsp.	15 mL
Vanilla	1 tsp.	5 mL
Milk	1/2 cup	125 mL
All-purpose flour	4 cups	1 L
Baking powder	1 tsp.	5 mL
Baking soda	1/2 tsp.	2 mL
Salt	1/2 tsp.	2 mL

Line 2 greased 9 x 5 x 3 inch (22 x 12 x 7 cm) loaf pans with brown paper. Grease paper. Combine first 7 ingredients in large bowl. Stir well.

Cream butter and sugar in large bowl. Beat in eggs, 1 at a time. Add lemon juice, flavorings and milk. Mix.

Add remaining ingredients. Stir to moisten. Add fruit mixture. Stir well. Divide between prepared pans. Bake in 275°F (140°C) oven for 2 1/4 to 2 1/2 hours until an inserted wooden pick comes out clean. Cool on rack. Remove from pans. Wrap in plastic to stand 2 to 3 weeks before freezing. Makes 2 cakes, 5 1/2 pounds (2.5 kg) total.

Pictured on page 79.

Steamed Cranberry Pudding

Appearance and texture are excellent. Flavor is not too sweet.

Cranberries, fresh or frozen, halved	2 cups	500 mL
All-purpose flour	1 1/3 cups	325 mL
Baking powder	1/2 tsp.	2 mL
Large egg	1	1
Mild molasses	1/4 cup	60 mL
Golden corn syrup	1/4 cup	60 mL
Vanilla	1 tsp.	5 mL
Baking soda	2 tsp.	10 mL
Hot water	1/3 cup	75 mL

Stir cranberries, flour and baking powder together in bowl.

Beat egg in mixing bowl. Beat in molasses, corn syrup and vanilla.

Dissolve baking soda in hot water in cup. Add to egg mixture. Mix. Add cranberry mixture. Stir to moisten. Turn into greased 8 cup (2 L) pudding pan. Cover with double square greased foil, tying sides down with string. Put in steamer with boiling water 2/3 up sides of pan. Cover. Steam for 1 1/2 hours, adding more boiling water as needed to keep level up. Remove pan from water. Let stand 1/2 hour. Turn out of pan. Cool on rack. Remove from pan. Wrap in plastic or foil. Freeze up to 2 months or keep in refrigerator 2 to 3 weeks. Reheat just before serving. Serve with Creamy Pudding Sauce, page 87. Serves 8 to 12.

Pictured below.

Steamed Cranberry Pudding, page 82
with Creamy Pudding
Sauce, page 87

Orange Gumdrop Loaf

Steamed Chocolate Pudding

A delightful change from the fruit steamed puddings.
Good with either sauce.

Butter or hard margarine, softened	½ cup	125 mL
Granulated sugar	¾ cup	175 mL
Large eggs	2	2
Vanilla	1 tsp.	5 mL
All-purpose flour	2 cups	500 mL
Baking powder	1 tbsp.	15 mL
Salt	¼ tsp.	1 mL
Milk	1 cup	250 mL
Unsweetened chocolate baking squares, cut up	2 × 1 oz.	2 × 28 g
Brown Sugar Sauce:		
Brown sugar, packed	1 cup	250 mL
All-purpose flour	¼ cup	60 mL
Salt	½ tsp.	2 mL
Water	2 cups	500 mL
Butter or hard margarine	1 tbsp.	15 mL
Vanilla	1 tsp.	5 mL

Cream butter and sugar in large bowl. Add eggs 1 at a time, beating well after each addition. Add vanilla. Mix.

Measure flour, baking powder and salt into separate bowl. Stir.

Add milk in 2 parts alternately with flour mixture in 3 parts, beginning and ending with flour.

Melt chocolate on low, stirring often. Stir into batter. Turn into greased 2 quart (2 L) pudding pan. Cover with double square greased foil, tying in place. Place in steamer with boiling water ⅔ up the side of pan. Cover steamer. Boil for 1 hour adding more boiling water as needed to keep level up. Makes 1 pudding.

Brown Sugar Sauce: Stir first 3 ingredients together in saucepan. Add water. Stir well. Heat and stir on medium until mixture boils and thickens.

Stir in butter and vanilla. Serve over Steamed Chocolate Pudding. Makes 2½ cups (625 mL) sauce.

Pictured on page 78 and 79.

Chocolate Pudding Sauce

Prepare Brown Sugar Sauce, adding 2 tbsp. (30 mL) cocoa to dry ingredients. Complete as above.

Orange Gumdrop Loaf

Nice and moist. Lots of orange throughout.

Gumdrop orange slices, cut up	⅓ lb.	150 g
Chopped dates	¾ cup	175 mL
All-purpose flour	⅛ cup	30 mL
Butter or hard margarine, softened	½ cup	125 mL
Granulated sugar	¾ cup	175 mL
Large eggs	2	2
All-purpose flour	1¾ cups	425 mL
Fine coconut	⅔ cup	150 mL
Baking soda	½ tsp.	2 mL
Chopped pecans	½ cup	125 mL
Salt	¼ tsp.	1 mL
Prepared orange juice	½ cup	125 mL

Toss first 3 ingredients together in small bowl. Set aside.

Beat butter and sugar together in large bowl. Beat in eggs, 1 at a time.

Stir next 5 ingredients together in separate bowl. Add to egg mixture. Stir.

Stir in orange juice then fruit mixture. Pour into greased 9 x 5 x 3 inch (22 x 12 x 7 cm) loaf pan. Bake in 350°F (175°C) oven for about 75 minutes until an inserted wooden pick comes out clean. Cool on rack. Remove from pan. Wrap in plastic or foil. Freeze up to 2 months or store in refrigerator 2 to 3 weeks. Makes 1 loaf.

Pictured above.

Loaves are easier to slice the next day. They are also easier to slice if frozen and slightly thawed. Return the unsliced portion to freezer. Keep muffins and loaves in the freezer for no longer than 3 months for best texture and taste.

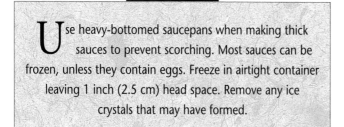

U se heavy-bottomed saucepans when making thick sauces to prevent scorching. Most sauces can be frozen, unless they contain eggs. Freeze in airtight container leaving 1 inch (2.5 cm) head space. Remove any ice crystals that may have formed.

Christmas Pudding Sauce

Beautiful caramel color with perfect blend of flavors. Serve with your favorite Christmas pudding.

Brown sugar, packed	½ cup	125 mL
Granulated sugar	½ cup	125 mL
Cornstarch	3 tbsp.	50 mL
Water	1 cup	250 mL
Butter or hard margarine	¼ cup	60 mL
Lemon juice, fresh or bottled	2 tbsp.	30 mL
Rum flavoring	1 tsp.	5 mL

Mix both sugars and cornstarch in saucepan.

Add water. Stir. Add butter, lemon juice and rum flavoring. Heat and stir until it boils and thickens. Makes 1⅔ cups (400 mL) sauce.

Pictured on page 85.

1. Creamy Pudding Sauce, page 87
2. Christmas Pudding Sauce, page 84
3. Rum Sauce, page 87
4. Carrot Pudding, page 86

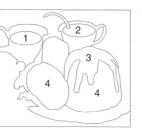

Pastel Hard Sauce

Try a variety of colors and shapes.
Make well in advance and store in fridge.
Layer between waxed paper.

Butter or hard margarine, softened	¼ cup	60 mL
Icing (confectioner's) sugar	1 cup	250 mL
Vanilla or brandy flavoring	1 tsp.	5 mL
Milk, for thinning		
Food coloring, if desired		

Beat butter, icing sugar and vanilla together. Add a bit of milk if needed, to make a touch softer. Work in food coloring with hands. Spread about ¼ inch (6 mm) thick on cookie sheet. Roll to smooth. Chill. Use cookie cutter to cut into Christmas trees, stars or balls. Remove with lifter. Soften scraps to room temperature. Repeat. Makes a scant 1 cup (250 mL) sauce.

Pictured on page 78.

Carrot Pudding

So moist, with a wonderful blend of flavors.

Grated carrot	1½ cups	375 mL
Chopped beef suet	1 cup	250 mL
All-purpose flour	2 cups	500 mL
Brown sugar, packed	1 cup	250 mL
Sultana raisins	1 cup	250 mL
Currants	1 cup	250 mL
Cut citron peel	1 cup	250 mL
Red or black currant jelly	½ cup	125 mL
Brandy flavoring	1 tsp.	5 mL
Ground ginger	1 tsp.	5 mL
Ground cinnamon	1 tsp.	5 mL
Baking powder	1 tsp.	5 mL
Baking soda	1 tsp.	5 mL
Ground allspice	½ tsp.	2 mL
Ground nutmeg	¼ tsp.	1 mL
Grated raw potato	1½ cups	375 mL

Combine first 7 ingredients in large bowl. Mix well.

Stir remaining 9 ingredients together in medium bowl. Add to first bowl. Stir well. Turn into greased 10 cup (2.5 L) pudding pan. Cover with double square greased foil, tying sides down with string. Put into steamer with boiling water ⅔ up sides of pan. Steam, covered, for 3 hours, adding more boiling water to keep level up. Cool. Remove from pan. Wrap in foil or plastic. Freeze for 2 months or store in refrigerator 2 to 3 weeks. Reheat just before serving. Serve with Rum Sauce, page 87. Serves 12 to 15.

Pictured on page 84 and 85.

For Gift Giving

Round Mini Loaves (Steamed Puddings)

Line bottoms of 3 greased 19 oz. (540 mL) cans with waxed paper. Divide pudding batter evenly among them. Top each with a glazed cherry placed in the center. Cover each can with double square greased foil, but first place foil over your fist to form a tent. Pudding tends to rise above the top of the can. Tie foil in place with string. Put all 3 cans into steamer or large pot (with bottom rack) with boiling water ⅔ way up sides of cans. Steam, covered, for 2¼ hours, adding more boiling water as needed to keep level up. Remove cans from steamer. While still warm, carefully loosen sides with table knife. Turn out onto rack to finish cooling. Wrap each pudding in plastic wrap and tie with decorative ribbon. Makes 3 small gift puddings.

Rectangular Mini Loaves (Fruitcakes)

Pour prepared fruitcake batter into 4 greased 2½ x 4 x 1 inch (6 x 10 x 2.5 cm) mini loaf pans. Bake in 350°F (175°C) oven for about 1 hour 15 minutes until an inserted wooden pick comes out clean. Cool on racks. Remove from pans. Wrap in plastic wrap and tie with decorative ribbon. Makes 4 mini gift loaves.

Christmas Cake

Nice hint of lemon. Not a heavy cake.

Raisins	2 cups	450 mL
Currants	2 cups	450 mL
Cut glazed mixed fruit	1 cup	225 mL
Glazed cherries, halved	½ cup	125 mL
Cut mixed peel	½ cup	125 mL
Chopped pecans or walnuts	1 cup	250 mL
Slivered almonds	¾ cup	175 mL
All-purpose flour	1 cup	250 mL
Butter or hard margarine	1 cup	250 mL
Brown sugar, packed	1 cup	250 mL
Granulated sugar	¼ cup	60 mL
Corn syrup	½ cup	125 mL
Large eggs	6	6
All-purpose flour	3½ cups	875 mL
Baking powder	1 tsp.	5 mL
Ground cinnamon	½ tsp.	2 mL
Ground nutmeg	½ tsp.	2 mL
Ground allspice	½ tsp.	2 mL
Ground cloves	⅛ tsp.	0.5 mL
Apple juice	1¾ cups	425 mL
Grated rind of 1 lemon		
Juice of 1 lemon		
Brandy flavoring	1 tbsp.	15 mL

Line 2 greased 9 x 5 x 3 inch (22 x 12 x 7 cm) loaf pans with brown paper or 2 layers of waxed paper. Grease paper. Measure first 8 ingredients into large bowl. Stir well to mix in flour.

Cream butter and both sugars well in separate bowl. Beat in corn syrup. Add eggs, 1 at a time, beating well after each addition.

Measure next 6 ingredients into medium bowl. Stir well.

Combine apple juice, lemon rind, lemon juice and brandy flavoring in small bowl. Add flour mixture in 2 parts alternately with apple juice mixture in 2 parts. Add fruit mixture. Mix well. Divide between prepared pans. Bake in 300°F (150°C) oven for about 2½ to 2¾ hours until an inserted wooden pick comes out clean. Let stand on rack to cool. Remove from pans. Wrap in plastic to store in cool place for 2 to 3 weeks before freezing for long-term storage. Makes 2 loaves, 8 pounds (3.6 kg) total.

Pictured on front cover.

Creamy Pudding Sauce

Serve with Steamed Cranberry Pudding, page 82.

Butter or hard margarine	½ cup	125 mL
All-purpose flour	2 tbsp.	30 mL
Evaporated skim milk (or light cream)	1 cup	250 mL
Granulated sugar	1 cup	250 mL
Vanilla	1 tsp.	5 mL
Salt	⅛ tsp.	0.5 mL

Melt butter in saucepan. Mix in flour.

Stir in milk. Heat and stir until it boils and thickens.

Add sugar, vanilla and salt. Stir to dissolve sugar. Makes 2 cups (500 mL) sauce.

Pictured on page 82 and on page 84.

Rum Sauce

Smooth and silky. Serve with Steamed Fruit Pudding, page 80 or Plum Pudding, page 81.

Butter or hard margarine	3 tbsp.	50 mL
All-purpose flour	3 tbsp.	50 mL
Salt	½ tsp.	2 mL
Water	1½ cups	375 mL
Brown sugar, packed	¾ cup	175 mL
Rum flavoring	1 tsp.	5 mL

Melt butter in saucepan. Mix in flour and salt.

Stir in water until it boils and thickens.

Add sugar and flavoring. Stir to dissolve sugar. Makes about 2 cups (500 mL) sauce.

Pictured on page 80 and on page 85.

Cookies & Confections

It's true that cookies come out of the oven year-round. But Christmas has a cookie collection all its own. That's when gingerbread men, shortbread and brightly-iced sugar cookies take shape by the dozen to be arranged on platters at home and beyond.

Likewise, confections are significant at this time of the year. Fudges, brittles and sweets by their very nature lend themselves to the holiday season because they look and taste great.

These holiday treats may be a bit more detailed than your usual efforts and definitely require a

> Use vegetable shortening or non-stick cooking spray rather than butter or margarine to grease baking sheets . This will help prevent burning. You may also line baking sheets with parchment paper. When reusing a baking sheet, be sure it has cooled before placing cookie dough on it. Leave 1 or 2 inches (2.5 or 5 cm) between each cookie.

shopping list of ingredients specific to the season. But the reaction they get makes the extra effort worth it.

Far Left: Divinity Drops, page 95   Left: Jolly Fruit Drops, page 89

Cherry Winks

So easy to make. Freezes well, too. Nice combination of cherry and coconut flavors.

Butter or hard margarine, softened	½ cup	125 mL
Icing (confectioner's) sugar	1½ cups	375 mL
Fine coconut	1 cup	250 mL
Maraschino cherries, halved, dried on paper towel	20	20
Graham cracker crumbs	¼ cup	60 mL

Mix butter, icing sugar and coconut well. Form into a long tube to make it easier to mark off into 40 pieces.

Wrap each piece around a cherry half. Shape into a ball.

Roll each ball in graham crumbs. Store in covered container in refrigerator. Makes about 40 winks.

Pictured on page 89.

Top Center: Chocolate Snowballs, page 93   Bottom Center: Cherry Winks, page 88   Right: Whipped Shortbread, page 89

Whipped Shortbread

These melt in your mouth!

Butter, softened (do not use margarine)	1 cup	250 mL
Granulated sugar	½ cup	125 mL
All-purpose flour	1½ cups	375 mL
Cornstarch	¼ cup	60 mL

Cream butter and sugar in medium bowl. Beat until light and fluffy.

Add flour and cornstarch gradually while beating continuously. Beat until light. Drop by teaspoonfuls onto ungreased cookie sheet. Bake in 375°F (190°C) oven for 12 to 14 minutes. Makes 2½ dozen cookies.

Pictured above.

Jolly Fruit Drops

Batter will be thick but the result is nice and chewy. Colorful. Make ahead and freeze.

Butter or hard margarine, softened	1 cup	225 mL
Granulated sugar	½ cup	125 mL
Brown sugar, packed	½ cup	125 mL
Vanilla	1 tsp.	5 mL
Medium coconut	1 cup	225 mL
Chopped dates	½ cup	125 mL
Chopped red glazed cherries	¼ cup	60 mL
Chopped green glazed cherries	¼ cup	60 mL
Quick cooking rolled oats	2 cups	450 mL
All-purpose flour	1 cup	225 mL
Baking soda	½ tsp.	2 mL
Salt	½ tsp.	2 mL

Cream butter and both sugars in large bowl. Beat in vanilla.

Stir in coconut, dates and both cherries.

Add remaining ingredients. Mix. Drop by teaspoonfuls onto ungreased baking sheet. Bake in 350°F (175°C) oven for 12 to 15 minutes. Makes about 5 dozen cookies.

Pictured above.

Coffee Perks

*Quick to make. Try different flavorings. Stir into
your evening coffee.*

Dipping chocolate wafers (available at craft stores)	2 cups	450 mL
Oil-based liqueur flavoring	1/8 tsp.	0.5 mL
Colored plastic spoons	18	18

Melt chocolate with liqueur flavoring in saucepan on
lowest heat, or in top of double boiler over warm water,
stirring often.

Dip ball of spoon in chocolate mixture. Hold above
chocolate so drips run back in saucepan. Lay spoon on
waxed paper on plate to harden. Dip 1 more time. When
hardened, wrap in decorative cellophane and tie with
pretty ribbons. Makes 18.

Pictured below.

Cookies being kept for several weeks or less can be stored
at room temperature in an airtight container. For longer
storage, keep in freezer up to 1 year. Cool cookies
completely before packing. Use a separate container for each
type of cookie. Crisp cookies will absorb moisture from
softer cookies. When stacking cookies, place a layer of
waxed paper or parchment paper between layers.

Merry Fruit Cookies

*These yummy, attractive cookies make an ideal cookie
exchange contribution.*

Glazed cherries, quartered	2 cups	500 mL
Dark raisins	1 1/2 cups	375 mL
Red pineapple rings, cut up	4	4
Green pineapple rings, cut up	4	4
Chopped dates	1 cup	250 mL
All-purpose flour	1/2 cup	125 mL
Butter or hard margarine, softened	1 lb.	454 g
Granulated sugar	2 cups	450 mL
Large eggs	3	3
Vanilla	1 tsp.	5 mL
Almond flavoring	1/2 tsp.	2 mL
Baking powder	1 tsp.	5 mL
Baking soda	1 tsp.	5 mL
Ground cinnamon	1/2 tsp.	2 mL
All-purpose flour	4 1/2 cups	1 L

Place first 6 ingredients in medium bowl. Stir to coat fruit
with flour.

Cream butter and sugar well in large bowl. Add eggs, 1 at
a time, beating well after each addition. Add vanilla and
almond flavoring.

Stir baking powder, baking soda and cinnamon into
second amount of flour in separate bowl. Add fruit mixture. Stir. Add to batter. Stir until it is too difficult to mix.
Work with your hands until flour is mixed in. Shape into
4 or 5 logs about 1 1/2 inches (4 cm) in diameter. Roll each
log in waxed paper. Chill for 1 hour or longer. Cut in 1/4 inch
(6 mm) slices. Arrange on greased baking sheet 1/2 inch
(12 mm) apart. Bake in 375°F (190°C) oven for about
10 minutes until golden. Makes about 9 dozen cookies.

Pictured above.

Nutty Cherry Shortbread

Keep refrigerated. Slice and bake as you need them.

Butter, softened	1 lb.	454 g
Brown sugar, packed	2 cups	450 mL
All-purpose flour	3½ cups	800 mL
Cornstarch	½ cup	125 mL
Quartered glazed cherries	1 cup	250 mL
Ground or finely chopped almonds	1 cup	250 mL

Cream butter and sugar well in large bowl.

Add remaining ingredients. Work into butter mixture. Shape into 4 rolls about 1½ inches (4 cm) in diameter. Roll each roll in waxed paper. Chill. Cut in ¼ inch (6 mm) slices. Arrange on ungreased baking sheet about 1 inch (2.5 cm) apart. Bake in 400°F (205°C) oven for 6 to 7 minutes until edges show some browning. Makes 6 dozen cookies.

Pictured on page 99.

Cocoa Cookies

Let the kids help you make and decorate these.

Butter or hard margarine, softened	¼ cup	60 mL
Granulated sugar	1 cup	250 mL
Large egg	1	1
Milk	6 tbsp.	100 mL
Vanilla	½ tsp.	2 mL
All-purpose flour	2 cups	500 mL
Cocoa	½ cup	125 mL
Baking soda	1 tbsp.	15 mL
Salt	¼ tsp.	1 mL

Cream butter and sugar in medium bowl. Add egg. Beat well. Add milk and vanilla. Beat in.

Add flour, cocoa, baking soda and salt. Mix. Roll ¼ inch (0.5 cm) thick on lightly floured surface. Cut into 2 inch (5 cm) rounds or use Christmas cookie cutters. Arrange on greased cookie sheet. Bake in 400°F (205°C) oven for about 10 minutes. Makes about 4 dozen cookies.

Pictured below.

Spritz

The cream cheese keeps these cookies soft.

Butter or hard margarine, softened	1 cup	250 mL
Cream cheese, softened	4 oz.	125 g
Granulated sugar	1 cup	250 mL
Large eggs	2	2
Vanilla	1½ tsp.	7 mL
Salt	¼ tsp.	1 mL
All-purpose flour	3 cups	750 mL
Sugar, sprinkles, colored sugar, red and green glazed cherries		

Cream butter, cream cheese and sugar in large bowl. Beat in eggs 1 at a time. Add vanilla and salt. Beat.

Add flour. Work into batter. Fill cookie press and press your choice of design onto ungreased cookie sheet. Decorate. Bake in 400°F (205°C) oven for 10 to 12 minutes until set and edges are showing a hint of brown. Makes 6 to 7 dozen cookies.

Chocolate Spritz

Exchange 6 tbsp. (100 mL) of flour with 6 tbsp. (100 mL) cocoa.

Orange Spritz

Add 2 tsp. (10 mL) finely grated orange rind and ½ tsp. (2 mL) orange flavoring.

Chocolate Orange Spritz

Exchange 6 tbsp. (100 mL) flour with an equal amount of cocoa. Add 2 tsp. (10 mL) orange flavoring.

Pictured on this page and on page 22.

Flake Macaroons

Light and crunchy. Can be made ahead and frozen.

Egg whites (large), room temperature	2	2
Granulated sugar	1 cup	250 mL
Vanilla	1 tsp.	5 mL
Corn flakes	2 cups	500 mL
Chopped pecans or walnuts	½ cup	125 mL
Fancy flake coconut	1 cup	250 mL

Beat egg whites in small bowl until stiff. Transfer to large bowl.

Sprinkle ⅓ sugar over at a time, folding in after each addition. Fold in vanilla.

Fold in corn flakes, pecans and coconut. Form mounds of about 1 rounded teaspoon. Place about 1 inch (2.5 cm) apart onto greased baking sheet. Bake in 350°F (175°C) oven for about 15 minutes. Makes 24 cookies.

Pictured below.

Caramel Popcorn Balls

Toffee-like chewiness. Kids will love these.

Popped corn (pop about ⅔ cup, 150 mL)	14 cups	3.15 L
Granulated sugar	1 cup	250 mL
Boiling water	¾ cup	175 mL
Brown sugar, packed	½ cup	125 mL

Put popped corn into large bowl.

Heat granulated sugar, stirring continually, in heavy saucepan until sugar melts and turns golden brown in color.

Gradually add boiling water, stirring until spattering quits and caramel mixture dissolves.

Add brown sugar. Stir on medium-low heat until dissolved. Cook and stir until it reaches soft ball stage 348°F (116°C) on candy thermometer or until a small spoonful dropped in cold water forms a soft ball. Pour over popcorn. Stir well to coat. Shape into 2½ inch (6 cm) balls, using buttered hands. Wrap each ball in plastic wrap. Makes 50 balls.

Pictured above.

Caramel Popcorn

Do not shape into balls. Let mixture dry on cookie sheets. Break apart and store in airtight container.

Pictured above.

Popcorn Balls

*Fun to make. Make it a second time but
with green food coloring.*

Popped corn (pop about 6 tbsp., 100 mL)	8 cups	1.8 L
White miniature marshmallows	3 cups	675 mL
Butter or hard margarine	2 tbsp.	30 mL
Salt	1/4 tsp.	1 mL

Red food coloring

Place popped corn in large bowl.

Heat marshmallows, butter and salt in large heavy saucepan, stirring often, until marshmallows are melted.

Add food coloring by drops to make a pretty pink color. Pour over popcorn. Stir well to coat every piece. Brush palms of hands with butter or margarine. Shape mixture into 3 inch (7.5 cm) balls. Cool. Wrap each ball in plastic wrap. Makes 8 balls.

Pictured below.

Crunchy Popcorn Balls

Try these with strawberry jelly powder and red food coloring.

Popped corn (pop about 1/2 cup, 125 mL)	16 cups	3.6 L
Light corn syrup	1 cup	250 mL
Granulated sugar	1/2 cup	125 mL
Lime flavored gelatin (jelly powder)	3 oz.	85 g

Green food coloring, if desired

Put popped corn into large bowl.

Heat and stir corn syrup and sugar in saucepan until it comes to a boil. Quit stirring. Let it reach a rolling boil (boils furiously). Remove from heat.

Stir in gelatin until it dissolves. Add a bit of green food coloring if you want a greener color. Pour over popcorn. Stir well to coat. Brush your hands with margarine. Shape into 2 1/2 inch (6 cm) balls. Cool. Wrap each ball in plastic wrap. Makes 21 balls.

Pictured on this page.

Chocolate Snowballs

Very tender and fragile. A melt-in-your-mouth cookie.

Butter or hard margarine, softened	1 1/4 cups	300 mL
Granulated sugar	2/3 cup	150 mL
Vanilla	1 1/2 tsp.	7 mL
All-purpose flour	2 cups	500 mL
Cocoa	1/2 cup	125 mL
Ground pecans (or walnuts)	1 1/2 cups	350 mL
Icing (confectioner's) sugar	1/2 cup	125 mL

Cream butter, granulated sugar and vanilla together well.

Mix in flour, cocoa and pecans. Shape into 1 inch (2.5 cm) balls. Arrange on ungreased baking sheet. Bake in 350°F (175°C) oven for about 20 minutes.

When balls are cool enough to handle, roll them in icing sugar. Cool completely before storing. Makes 7 dozen snowballs.

Pictured on page 89.

Crunchy Popcorn Balls

Popcorn Balls

Alfajores

Alfajores

These alfa-HORE-ez are really different and delicious, but take extra time.

Sweetened condensed milk	11 oz.	300 mL
Boiling water		
Cookies:		
Butter or hard margarine, softened	½ cup	125 mL
Granulated sugar	¾ cup	175 mL
Large egg	1	1
Egg yolk (large)	1	1
Finely grated lemon peel	1 tsp.	5 mL
Cornstarch	1¼ cups	300 mL
All-purpose flour	¾ cup	175 mL
Baking powder	1 tsp.	5 mL
Caramelized sweetened condensed milk		
Thread coconut	½ cup	125 mL

Empty milk into 8 inch (20 cm) glass pie plate. Put ¼ inch (6 mm) hot water into 2 quart (2 L) shallow casserole. Set pie plate in water. Bake at 425°F (220°C) for about 1 hour 20 minutes to caramelize.

Cookies: Cream butter and sugar in medium bowl. Beat in egg and egg yolk. Add lemon peel, cornstarch, flour and baking powder. Stir. Work with your hands until dough sticks together. Let dough rest for 15 minutes. Roll dough a scant ¼ inch (6 mm) thick on floured surface. Cut into 1½ inch (4 cm) circles. Arrange on greased baking sheet. Bake in 325°F (160°C) oven for 10 to 15 minutes. They should be dry but not brown. Cool.

Sandwich 2 cookies together with a layer of caramelized condensed milk. Spread a thin layer of caramelized condensed milk around outside edge of alfajores. Roll edge in coconut. Makes 30 alfajores.

Pictured above.

Christmas Trees

"Plant" these trees in and around other cookies on your cookie tray. But be prepared—they'll disappear quickly.

Butter or hard margarine	½ cup	125 mL
Icing (confectioner's) sugar	2 cups	450 mL
Milk	3 tbsp.	50 mL
Medium coconut	3 cups	675 mL
Vanilla or mint flavoring	½ tsp.	2 mL
Green flood coloring		
White baking chocolate squares, cut up	4 × 1 oz.	4 × 28 g

Melt butter in large saucepan. Remove from heat. Stir in icing sugar and milk.

Mix in coconut and vanilla. Add enough food coloring to tint a pretty green. Shape into small balls about 1 inch (2.5 cm) in diameter. Squeeze top to form an upside down cone shape. Put on tray in refrigerator overnight, uncovered, to dry.

Melt chocolate in saucepan on lowest heat, stirring often. Dip tops of trees in chocolate to look like snow. Makes 30 "trees".

Pictured on page 105.

Sugar Cookies

Everyone's favorite. Make and freeze well ahead of time.

Butter or hard margarine, softened	¾ cup	175 mL
Granulated sugar	¾ cup	175 mL
Large egg	1	1
Vanilla	1 tsp.	5 mL
All-purpose flour	2 cups	450 mL
Baking soda	1 tsp.	5 mL
Cream of tartar	1 tsp.	5 mL
Cardamom (optional but good)	¼ tsp.	1 mL
Salt	¼ tsp.	1 mL

Cream butter and sugar in large bowl. Add egg and vanilla. Beat.

Mix remaining ingredients in separate bowl. Stir into batter. Roll out ⅛ inch (3 mm) thick on lightly floured surface. Cut into rounds or different shapes. Bake on greased cookie sheet in 350°F (175°C) oven for about 10 minutes. Cool. Decorate. Makes 7 dozen cookies.

Variation: For plain sugar cookies, sprinkle with granulated sugar before baking.

Variation: For decorated cookies, sprinkle with colored sugar or sprinkles before baking or decorate baked cookies with icing.

Pictured below and on page 22.

Sugar Cookies

Cookies are usually baked on the middle rack in the oven. However, if your cookies appear to be burning on the bottom, move them up one rack; if the tops are browning too much, move them down one rack. For delicate cookies (Whipped Shortbread, page 89) try stacking 2 cookie sheets together. When baking 2 sheets of cookies at the same time, put one on the middle rack to one side and one on the lower rack to the other side. Set your timer to switch them halfway through baking.

Divinity Drops

So white, with red and green flecks peeking through. Smooth melt-in-your-mouth texture.

Granulated sugar	3 cups	700 mL
White corn syrup	½ cup	125 mL
Hot water	¾ cup	175 mL
Salt	⅛ tsp.	0.5 mL
Egg whites (large), room temperature	2	2
Vanilla	1 tsp.	5 mL
Candied cherries, cut up, or finely chopped walnuts or pecans	½ cup	125 mL

Measure sugar, corn syrup, water and salt into 3 quart (3 L) heavy saucepan. Heat and stir constantly as you slowly bring it to a boil. Sugar should be dissolved before it starts to boil. Boil, without stirring, until candy thermometer reaches hard ball stage or until a small spoonful dropped in cold water forms a hard ball that is still pliable and plastic-like.

Meanwhile, beat egg whites in a large bowl until stiff. Pour hot syrup mixture in a thin stream over beaten egg whites, beating continually. Beat until fairly stiff and it loses its gloss. A small amount dropped on saucer should hold its shape.

Quickly stir in vanilla and cherries or walnuts. Work quickly with greased spoons and drop onto greased waxed paper. Makes 36 drops.

Pictured on page 88.

Christmas Fudge

A very pretty fudge—Christmas colors.
Freeze ahead. Keeps well in refrigerator.

Granulated sugar	3 cups	675 mL
Light cream	¾ cup	175 mL
Corn syrup	3 tbsp.	45 mL
Butter (do not use margarine)	1 tbsp.	15 mL
Vanilla	1 tsp.	5 mL
Almond flavoring	1 tsp.	5 mL
Chopped candied red cherries	¼ cup	60 mL
Chopped candied green cherries	¼ cup	60 mL
Chopped pecans	½ cup	125 mL
Sliced Brazil nuts	½ cup	125 mL
Chopped candied yellow pineapple	⅓ cup	75 mL

Put sugar, cream, syrup and butter into 3 quart (3 L) heavy saucepan. Heat on medium-low, stirring often, until it starts to boil. Boil gently, stirring occasionally to prevent sticking, until it reaches soft ball on candy thermometer or until a small spoonful forms a soft ball in cold water. Remove from heat. Remove thermometer. Let stand until crust forms on top but liquid is still warm, about 10 minutes. Beat until slightly thickened and a little lighter in color.

Add vanilla and almond flavoring. Beat until it has lost its gloss.

Mix in remaining 5 ingredients quickly. Press with greased hands into 8 x 8 inch (20 x 20 cm) pan. Cool. Cuts into 36 pieces. Makes 2½ pounds (1.1 kg).

Pictured on page 97.

1. Condensed Fudge, page 96
2. Christmas Fudge, page 96
3. Special Chocolate Fudge, page 96

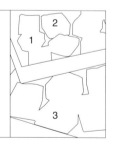

Special Chocolate Fudge

Sweet—like fudge should be!

Granulated sugar	3 cups	675 mL
Light cream	1 cup	225 mL
Unsweetened chocolate baking squares, cut up	3 x 1 oz.	3 x 28 g
Corn syrup	2 tbsp.	30 mL
Butter or hard margarine	2 tbsp.	30 mL
Salt	⅛ tsp.	0.5 mL
Vanilla	1 tsp.	5 mL
Chopped walnuts	¾ cup	175 mL

Combine first 6 ingredients in 3 quart (3 L) heavy saucepan. Heat and stir slowly until sugar is dissolved. Bring to a boil. Boil slowly until soft ball stage is reached on candy thermometer or until a small spoonful dropped in cold water forms a soft ball. Remove from heat. Remove thermometer. Let stand 40 minutes to cool slightly.

Add vanilla. Beat until it loses its gloss and starts to thicken. Quickly add walnuts. Pour into greased 8 x 8 inch (20 x 20 cm) pan. Cool. Cuts into 36 pieces.

Pictured on page 97.

Condensed Fudge

Great brown sugar taste.

Sweetened condensed milk	11 oz.	300 mL
Brown sugar, packed	2 cups	450 mL
Granulated sugar	1 cup	225 mL
Milk	½ cup	125 mL
Butter or hard margarine	3 tbsp.	50 mL
Corn syrup	2 tbsp.	30 mL
Vanilla	1 tsp.	5 mL

Combine first 6 ingredients in 3 quart (3 L) saucepan. Heat on medium-low, stirring often as it comes to a boil. Boil, stirring occasionally to prevent sticking, until soft ball stage on candy thermometer or until a small spoonful dropped in cold water forms a soft ball. Remove from heat. Remove thermometer. Let stand 40 minutes.

Add vanilla. Beat until it gets thick. Pour into greased 9 x 9 inch (22 x 22 cm) pan. Cool. Cuts into 36 pieces. Makes 2 pounds (900 g).

Pictured on page 97.

Shortbread Squares

Crunchy and crisp.

Butter, softened (do not use margarine)	½ lb.	225 g
All-purpose flour	2½ cups	575 mL
Granulated sugar	¾ cup	175 mL
Granulated sugar (plain or colored)	½ cup	125 mL

Melt butter in small saucepan.

Stir flour and first amount of sugar well in bowl. Add melted butter. Mix well. Pat out flat about ¼ inch (6 mm) thick on ungreased cookie sheet. Bake in 325°F (160°C) oven for about 25 minutes until golden.

Cut into squares while hot. Coat with remaining sugar. Makes 36 squares.

Pictured on this page.

Top: Peanut Butter Treats
Bottom: Scotch Shortbread

Center: Shortbread Squares

Peanut Butter Treats

These no-bake treats freeze well. Very rich.

Butter or hard margarine	½ cup	125 mL
Smooth peanut butter	1 cup	250 mL
Graham cracker crumbs	1 cup	250 mL
Icing (confectioner's) sugar	2 cups	500 mL
Chopped walnuts	⅓ cup	75 mL
Icing:		
Semisweet chocolate chips	1 cup	250 mL
Butter or hard margarine	3 tbsp.	50 mL

Heat and stir butter and peanut butter in large saucepan until smooth.

Add graham crumbs, icing sugar and walnuts. Mix well. Press into ungreased 8 x 8 inch (20 x 20 cm) pan.

Icing: Heat and stir chocolate chips and butter in saucepan on low until smooth. Spread over top. Let stand until set. Cuts into 25 squares.

Pictured above.

Jean's Favorite

Scotch Shortbread

Perfect! Lightly golden squares with a dusting of icing sugar. Try the variation too.

Butter, softened (do not use margarine)	½ lb.	225 g
Icing (confectioner's) sugar	½ cup	125 mL
All-purpose flour	2 cups	450 mL
Baking powder	¼ tsp.	1 mL
Salt	⅛ tsp.	0.5 mL

Icing (confectioner's) sugar

Cream butter and icing sugar in medium bowl.

Mix in flour, baking powder and salt. Press into 9 x 9 inch (22 x 22 cm) pan. Prick dough, using fork, every 2 inches (5 cm). Bake in 350°F (175°C) oven for about 30 minutes until golden.

Cut into squares while hot. Sprinkle with icing sugar. Store in airtight container. Makes 36 squares.

Variation: Press into large ceramic shortbread mold. Bake in 350°F (175°C) oven for about 30 minutes until golden. Unmold carefully when cool. Makes 1 large mold.

Pictured on this page.

Top: Beer Nuts, page 99
Center: Nutty Cherry Shortbread, page 91
Bottom: Chocolate Drop Cookies, page 99

Chocolate Drop Cookies

A soft, tasty cookie.

Butter or hard margarine	½ cup	125 mL
Unsweetened baking chocolate squares, cut up	2 × 1 oz.	2 × 28 g
Brown sugar, packed	1 cup	250 mL
Large egg	1	1
Milk	¾ cup	175 mL
Vanilla	1 tsp.	5 mL
All-purpose flour	2¼ cups	500 mL
Baking soda	½ tsp.	2 mL
Topping:		
Semisweet baking chocolate squares, melted	2 × 1 oz.	2 × 28 g

Melt butter and chocolate in large saucepan over low heat, stirring often. Remove from heat.

Using spoon, beat in sugar, egg, milk and vanilla.

Stir flour and baking soda together. Add and stir to moisten. Drop by rounded teaspoonfuls onto greased cookie sheet about 1 inch apart. Bake in 350°F (175°C) oven for 8 to 10 minutes. Cool.

Topping: Drizzle with melted chocolate. Makes 4 dozen cookies.

Pictured above.

Beer Nuts

Nice, toasty flavor. Keep a good supply on hand.

Large peanuts, with skins	4 cups	1 L
Butter or hard margarine	½ cup	125 mL
Brown sugar, packed	1 cup	250 mL
Corn syrup	¼ cup	60 mL
Salt	½ tsp.	2 mL
Baking soda	¼ tsp.	1 mL

Place peanuts in shallow non-stick baking pan. Keep warm in 225°F (110°C) oven.

Combine butter, brown sugar, corn syrup and salt in saucepan. Cook to firm ball, 250°F (120°C), or until a small spoonful dropped in cold water retains a round shape when rolled between fingers. Remove from heat.

Stir in baking soda. Pour slowly over peanuts, stirring gently to coat. Return to 250°F (120°C) oven for about 1 hour. Stir every 15 minutes. Cool. Stir several times while cooling. Keep in airtight container. Makes 5 cups (1.25 L) nut mixture.

Pictured on this page.

Gingerbread Figures

A treat for little (or big) kids! Leave as is or glaze or decorate with icing and small candy silver balls.

Butter or hard margarine, softened	½ cup	125 mL
Granulated sugar	½ cup	125 mL
Fancy molasses	½ cup	125 mL
Egg yolk (large)	1	1
All-purpose flour	2 cups	500 mL
Baking powder	½ tsp.	2 mL
Baking soda	½ tsp.	2 mL
Ground cinnamon	1 tsp.	5 mL
Ground ginger	1 tsp.	5 mL
Ground cloves	½ tsp.	2 mL
Ground nutmeg	¼ tsp.	1 mL
Salt	¼ tsp.	1 mL
Frosting:		
Egg white, large	1	1
Icing (confectioner's) sugar	2 cups	500 mL

Gingerbread Figures

Cream butter, sugar, molasses and egg yolk together until light.

Add next 8 ingredients. Mix well. Wrap in plastic and chill at least 1 hour. Roll out. Cut into shapes with cookie cutters. Arrange on baking sheet. Bake in 350°F (175°C) oven for 10 to 15 minutes. Cool.

Frosting: Beat egg white with spoon in medium bowl. Beat in as much icing sugar as needed until icing will hold its shape. Ice cookies. Makes 12 to 16 gingerbread men cookies or a variety of other shapes.

Pictured below.

Gingerbread Lollipops

Shape ¼ to ⅓ cup (60 to 75 mL) dough into ball. Insert wooden stick. Place on greased cookie sheet. Press with bottom of tumbler to ¼ inch (6 mm) thick. Bake for 10 to 12 minutes. Cool.

Chocolate Oat Balls

A no-bake confection. These can also be a drop cookie, if desired.

Butter or hard margarine	½ cup	125 mL
Granulated sugar	2 cups	500 mL
Milk	½ cup	125 mL
Quick cooking rolled oats	2 cups	500 mL
Cocoa	½ cup	125 mL
Vanilla	1 tsp.	5 mL
Toasted chopped pecans or walnuts (see Note)	1 cup	250 mL
Toasted finely chopped pecans or walnuts (see Note)	1 cup	250 mL

Heat butter, sugar and milk in saucepan, stirring often, until mixture comes to a simmer. Simmer 3 minutes. Remove from heat.

Add rolled oats, cocoa and vanilla. Stir well. Add first amount of pecans. Mix. Cool slightly. Shape into 1 inch (2.5 cm) balls.

Roll balls in remaining nuts. Store in airtight container. Makes 3 dozen cookies.

Note: To toast pecans or walnuts, spread on baking sheet. Bake in 350°F (175°C) oven for 5 to 8 minutes until "toasty" aroma.

Pictured on page 104.

Cherry Surprise

Very impressive and so easy to make. Freezes well.

Sweetened condensed milk	11 oz.	300 mL
Unsweetened chocolate baking squares, cut up	2 × 1 oz.	2 × 28 g
Graham wafer crumbs	2 cups	450 mL
Glazed cherries, red and green	32	32
Fine coconut	¾ cup	175 mL

Put milk and chocolate in top of double boiler. Cook over boiling water, stirring often, until thick, about 5 minutes.

Stir in graham crumbs. Chill for 1 hour.

Mold 1 tbsp. (15 mL) around each cherry.

Roll in coconut. Makes 32 confections.

Pictured on page 104.

Rum Balls

Rum Balls

Always a favorite. Roll in chocolate sprinkles, icing sugar or cocoa for variety.

Vanilla wafer crumbs	3 cups	675 mL
Finely ground almonds or pecans	½ cup	125 mL
Cocoa	3 tbsp.	50 mL
Icing (confectioner's) sugar	1 cup	250 mL
Corn syrup	3 tbsp.	50 mL
Water	⅓ cup	75 mL
Rum flavoring	2 tsp.	10 mL
Icing (confectioner's) sugar	¼ cup	60 mL

Mix first 7 ingredients well in medium bowl. Shape into 1 inch (2.5 cm) balls.

Roll balls in remaining icing sugar. Store in covered container for several days before serving. Makes 36 balls.

Pictured above.

Taffy

Have a taffy pull party. Loads of fun!

Granulated sugar	2 cups	450 mL
Water	½ cup	125 mL
White vinegar	¼ cup	60 mL
Butter or hard margarine	2 tsp.	10 mL
Salt	⅛ tsp.	0.5 mL
Vanilla	1 tsp.	5 mL

Place sugar, water, vinegar, butter and salt in 3 quart (3 L) heavy saucepan. Heat and stir on medium until sugar dissolves. Bring to a boil. Boil, without stirring, until it reaches hard-ball stage 250°F (120°C) on candy thermometer. A teaspoonful dropped in some cold water will become hard. Remove from heat. Remove thermometer.

Stir in vanilla. Pour into buttered 9 x 13 inch (22 x 33 cm) pan to cool. When it has cooled enough to handle, divide among helpers. Pull with buttered fingertips. It will become much lighter in color. When it gets hard to pull, stretch into ropes about ½ to ¾ inch (12 to 18 mm) wide. Butter edges of scissors. Cut quickly into 1 inch (2.5 cm) lengths. Wrap each piece in waxed paper or plastic wrap. Makes about 100 pieces or 1¼ pounds (500 g).

Pictured below.

Breton Brittle

Fantastic people-pleaser. Quick and easy.

Dare Breton crackers (see Note)	28	28
Butter or hard margarine	1 cup	250 mL
Brown sugar, packed	1 cup	250 mL
Topping:		
Semisweet chocolate chips	1⅔ cups	400 mL
Finely chopped pecans or walnuts	⅓ cup	75 mL

Overlap crackers in foil-lined 9 x 13 inch (22 x 33 cm) pan so bottom is covered. Use 4 crackers across and 7 crackers lengthwise.

Stir butter and brown sugar together in saucepan until it comes to a boil. Pour carefully over crackers. Bake in 400°F (205°C) oven for 5 minutes.

Topping: Scatter chocolate chips over top. Let stand until soft. Spread to cover. Sprinkle with pecans. Cool. Store in refrigerator. Break or cut into pieces to serve. Makes 8 cups (2 L) brittle.

Pictured below.

Note: If Dare Breton crackers aren't available in your area, use thin round 2½ inch (6 cm) crackers (not soda) to line your pan.

Top Left: Peanut Brittle, page 103
Top Right: Almond Roca, page 103
Center: Breton Brittle, page 102
Bottom: Taffy, page 102

Almond Roca

Absolutely the best! Store in container in cool place—but keep handy.

Butter (do not use margarine)	1 lb.	454 g
Granulated sugar	2 cups	450 mL
Water	1/4 cup	60 mL
Corn syrup	2 tbsp.	30 mL
Toasted, slivered almonds (see Note)	1 1/3 cups	300 mL
Semisweet chocolate baking squares, cut up	4 x 1 oz.	4 x 28 g
Toasted, slivered almonds, finely chopped (see Note)	2/3 cup	300 mL
Semisweet baking chocolate squares, cut up	4 x 1 oz.	4 x 28 g

Melt butter in heavy saucepan over low heat. Add sugar. Stir to dissolve. Stir in water and corn syrup. Cook over low heat, stirring often but gently, until candy thermometer reads 290°F (142°C). Be patient. This will take 30 to 40 minutes. Remove from heat. Remove thermometer.

Add first amount of slivered almonds. Pour into greased 10 x 15 inch (25 x 30 cm) jelly roll pan about 1/4 inch (6 mm) deep. Let cool.

Melt first amount of chocolate squares in saucepan over lowest heat, stirring often. Cool until you can hold your hand on saucepan but pan feels hot. Spread over candy.

Sprinkle with 1/2 remaining chopped almonds. Wait until chocolate hardens. Cover with waxed paper. Place another pan over top. Invert. Melt second amount of chocolate squares in saucepan over lowest heat. Cool until you can hold your hand on saucepan but pan feels hot. Spread over candy. Sprinkle with remaining chopped almonds. Allow to harden. Break into pieces to serve and to store. Makes 2.5 pounds (1.2 kg).

Note: To toast almonds, spread on baking sheet. Bake in 350°F (175°C) oven for 5 to 8 minutes until lightly browned.

Pictured on page 102.

Peanut Brittle

Include a box of this in your out-of-town parcels.

Granulated sugar	1 1/2 cups	350 mL
Water	1/3 cup	75 mL
White corn syrup	2/3 cup	150 mL
Spanish peanuts	2 cups	450 mL
Butter (do not use margarine)	2 tbsp.	30 mL
Vanilla	1 tsp.	5 mL
Baking soda	2 tsp.	10 mL

Measure first 3 ingredients into heavy 3 quart (3 L) saucepan. Heat and stir until sugar dissolves and it starts to boil. Boil without stirring until it reaches soft-ball stage on candy thermometer or until a small spoonful dropped in cold water forms a soft ball.

Add peanuts and butter. Stir frequently until it reaches hard-crack or until a small spoonful dropped in cold water separates into threads and are hard and brittle and break between your fingers. Remove from heat. Grease baking sheet.

Add vanilla and baking soda. Work quickly and stir into mixture. It will foam. Immediately pour onto greased baking sheet. Spread evenly using greased pancake turner or spoon. Cool completely. Break into pieces. Makes 1 1/2 pounds (680 g).

Pictured on page 102.

Butterscotches

Let the kids make these. Make as either a drop cookie or a rolled ball.

Granulated sugar	1 1/2 cups	350mL
Butter or hard margarine	1/2 cup	125 mL
Evaporated milk (small can)	2/3 cup	150 mL
Butterscotch chips	1 cup	250 mL
Quick cooking rolled oats	3 1/2 cups	800 mL
Medium coconut	1/2 cup	125 mL

Stir sugar, butter and milk in saucepan. Heat stirring constantly while it comes to a boil and boils for 1 minute. Remove from heat.

Add butterscotch chips. Stir until melted.

Mix in rolled oats and coconut. Stir well. Cool for 5 to 10 minutes. Drop by rounded teaspoonfuls onto waxed paper. Chill until firm. Makes about 6 dozen.

Pictured on page 104.

Dipped Vanillas

These are so pretty on a tray of mixed cookies. Freeze ahead.

Butter	½ cup	125 mL
Ground almonds	½ cup	125 mL
Granulated sugar	¼ cup	60 mL
Vanilla	1 tsp.	5 mL
All-purpose flour	1 cup	250 mL
Cornstarch	2 tbsp.	30 mL
Dip:		
Semisweet chocolate baking squares, cut up	2 x 1 oz.	2 x 28 g
Grated paraffin wax	2 tbsp.	30 mL

Cream butter, almonds, sugar and vanilla in mixing bowl.

Mix in flour and cornstarch. Shape into 1 inch (2.5 cm) balls. Roll each ball into a crescent shape. Place on greased baking sheet. Bake in 375°F (190°C) oven for 8 to 10 minutes. Cool.

Dip: Melt chocolate and wax in saucepan on lowest heat, stirring often. Dip top sides of crescents or 1 or both ends. Place on waxed paper to harden. Makes 30.

Pictured on page 104.

1. Cherry Surprise, page 101
2. Butterscotches, page 103
3. Dipped Vanillas, page 105
4. Chocolate Oat Balls, page 101
5. Christmas Trees, page 94

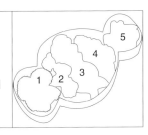

Desserts

Desserts

Special meals call for special desserts. You'll find the perfect finale for any of your holiday meals in this selection of squares, cakes and fancy desserts.

You can't go wrong with squares when it comes time for dessert. The variety is endless and they look and taste good.

Keep the pieces small for more variety on the plate. For easier cutting and serving, line the baking pan with foil. That makes it easier to lift the squares out for cutting.

If you think you will be serving a lot of squares during the season, cool and cut before freezing. That lets you scoop out the number you need without having to defrost the entire pan.

Cakes are another versatile and attractive choice. Some can be frozen and iced when defrosted. Depending on the icing, some cakes can be frosted ahead of time. Just be sure to use toothpicks to keep the wrap away from the icing.

Angel food and some kinds of tube cakes slice better when slightly frozen, while some other cakes cut better when defrosted a bit.

If you're looking for something different and a bit fun, try a fancy dessert. These whimsical concoctions will delight your guests to no end.

A fitting end is what you're looking for and that's what you get with these tempting dessert recipes.

Strawberry Cream Dessert

Very strawberry! A pretty ending to a meal.

Crust:		
Butter or hard margarine	½ cup	125 mL
Graham cracker crumbs	2 cups	500 mL
Brown sugar, packed	¼ cup	60 mL
Filling:		
Frozen strawberries in syrup, thawed, syrup reserved	15 oz.	425 g
Reserved strawberry syrup		
Strawberry-flavored gelatin (jelly powder)	3 oz.	85 g
Granulated sugar	½ cup	125 mL
Lemon juice, fresh or bottled	2 tbsp.	30 mL
Whipping cream (or 1 envelope topping)	1 cup	250 mL
Topping:		
Whipping cream (or 1 envelope topping)	1 cup	250 mL
Granulated sugar	2 tsp.	10 mL
Vanilla	½ tsp.	2 mL
Reserved crumbs	½ cup	125 mL

Crust: Melt butter in saucepan. Stir in graham crumbs and sugar. Reserve ½ cup (125 mL) for topping. Press remaining crumbs in ungreased 9 x 9 inch (22 x 22 cm) pan. Bake in 350°F (175°C) oven for 10 minutes. Cool.

Filling: Strain strawberries. Reserve syrup.

Pour reserved syrup into saucepan over medium heat. Stir gelatin into hot syrup to dissolve.

Stir in sugar and lemon juice. Cool. Add strawberries. Stir. Chill, stirring and scraping down sides often, until it starts to thicken.

Beat cream in small bowl until stiff. Fold into strawberry mixture. Pour over crust. Chill.

Topping: Beat cream, sugar and vanilla in small bowl until stiff. Spread over all. Sprinkle with reserved crumbs. Chill. Cuts into 9 or 12 pieces.

Pictured on page 107.

Profiteroles

You've seen them on restaurant menus—but these are chocolate! Make pro-FIT-er-ohls at home.

Cream Puffs:

Hot water	1 cup	250 mL
Butter or hard margarine	½ cup	125 mL
Semisweet chocolate baking square, cut up	1 × 1 oz.	1 × 28 g
Salt	½ tsp.	2 mL
All-purpose flour	1 cup	250 mL
Granulated sugar	1 tbsp.	15 mL
Large eggs	4	4

Chocolate Filling:

Instant chocolate pudding powder, 4 serving size	1	1
Milk	1 cup	250 mL
Whipping cream (or 1 envelope topping)	1 cup	250 mL

Chocolate Glaze:

Semisweet chocolate baking squares, cut up	2 × 1 oz.	2 × 28 g
Milk	2 tbsp.	30 mL
Corn syrup	1 tbsp.	15 mL
Vanilla	¼ tsp.	1 mL

Cream Puffs: Combine first 4 ingredients in medium saucepan. Stir often over medium heat as mixture comes to a boil.

Add flour and sugar all at once. Cook and stir until it forms a ball of dough that won't stick to edge of saucepan. Remove from heat.

Add eggs 1 at a time, beating well after each addition. Divide dough into 4 equal portions. Spoon onto greased baking sheet getting 12 from each portion. Bake in 450°F (230°C) oven for 10 minutes. Reduce heat to 350°F (175°C). Bake about 5 minutes more until risen and browned. Cool.

Chocolate Filling: Beat pudding and milk together until smooth.

Beat cream until stiff. Fold into pudding. Cut tops not quite off puffs. Spoon in filling. Place on platter in shape of a bunch of grapes.

Chocolate Glaze: Combine all ingredients in saucepan. Heat and stir on medium-low until smooth. Drizzle over puffs. Makes 48. Serves 6 each to 8 guests.

Pictured on page 106.

Chocolate Truffle

Pure ecstacy!

Crust:

Butter or hard margarine	¼ cup	60 mL
Chocolate wafer crumbs	1¼ cups	300 mL
Granulated sugar	1 tbsp.	15 mL

Filling:

Butter or hard margarine	1 cup	250 mL
Semisweet chocolate chips	3 cups	750 mL
Large eggs, room temperature	5	5
Vanilla	1 tsp.	5 mL

Chocolate Glaze:

Semisweet chocolate chips	½ cup	125 mL
Evaporated milk or whipping cream	3 tbsp.	50 mL

Topping:

Whipping cream (or 1 envelope topping)	1 cup	250 mL
Granulated sugar	2 tsp.	10 mL
Vanilla	½ tsp.	2 mL
Cocoa, or grated chocolate, for dusting		

Crust: Melt butter in medium saucepan. Stir in crumbs and sugar. Press into bottom of ungreased 8 inch (20 cm) springform pan. Set pan on a piece of foil. Press foil up all around to prevent water leaking into pan. Set pan in roaster or other wide pan.

Filling: Melt butter in large saucepan on low. Add chocolate chips. Stir often until they melt. Pour into medium bowl.

Add eggs 1 at a time, beating well after each addition. Mix in vanilla. Pour over crust in pan. Pour boiling water in roaster about ½ to ⅔ up side of springform pan. Bake in 425°F (220°C) oven for about 15 minutes until outer edge is set. Center will still be soft. Lift springform out of water and place on rack. Cool. Chill for at least 4 hours. Remove sides of springform pan.

Chocolate Glaze: Melt chocolate chips with milk in small saucepan on low. Stir often until smooth. Pour on top of filling. Smooth to glaze top and sides. Let stand a few minutes to dry before adding topping.

Topping: Beat cream, sugar and vanilla in small mixing bowl until stiff. Drop in puff balls around outside edge of cake.

Dust puffs with cocoa or sprinkle with grated chocolate. Chill until ready to serve. Serves 8 to 12.

Pictured on page 106.

Buttermilk Cake

Luscious Chocolate Cake

Buttermilk Cake

Nice large cake. Freezes well. Very moist.

Butter or hard margarine, softened	1 cup	250 mL
Granulated sugar	3 cups	675 mL
Egg yolks (large)	5	5
Vanilla	1 tsp.	5 mL
Salt	1/8 tsp.	0.5 mL
Buttermilk, fresh or reconstituted from powder	1 cup	250 mL
Baking soda	3/4 tsp.	4 mL
All-purpose flour	3 cups	750 mL
Egg whites (large), room temperature	5	5

Cream butter and sugar well in large bowl. Add egg yolks, 1 at a time, beating well after each. Stir in vanilla and salt.

Measure buttermilk into separate bowl. Stir in baking soda.

Add flour in 3 parts alternately with buttermilk in 2 parts, beginning and ending with flour.

Beat egg whites until stiff. Fold into batter. Turn into greased (bottom only) 10 inch (25 cm) angel food pan. Bake in 325°F (160°C) oven for about 1 hour. There will be tiny cracks in top. Cool completely in pan before removing. Makes 1 cake.

Pictured on this page.

Luscious Chocolate Cake

"This is to die for," it has been said.

Chocolate cake mix, 2 layer size	1	1
Instant chocolate pudding powder, 4 serving size	1	1
Large eggs	4	4
Cooking oil	1/2 cup	125 mL
Warm water	1/2 cup	125 mL
Sour cream	1 cup	250 mL
Semisweet chocolate chips	1 1/2 cups	375 mL
Chocolate Glaze:		
Semisweet chocolate chips	1/2 cup	125 mL
Butter or hard margarine	1 tbsp.	15 mL

Combine first 6 ingredients in large bowl. Beat on low to moisten, scraping down sides 2 or 3 times. Beat on medium for 2 minutes.

Stir in chocolate chips. Turn into greased and floured 12 cup (2.7 L) bundt pan. Bake in 350°F (175°C) oven for 50 to 60 minutes until an inserted wooden pick comes out clean. Let stand for 20 minutes. Invert onto plate or rack to cool.

Chocolate Glaze: Melt chocolate chips and butter in saucepan over low heat, stirring often. Remove from heat. Spread over top of cake allowing some to run down sides. Makes 1 cake.

Pictured above.

Prune Cake

Nice spicy flavor but not strong. This will be a winner.

Cooking oil	½ cup	125 mL
Granulated sugar	1 cup	250 mL
Large eggs	2	2
Stewed, pitted and chopped prunes, drained, juice reserved	⅔ cup	150 mL
All-purpose flour	1½ cups	375 mL
Baking powder	½ tsp.	2 mL
Baking soda	½ tsp.	2 mL
Salt	½ tsp.	2 mL
Ground cinnamon	½ tsp.	2 mL
Ground nutmeg	½ tsp.	2 mL
Ground allspice	½ tsp.	2 mL
Sour milk (or 2 tsp. 10 mL, white vinegar plus milk, stand 5 minutes)	⅔ cup	150 mL

Prune Icing:

Icing (confectioner's) sugar	3 cups	750 mL
Butter or hard margarine, softened	6 tbsp.	100 mL
Reserved prune juice	¼ cup	60 mL
Vanilla	½ tsp.	2 mL

Beat cooking oil, sugar and 1 egg together in large bowl. Beat in second egg. Add prunes and stir with spoon.

Stir next 7 ingredients in separate bowl.

Add flour mixture in 3 parts alternately with sour milk in 2 parts beginning and ending with flour. Divide between 2 greased 8 inch (20 cm) round layer pans. Bake in 350°F (175°C) oven for about 25 minutes. An inserted wooden pick should come out clean. Cool. Remove from pans.

Prune Icing: Beat all ingredients in medium bowl on low to moisten. Beat on medium, adding more juice or icing sugar if needed to make proper spreading consistency. Makes about 1½ cups (375 mL), enough to fill and ice Prune Cake. Makes 1 cake.

Pictured on page 107.

Chocolate Crêpes

Put dessert under wraps.

Large eggs	3	3
Milk	1 cup	250 mL
Water	½ cup	125 mL
All-purpose flour	1¼ cups	300 mL
Granulated sugar	¼ cup	60 mL
Cocoa	2 tbsp.	30 mL
Cooking oil	2 tbsp.	30 mL
Rum flavoring (optional)	½ tsp.	2 mL
Filling:		
Cottage cheese	2 cups	500 mL
Icing (confectioner's) sugar	⅔ cup	150 mL
Topping:		
Frozen raspberries (or strawberries), in syrup	15 oz.	425 g

Beat eggs in mixing bowl until frothy. Add remaining ingredients. Beat until smooth. Add a bit more milk if too thick. Spoon 2 tbsp. (30 mL) batter into hot greased crêpe pan or use crêpe pan that dips into batter. Tip pan quickly so batter covers bottom. When underside is brown, remove crêpe to plate. Repeat. Makes about 24 crêpes.

Filling: Beat cottage cheese and icing sugar in small bowl until quite smooth. Place 1½ tbsp. (25 mL) down center of each crêpe. Fold sides over.

Topping: Spoon raspberries with juice across center of folded crêpes.

Pictured below.

Chocolate Crêpes

Bread Pudding

Everyone will love the taste. Raisins can be substituted for the currants, if preferred. Serve with cream.

Evaporated skim milk	13½ oz.	385 mL
Milk	¼ cup	60 mL
Raisin bread slices, cut bite size	5	5
Butter or hard margarine	2 tbsp.	30 mL
Large eggs, beaten	2	2
Brown sugar, packed	⅔ cup	150 mL
Salt	½ tsp.	2 mL
Vanilla	1 tsp.	5 mL
Currants	½ cup	125 mL
Ground cinnamon	¼ tsp.	1 mL

Heat both milks in heavy saucepan until steaming. Remove from heat.

Add bread and butter.

Beat eggs in small bowl. Add brown sugar, salt and vanilla. Stir in currants and cinnamon. Pour into milk mixture. Stir well. Turn into greased 1 quart (1 L) casserole. Bake, uncovered, in 350°F (175°C) oven for 40 to 45 minutes until set. Serves 6.

Pictured below.

Bread Pudding

Angel Mint Roll

The roll can be frozen in the towel in a plastic bag, then thawed and filled the day of serving.

Angel food cake mix	1	1
Icing (confectioner's) sugar	¼ cup	60 mL
Filling:		
Milk	½ cup	125 mL
Large marshmallows	36	36
Whipping cream (or 2 envelopes topping)	2 cups	500 mL
Crème De Menthe, green	⅓ cup	75 mL
Chocolate crumbs	¼ cup	60 mL
Coating:		
Whipping cream (or 2 envelopes topping)	2 cups	500 mL
Granulated sugar	2 tbsp.	30 mL
Vanilla	1 tsp.	5 mL

Prepare cake mix according to package directions. Line greased 10 × 15 inch (25 × 38 cm) jelly roll pan with waxed paper. Spread cake batter in pan. Bake in 375°F (190°C) oven for about 20 minutes until an inserted wooden pick comes out clean. Cool.

Turn out onto tea towel that has been well sprinkled with icing sugar. Carefully peel off waxed paper. Roll up with towel, starting from short side.

Filling: Heat, stirring often, milk and marshmallows in large saucepan until marshmallows melt. Cool thoroughly.

Beat whipping cream in large bowl until stiff. Add Crème De Menthe. Fold into cooled marshmallow mixture. Chill until fairly thick. Unroll angel cake. Spread with filling.

Sprinkle with chocolate crumbs. Roll up without towel.

Coating: Beat whipping cream, sugar and vanilla until stiff. Spread over roll covering sides, top and ends. Cuts into 12 slices.

Pictured on page 113.

Angel Mint Roll, page 112

Chocolate Roulade Yule Log, page 113

Chocolate Roulade Yule Log

A delicate roll.

Egg whites (large), room temperature	6	6
Cream of tartar	½ tsp.	2 mL
Egg yolks (large)	6	6
Granulated sugar	1 cup	250 mL
Cocoa	⅓ cup	75 mL
Vanilla	1 tsp.	5 mL
Salt, just a pinch		
Cocoa, sprinkle		
Filling:		
Whipping cream	2 cups	500 mL
Cocoa	½ cup	125 mL
Granulated sugar	½ cup	125 mL
Chocolate or coffee liqueur	¼ cup	60 mL
Large marshmallow	1	1
Pecan halves	6	6

Line greased 10 x 15 inch (25 x 38 cm) jelly roll pan with waxed paper. Beat egg whites in large bowl until soft peaks form. Add cream of tartar. Beat until stiff.

Using same beaters beat egg yolks, sugar, cocoa, vanilla and salt in medium bowl until frothy. Fold in egg whites. Spread in prepared pan. Bake in 350°F (175°C) oven for 15 to 20 minutes until an inserted wooden pick comes out clean.

Sift cocoa over a tea towel. Turn out cake onto cocoa. Peel off waxed paper. Begin at shorter side. Roll both towel and cake together, continuing to dust with cocoa. Cool. When cool, unroll and spread with filling.

Filling: Beat cream, cocoa, sugar and liqueur in small bowl until thick.

Unroll cake. Spread with ½ filling. Roll up again without the towel. Chill. Spread outside with remaining filling, using large marshmallow to form "knot" on "log". Place pecan halves at random. Cuts into 12 slices.

Pictured above.

Cookies 'N Cake

The kids will love this even without the icing and chocolate drizzle.

White cake mix, 2 layer size	1	1
Cooking oil	½ cup	125 mL
Large eggs	4	4
Water	1 cup	250 mL
Coarsely crushed cream filled chocolate cookies	1 cup	250 mL
Icing:		
Icing (confectioner's) sugar	1 cup	250 mL
Butter or hard margarine, softened	2 tbsp.	30 mL
Water	1½ tbsp.	25 mL
Vanilla	½ tsp.	2 mL
Unsweetened baking chocolate square, cut up, melted	1 × 1 oz.	1 × 28 g

Place cake mix, cooking oil, eggs and water into large bowl. Beat on low to moisten. Beat on medium for 2 minutes until smooth.

Carefully stir in crushed cookies. Turn into greased and floured 12 cup (2.7 L) bundt pan. Bake in 350°F (175°C) oven for about 45 to 55 minutes until an inserted wooden pick comes out clean. Cool. Turn out onto rack.

Icing: Stir all 4 ingredients together vigorously. Add more or less icing sugar or water to make a little softer than a spreading consistency. Spoon over cake allowing some to run down sides.

Drizzle chocolate over icing. Makes 1 cake.

Pictured on page 115.

Sherry Trifle

Be sure and use a see-through dish or special trifle bowl. The layers are so eye-catching.

White cake mix, 2 layer size	1	1
Raspberry jam	½ cup	125 mL
Custard:		
Milk	2⅔ cups	650 mL
Custard powder	¼ cup	60 mL
Granulated sugar	¼ cup	60 mL
Milk	⅓ cup	75 mL
Vanilla	¾ tsp.	4 mL
Sherry (or alcohol-free sherry)	⅓ cup	75 mL
Reserved raspberry syrup		
Frozen raspberries in syrup, thawed, syrup reserved	15 oz.	425 g
Whipped Cream:		
Whipping cream (or 1 envelope topping)	1 cup	250 mL
Granulated sugar	1 tbsp.	15 mL
Vanilla	½ tsp.	2 mL

Maraschino cherries, for garnish

Make cake mix according to directions on box, using two 8 inch (20 cm) round cake pans. Cool completely. Slice cake layers in half horizontally to make 2 thin layers each. Spread 2 layers with ¼ cup (60 mL) jam each. Cut all 4 layers into cubes.

Custard: Heat first amount of milk in heavy saucepan until it simmers.

Stir custard powder and sugar together well in small bowl. Mix in remaining milk and vanilla. Stir slowly into hot milk until mixture boils and thickens. Cool completely.

Mix sherry and reserved raspberry syrup in small bowl.

Spread ½ the cake cubes in bottom of 2 quart (2 L) glass bowl. Pour ½ the sherry mixture over the cubes. Sprinkle with ½ the raspberries. Spread ½ custard over raspberries. Repeat with remaining cubes, sherry mixture, raspberries and custard. Chill until cold.

Whipped Cream: Beat cream, sugar and vanilla in small bowl until stiff. Spread over top layer of custard.

Garnish with cherries. Serves 6 to 8.

Pictured on page 115.

Left: Sherry Trifle, page 114
Right: Cookies 'N Cake, page 114

Pineapple Cake

Refreshing taste. Ice with Fluffy Frosting, page 122, and sprinkle with crushed rock candy.

Butter or hard margarine, softened	½ cup	125 mL
Granulated sugar	1½ cups	375 mL
Egg yolks, large	3	3
Crushed pineapple, with juice to measure	1 cup	250 mL
Vanilla	1½ tsp.	7 mL
Water	¼ cup	60 mL
Salt	½ tsp.	2 mL
Cake flour, sift before measuring	2½ cups	575 mL
Baking powder	1 tbsp.	15 mL
Egg whites (large), room temperature	3	3

Cream butter and sugar well in large bowl. Beat in egg yolks.

Add pineapple, juice, vanilla, water and salt. Stir to mix.

Add flour and baking powder. Stir slowly until moistened.

Beat egg whites with clean beater until stiff. Fold into cake batter. Turn into 2 greased 8 inch (20 cm) round layer pans. Bake in 350°F (175°C) oven for about 30 to 35 minutes. An inserted wooden pick should come out clean. Cool. Makes 1 cake.

Pictured below.

Pineapple Cake, page 116 with Fluffy Frosting, page 122

Creamy Chilled Dessert

Nice and creamy with a thick nutty shortbread crust.

Bottom Layer:		
All-purpose flour	2 cups	500 mL
Granulated sugar	⅓ cup	75 mL
Butter or hard margarine	1 cup	250 mL
Chopped pecans or walnuts	½ cup	125 mL
Second Layer:		
Cream cheese, softened	8 oz.	250 g
Icing (confectioner's) sugar	1 cup	250 mL
Vanilla	1½ tsp.	7 mL
Envelope dessert topping (to make 1½ cups, 375 mL)	1	1
Third Layer:		
Instant vanilla pudding powder, 6 serving size	1	1
Milk	2 cups	450 mL
Topping:		
Whipping cream (or 2 envelopes topping)	2 cups	500 mL
Granulated sugar	2 tbsp.	30 mL
Vanilla	2 tsp.	10 mL

Bottom Layer: Mix flour and sugar in medium bowl. Cut in butter until mixture is crumbly.

Add pecans. Stir. Pack into 9 x 13 inch (22 x 33 cm) pan. Bake in 350°F (175°C) oven for about 15 minutes. Cool.

Second Layer: Beat cream cheese, icing sugar and vanilla until smooth.

Prepare dessert topping as directed on envelope. Fold into cream cheese mixture. Spread over bottom layer.

Third Layer: Empty pudding mix into small bowl. Beat in milk for about 1½ minutes until smooth. Pour over second layer.

Topping: Beat whipping cream, sugar and vanilla until stiff. Spread over all. Chill. Cuts into 15 to 18 pieces.

Pictured on page 119.

Variation: Use frozen strawberries (or raspberries) in syrup, thawed, instead of whipped cream topping. Spoon over dessert.

Chocolate Cheesecake

A luscious, rich dessert.

Chocolate Cracker Crust:

Butter or hard margarine	6 tbsp.	100 mL
Graham cracker crumbs	1½ cups	375 mL
Cocoa	3 tbsp.	50 mL
Granulated sugar	3 tbsp.	50 mL

Filling:

Unsweetened chocolate baking squares, cut up	2 × 1 oz.	2 × 28 g
Semisweet chocolate baking squares, cut up	3 × 1 oz.	3 × 28 g
Cream cheese, softened	3 × 8 oz.	3 × 250 g
Granulated sugar	1¼ cups	300 mL
Large eggs	4	4
Sour cream	½ cup	125 mL
Vanilla	1 tsp.	5 mL
Rum flavoring	1 tsp.	5 mL

Chocolate Cracker Crust: Melt butter in medium saucepan. Stir in graham crumbs, cocoa and sugar. Press in bottom of ungreased 9 inch (22 cm) springform pan. Bake in 350°F (175°C) oven for 10 minutes.

Filling: Melt both chocolates in heavy saucepan over lowest heat, stirring often as it melts. Remove from heat.

Beat cream cheese and sugar in bowl until smooth. Add chocolate. Beat.

Add eggs 1 at a time beating slowly after each addition just to mix. Mix in sour cream, vanilla and rum flavoring slowly to mix. Pour over chocolate crust. Bake in 300°F (150°C) oven for about 50 minutes until set. Center will wobble a bit when jiggled. Place pan on wire rack. Run knife around top edge to allow cake to settle evenly. Cool. Chill, uncovered, overnight for best flavor. Serves 12.

Pictured above.

Coconut Cream Delight

*Not too sweet. Crumb layer has a nice "toasty" flavor.
A real delight!*

Bottom Layer:

All-purpose flour	1 cup	250 mL
Fine coconut	1 cup	250 mL
Brown sugar, packed	¼ cup	60 mL
Butter or hard margarine	½ cup	125 mL

Filling:

Milk	2¼ cups	500 mL
Granulated sugar	½ cup	125 mL
All-purpose flour	½ cup	125 mL
Salt	¼ tsp.	1 mL
Coconut flavoring	2 tsp.	10 mL
Large eggs	2	2
Flake coconut	1 cup	225 mL

Topping:

Whipping cream (or 1 envelope topping)	1 cup	250 mL
Granulated sugar	2 tsp.	10 mL
Vanilla	½ tsp.	2 mL
Reserved crumbs	¼ cup	60 mL

Bottom Layer: Mix all 4 ingredients together until crumbly. Spread in jelly roll pan. Bake in 400°F (205°C) oven for about 5 to 10 minutes until lightly browned. Reserve ¼ cup (60 mL) for topping. Press remaining crumbs into ungreased 9 x 9 inch (22 x 22 cm) pan.

Filling: Heat milk in heavy saucepan.

Stir sugar, flour and salt in bowl. Add flavoring and eggs. Stir well. Beat with spoon. Stir into hot milk until it boils and thickens. Remove from heat.

Stir in coconut. Pour over bottom layer. Cool.

Topping: Beat cream, sugar and vanilla in small bowl until stiff. Spread over cooled filling.

Sprinkle with reserved crumbs. Chill. Cuts into 9 to 12 pieces.

Pictured on page 119.

For a graham crumb crust that cuts nicely and doesn't crumble, mix the butter and crumbs together thoroughly and then pack the crumbs very well using the tips of your fingers or the bottom of a glass.

Raspberry Dessert

Try various combinations of strawberry or raspberry gelatin and frozen strawberries or raspberries. All are delicious!

Graham Crust:

Butter or hard margarine	½ cup	125 mL
Graham cracker crumbs	2 cups	500 mL
Brown sugar, packed	¼ cup	60 mL

Second Layer:

Cream cheese, softened	8 oz.	250 g
Icing (confectioner's) sugar	½ cup	125 mL
Vanilla	1 tsp.	5 mL
Salt	½ tsp.	2 mL

Third Layer:

Boiling water	1¼ cups	275 mL
Strawberry flavored gelatin (jelly powder)	6 oz.	170 g
Granulated sugar	¼ cup	60 mL
Frozen raspberries in syrup, thawed	15 oz.	425 g
Lemon juice, fresh or bottled	1 tsp.	5 mL

Top Layer:

Whipping cream (or 2 envelopes topping)	2 cups	500 mL
Icing (confectioner's) sugar	¼ cup	60 mL
Vanilla	1 tsp.	5 mL

Graham Crust: Melt butter in saucepan. Stir in graham crumbs and brown sugar. Reserve ½ cup (125 mL) for topping. Pack remaining mixture into ungreased 9 x 13 inch (22 x 33 cm) pan. Bake in 350°F (175°C) oven for 10 minutes. Cool.

Second Layer: Beat cream cheese, icing sugar, vanilla and salt in small bowl until smooth. Spread over cooled graham crust.

Third Layer: Pour boiling water into separate small bowl. Add gelatin powder and sugar. Stir until dissolved.

Add raspberries in syrup and lemon juice. Stir. Chill, stirring and scraping down sides of bowl every 10 minutes until it shows definite signs of thickening. Pour over cream cheese layer. Chill until set.

Top Layer: Beat cream, icing sugar and vanilla in small bowl until mixture holds stiff peaks. Smooth over red layer. Sprinkle with reserved crumbs. Chill. Cuts into 15 pieces.

Pictured on page 119.

Glimmering Slice

This looks spectacular.

Graham Crust:

Butter or hard margarine	½ cup	125 mL
Graham cracker crumbs	2 cups	500 mL
Brown sugar, packed	¼ cup	60 mL

Second Layer:

Unflavored gelatin	1 x ¼ oz.	1 x 7 g
Cold water	¼ cup	60 mL
Cold water	½ cup	125 mL
Lemon juice, fresh or bottled	½ cup	125 mL
Sweetened condensed milk (or 14 oz., 398 mL)	11 oz.	300 mL

Third Layer:

Raspberry flavored gelatin (jelly powder)	2 x 3 oz.	2 x 85 g
Boiling water	3 cups	675 mL

Graham Crust: Melt butter in saucepan. Stir in graham crumbs and sugar. Pack into ungreased 9 x 13 inch (22 x 33 cm) pan. Bake in 350°F (175°C) oven for 10 minutes. Cool.

Second Layer: Sprinkle gelatin over first amount of cold water in small saucepan. Let stand 1 minute. Heat and stir on medium-low to dissolve. Remove from heat.

Combine second amount of cold water, lemon juice and condensed milk in small bowl. Add dissolved gelatin mixture. Beat well. Smooth over graham crust.

Third Layer: Pour raspberry gelatin into small bowl. Add water. Stir until gelatin dissolves. Cool by placing bowl in cold water in sink. Stir as it cools. Chill in refrigerator, stirring and scraping down sides often with spatula, until it begins to thicken. Pour over second layer. Chill. Cuts into 15 pieces.

Pictured below.

Left: Coconut Cream Delight, page 118   Top Center: Creamy Chilled Dessert, page 116   Bottom Center: Glimmering Slice, page 119   Right: Raspberry Dessert, page 118

Date Cake

Rich and delicious. Very moist. Freezes well.

Chopped dates	1½ cups	375 mL
Baking soda	1½ tsp.	7 mL
Boiling water	1½ cups	375 mL
Butter or hard margarine, softened	¾ cup	175 mL
Brown sugar, packed	1 cup	250 mL
Granulated sugar	½ cup	125 mL
Large eggs	2	2
Vanilla	1 tsp.	5 mL
All-purpose flour	2½ cups	625 mL
Baking powder	1½ tsp.	7 mL
Salt	½ tsp.	2 mL
Topping:		
Butter or hard margarine	⅓ cup	75 mL
Brown sugar, packed	1 cup	250 mL
Cream or milk	3 tbsp.	50 mL
Fine coconut	1 cup	250 mL

Put dates into small bowl. Add baking soda. Pour boiling water over top. Cool.

Cream butter and both sugars in large bowl. Beat in eggs and vanilla.

Stir flour, baking powder and salt together. Add flour mixture in 3 parts alternately with date mixture in 2 parts beginning and ending with flour. Turn into greased 9 x 13 inch (22 x 33 cm) pan. Bake in 325°F (160°C) oven for 40 to 50 minutes until an inserted wooden pick comes out clean.

Topping: Measure butter, brown sugar and cream into saucepan. Heat and stir until it comes to a full rolling boil. Remove from heat.

Add coconut. Stir. Spoon over cake as soon as it is done. Broil until golden brown, 2 to 3 minutes. Makes 1 cake.

Pictured on page 121.

Dream Cake, page 120

Dream Cake

Festive square.

Bottom Layer:		
All-purpose flour	1½ cups	375 mL
Brown sugar, packed	¾ cup	175 mL
Butter or hard margarine	¾ cup	175 mL
Top Layer:		
Sweetened condensed milk	11 oz.	300 mL
Vanilla	½ tsp.	2 mL
Chopped walnuts	½ cup	125 mL
Chopped glazed cherries	⅓ cup	75 mL
Medium coconut	1½ cups	375 mL

Bottom Layer: Mix flour and sugar well. Cut in butter until crumbly. Pack into ungreased 9 x 13 inch (22 x 33 cm) pan. Bake in 350°F (175°C) oven for about 10 minutes until golden.

Top Layer: Stir all 5 ingredients together in bowl. Spoon dabs here and there over bottom layer. Spread. Bake in 350°F (175°C) oven for about 25 to 30 minutes until set and golden color. Cool. Cuts into 54 squares.

Pictured above.

Date Cake, page 120

Velvet Fruit Torte

Very smooth. Pears are a nice change. Drizzle with chocolate just before serving if desired.

First Layer:

All-purpose flour	1 cup	250 mL
Granulated sugar	¼ cup	60 mL
Butter or hard margarine	½ cup	125 mL
Chopped pecans or walnuts	½ cup	125 mL

Second Layer:

Cream cheese, softened	8 oz.	250 g
Large egg	1	1
Granulated sugar	½ cup	75 mL
Vanilla	½ tsp.	2 mL

Third Layer:

Canned pears, drained, cut in wedges	14 oz.	398 mL
Cinnamon, sprinkle		

First Layer: Mix flour and sugar. Cut in margarine until mixture resembles small crumbs. Add pecans. Press well into ungreased 9 x 9 inch (22 x 22 cm) pan. Bake in 350°F (175°C) oven for 12 minutes. Set aside.

Second Layer: Beat cream cheese, egg, sugar and vanilla in small mixing bowl until smooth. Spread over first layer.

Third Layer: Arrange pear wedges on top of second layer. Sprinkle with cinnamon. Bake in 350°F (175°C) oven for 35 to 40 minutes until set. Cool completely. Serves 9 to 12.

Pictured on page 107.

Pudding Brownies

Instant pudding adds the flavor.

Butter or hard margarine, softened	6 tbsp.	100 mL
Granulated sugar	2/3 cup	150 mL
Large eggs	2	2
Vanilla	1 tsp.	5 mL
All-purpose flour	1/2 cup	125 mL
Instant chocolate pudding powder, 4 serving size	1	1
Chopped walnuts	1/2 cup	125 mL

Cream butter and sugar in medium bowl. Beat in eggs 1 at a time. Add vanilla. Mix.

Add flour, pudding powder and walnuts. Stir until moistened. Spread in greased 8 x 8 inch (20 x 20 cm) pan. Bake in 350°F (175°C) oven for about 30 minutes until a wooden pick inserted in center comes out clean but moist. Cuts into 25 squares.

Pictured on page 125.

Fluffy Frosting

A glossy white finish.

Egg white (large), room temperature	1	1
Salt	1/8 tsp.	0.5 mL
Granulated sugar	2 tbsp.	30 mL
White corn syrup	1/3 cup	75 mL
Vanilla	1/2 tsp.	2 mL

Beat egg white and salt in small mixing bowl until frothy.

Add sugar gradually while beating until smooth and glossy.

Drizzle corn syrup in as you continue to beat. Beat until icing will stand in very stiff peaks.

Fold in vanilla. Makes 2 cups (500 mL) frosting.

Pictured on page 116.

Frozen Fast Forward

A hint of vanilla. This can be made and frozen well in advance.

Crust:		
Butter or hard margarine	6 tbsp.	100 mL
Graham cracker crumbs	1 1/3 cups	325 mL
Filling:		
Vanilla instant pudding powder, 4 serving size	1	1
Milk	2/3 cup	150 mL
Butter pecan ice cream, slightly softened	4 cups	1 L
Whipping cream (or 1 envelope topping)	1 cup	250 mL
Topping:		
Skor or Heath candy bars, finely crushed or ground	2 x 1 1/2 oz.	2 x 38 g

Crust: Melt butter in saucepan. Stir in graham crumbs. Pack into ungreased 10 inch (25 cm) springform pan. Chill.

Filling: Beat pudding powder with milk in large bowl until smooth.

Fold in ice cream.

Beat cream in small bowl until stiff. Fold into pudding mixture. Pour over crust.

Topping: Sprinkle with crushed candy bars. Freeze. Remove from freezer about 15 minutes before serving. Cuts into 12 wedges.

Pictured on page 123.

Maple Nut Sauce

Quick to make. Store in refrigerator up to three weeks. Serve over ice cream.

Sweetened condensed milk	11 oz.	300 mL
Chopped pecans or walnuts	2 tbsp.	30 mL
Maple flavoring	1/2 tsp.	2 mL

Stir milk, pecans and maple flavoring together in bowl. Makes 1 1/2 cups (375 mL).

Pictured on page 125.

Frozen Fast Forward, page 122

Candy Cake

Easy. Delicious. Light texture.

All-purpose flour	2 cups	500 mL
Brown sugar, packed	2 cups	500 mL
Butter or hard margarine	½ cup	125 mL
Large egg, beaten	1	1
Milk	1 cup	250 mL
Baking soda	1 tsp.	5 mL
Salt	½ tsp.	2 mL
Vanilla	1 tsp.	5 mL

Topping:		
Reserved crumbs	1 cup	250 mL
Skor or Heath bars, (39 g size)	4	4

Mix flour and brown sugar in medium bowl. Cut in butter until crumbly. Measure out 1 cup (225 mL) and reserve.

Add egg, milk, baking soda, salt and vanilla to remaining crumb mixture. Beat well. Turn into greased 9 x 13 inch (22 x 33 cm) pan.

Topping: Stir reserved crumbs and Skor crumbs together. Sprinkle over cake batter. Bake in 350°F (175°C) oven for about 30 minutes until an inserted wooden pick comes out clean. Serve warm or cool. Makes 1 cake.

Pictured on page 125.

Six Layer Squares

Very quick to assemble. Freezes well. Great taste!

Butter or hard margarine	½ cup	125 mL
Graham cracker crumbs	1 cup	225 mL
Semisweet chocolate chips	1 cup	225 mL
Butterscotch chips	1 cup	225 mL
Flake coconut	1 cup	225 mL
Sweetened condensed milk	11 oz.	300 mL

Melt butter in 9 x 13 inch (22 x 33 cm) pan over low heat.

Sprinkle next 4 ingredients over butter in order given.

Heat condensed milk on low in small saucepan until just warm. Pour evenly over top. Bake in 350°F (175°C) oven for about 30 minutes. Cool. Cuts into 54 squares.

Pictured on page 125.

Maraschino Chocolate Cake

Rich chocolate flavor with moist texture.

Butter or hard margarine, softened	½ cup	125 mL
Granulated sugar	1 cup	250 mL
Large egg	1	1
Vanilla	1 tsp.	5 mL
Almond flavoring	½ tsp.	2 mL
Syrup, from 8 oz. (224 g) bottle of maraschino cherries	½ cup	125 mL
Unsweetened baking chocolate squares, cut up	2 × 1 oz.	2 × 28 g
All-purpose flour	2 cups	500 mL
Baking soda	1 tsp.	5 mL
Salt	¼ tsp.	1 mL
Buttermilk (fresh or reconstituted from powder)	1 cup	250 mL
Maraschino cherries, from 8 oz. (224 g) bottle, halved	¾ cup	175 mL
Chopped walnuts	½ cup	125 mL

Cream butter and sugar well in large bowl. Beat in egg, vanilla and almond flavoring. Mix in cherry syrup.

Heat chocolate in saucepan on low, stirring often, until smooth. Beat into batter.

Stir flour, baking soda and salt together in separate bowl.

Add flour in 3 additions alternately with buttermilk in 2 additions beginning and ending with flour.

Add cherries and walnuts. Mix in. Turn into greased 9 × 13 inch (22 × 33 cm) pan. Bake in 350°F (175 °C) oven for about 55 minutes until an inserted wooden pick comes out clean. Cool. Ice with Chocolate Icing, this page. Makes 1 cake.

Pictured below.

Maraschino Chocolate Cake with Chocolate Icing

Chocolate Icing

Rich chocolate brown. Satin-like appearance. Delicious.

Icing (confectioner's) sugar)	2 cups	500 mL
Cocoa	⅓ cup	75 mL
Butter or hard margarine, softened	¼ cup	60 mL
Water	3 tbsp.	50 mL
Vanilla	1 tsp.	5 mL

Beat all ingredients together in mixing bowl until smooth, adding more water or icing sugar as needed for proper spreading consistency. Makes about 1¼ cups (300 mL).

Pictured on this page.

Pineapple Squares

Meringue-like top. Do not freeze.

Bottom Layer:		
Butter or hard margarine, softened	½ cup	125 mL
Granulated sugar	½ cup	125 mL
All-purpose flour	1½ cups	375 mL
Baking powder	1 tsp.	5 mL
Salt	¼ tsp.	1 mL
Crushed pineapple, drained	14 oz.	398 mL
Top Layer:		
Large eggs	2	2
Granulated sugar	1 cup	250 mL
Medium coconut	1 cup	250 mL
Butter or hard margarine, melted	1 tbsp.	15 mL

Bottom Layer: Mix all 5 ingredients well in small bowl. Press firmly into ungreased 9 × 9 inch (22 × 22 cm) pan.

Scatter pineapple over top as evenly as you can.

Top Layer: Beat eggs in small bowl until smooth. Beat in sugar.

Stir in coconut and butter. Spread over pineapple. Bake in 350°F (175°C) oven for 30 to 40 minutes. Cut while warm. Cuts into 36 squares.

Pictured on page 127.

Top Left: Candy Cake, page 123
Bottom Left: Six Layer Squares, page 123

Center: Pudding Brownies, page 122

Top Right: Maple Nut Sauce, page 122
Bottom Right: Bees Knees Squares, page 125

Bees Knees Squares

Good eye appeal. Make ahead and freeze.

Butter or hard margarine, softened	1 cup	250 mL
Honey	⅓ cup	75 mL
Vanilla	1 tsp.	5 mL
Quick cooking rolled oats	1½ cups	375 mL
All-purpose flour	1½ cups	375 mL
Salt	½ tsp.	2 mL
Butterscotch chips	1 cup	250 mL
Slivered almonds	½ cup	125 mL
Honey	2 tbsp.	30 mL

Beat butter, first amount of honey and vanilla in mixing bowl until smooth.

Stir in rolled oats, flour and salt. Add butterscotch chips. Stir. Spread in greased 9 x 13 inch (22 x 33 cm) pan.

Sprinkle with almonds. Push down to make them stick.

Heat remaining honey slightly until it is runny. Brush or dab over surface. Bake in 350°F (175°C) oven for 25 to 30 minutes until golden browned. Cool before cutting into 54 squares.

Pictured above.

Chocolate Date Squares

Yummy combination of flavors.

Large egg	1	1
Butter or hard margarine, melted	¼ cup	60 mL
Granulated sugar	¼ cup	60 mL
Brown sugar	2 tbsp.	30 mL
Salt	⅛ tsp.	0.5 mL
All-purpose flour	⅔ cup	150 mL
Baking soda	½ tsp.	2 mL
Milk	¼ cup	60 mL
Prepared orange juice	¼ cup	60 mL
Chopped walnuts	½ cup	125 mL
Semisweet chocolate chips	½ cup	125 mL
Chopped dates	½ cup	125 mL
Icing:		
Icing (confectioner's) sugar	1 cup	250 mL
Butter or margarine, softened	2 tbsp.	30 mL
Prepared orange juice	1½ tbsp.	25 mL
Dry orange rind	¼ tsp.	1 mL

Beat egg well in large bowl.

Add next 6 ingredients. Mix.

Add next 5 ingredients. Stir well. Turn into greased 8 × 8 inch (20 × 20 cm) pan. Bake in 350°F (175°C) oven for about 25 minutes until an inserted wooden pick comes out clean. Cool.

Icing: Mix all ingredients in small bowl adding more or less orange juice to make spreading consistency. Spread over cooled squares. Let stand to firm icing a bit. Cuts into 36 squares.

Pictured on page 127.

Cinnanut Squares

Cinnamon flavor comes through.

Bottom Layer:		
Butter or hard margarine, softened	½ cup	125 mL
Granulated sugar	½ cup	125 mL
Brown sugar, packed	¼ cup	60 mL
Large egg	1	1
All-purpose flour	1¼ cups	300 mL
Salt	½ tsp.	2 mL
Baking soda	½ tsp.	2 mL
Coarsely crushed corn flakes	1 cup	250 mL
Filling:		
Butter or hard margarine, softened	¼ cup	60 mL
Brown sugar, packed	½ cup	125 mL
Corn syrup	2 tbsp.	30 mL
Ground cinnamon	1 tsp.	5 mL
Chopped dates	½ cup	125 mL
Chopped walnuts	½ cup	125 mL

Bottom Layer: Mix butter, both sugars and egg in bowl.

Add flour, salt and baking soda. Stir well. Mix in corn flakes. Spread ½ in greased 8 × 8 inch (20 × 20 cm) pan.

Filling: Mix butter, sugar, syrup and cinnamon well in bowl.

Add dates and walnuts. Spread over layer in pan. Sprinkle with second ½ corn flake mixture. Bake in 350° (175°C) oven for about 30 minutes. Cuts into 25 squares.

Pictured on page 127.

Chewy Chip Squares

Nice and chewy—just like its name! Drizzle with melted chocolate to dress it up.

Graham cracker crumbs	1½ cups	350 mL
Semisweet chocolate chips	1 cup	225 mL
Butterscotch chips	1 cup	225 mL
Chopped walnuts	1 cup	225 mL
Sweetened condensed milk	11 oz.	300 mL

Measure all ingredients in bowl. Stir together well. Turn into greased 9 × 9 inch (22 × 22 cm) pan. Smooth with back of greased spoon. Bake in 350°F (175°C) oven for 30 to 35 minutes. Cool for 45 minutes. Cuts into 36 squares.

Pictured on page 127.

Almond Flake Squares

Orange Chocolate Squares

Shortbread-type crust. A slightly chewy square.
An all-round winner!

Bottom Layer:		
All-purpose flour	2 cups	500 mL
Brown sugar, packed	½ cup	125 mL
Butter or hard margarine, softened	1 cup	250 mL
Second Layer:		
Large eggs	4	4
Grated rind of 2 oranges		
Prepared orange juice	⅓ cup	75 mL
Granulated sugar	2 cups	500 mL
All-purpose flour	¼ cup	60 mL
Baking powder	1 tsp.	5 mL
Drizzle:		
Semisweet chocolate chips	½ cup	125 mL

Bottom Layer: Mix all ingredients together in bowl until crumbly. Pack in 9 x 13 inch (22 x 33 cm) ungreased pan. Bake in 350°F (175°C) oven for 15 to 20 minutes until golden.

Second Layer: Beat eggs in medium bowl until blended. Add orange rind, orange juice, sugar, flour, and baking powder. Mix. Pour over bottom layer. Bake in 325°F (160°C) oven for about 25 minutes until firm.

Drizzle: Melt and stir chocolate chips in small saucepan over lowest heat until smooth. Drizzle over top. Cool. Cuts into 54 squares.

Pictured on page 127.

Almond Flake Squares

Decadent. Sweet, buttery and nutty.

Miniature marshmallows	9 oz.	250 g
Butter or hard margarine	½ cup	125 mL
Vanilla	1 tsp.	5 mL
Medium coconut	1 cup	250 mL
Flaked almonds, toasted (bake in 350°F, 175°C oven for about 5 minutes)	1 cup	250 mL
Corn flakes	5 cups	1.25 L
Reserved flaked almonds	¼ cup	60 mL

Heat and stir marshmallows, butter and vanilla in large saucepan until melted. Remove from heat.

Stir in coconut, ¾ cup (175 mL) almonds and corn flakes. Press lightly into greased 9 x 9 inch (22 x 22 cm) pan.

Sprinkle with reserved almonds. Press down slightly so they will stick. Cool. Cuts into 36 squares.

Pictured above.

To drizzle chocolate, put melted chocolate in small freezer bag (do not use a sandwich bag). Do not close top. Push chocolate to one corner. Twist bag closed. Snip off the very tip of corner. Squeeze and drizzle over squares, cookies or cake.

Coconut Squares

*The sides rise higher on these—but every bite
is delicious nonetheless.*

Butter or hard margarine	½ cup	125 mL
Brown sugar, packed	2 cups	500 mL
Large eggs	2	2
Vanilla	2 tsp.	10 mL
All-purpose flour	1 cup	250 mL
Baking powder	2 tsp.	10 mL
Salt	1 tsp.	5 mL
Flaked coconut	1½ cups	375 mL
Chopped walnuts	½ cup	125 mL

Melt butter in large saucepan. Stir in brown sugar. Beat in eggs and vanilla.

Stir flour, baking powder and salt together in bowl. Add to saucepan. Mix.

Stir in coconut and walnuts. Turn into greased 9 x 13 inch (22 x 33 cm) pan. Bake in 350°F (175°C) oven for 25 to 30 minutes. Cuts into 54 squares.

Pictured on page 127.

Back To Square One

*Rich and gooey! Strong peanut flavor with
an underlying sweetness.*

Butter or hard margarine	6 tbsp.	100 mL
Creamy peanut butter	½ cup	125 mL
Brown sugar, packed	½ cup	125 mL
Corn syrup	½ cup	125 mL
Crisp rice cereal	2 cups	500 mL
Ground peanuts	1 cup	250 mL
Semisweet chocolate chips	1 cup	250 mL
Creamy peanut butter	⅓ cup	75 mL

Put butter, first amount of peanut butter, brown sugar and syrup into saucepan. Heat and stir until smooth.

Add cereal and peanuts. Mix. Pack into greased 9 x 9 inch (22 x 22 cm) pan.

Combine chocolate chips with last amount of peanut butter in saucepan. Heat, stirring often, on lowest heat until smooth. Spread over cereal mixture in pan. Chill. Cuts into 36 squares.

Pictured on page 127.

Jean's Favorite

Turtle Oat Squares

Chocolate and caramel go together nicely.

Butter or hard margarine	1 cup	250 mL
Vanilla	½ tsp.	2 mL
Quick cooking rolled oats	2 cups	500 mL
All-purpose flour	2 cups	500 mL
Brown sugar, packed	½ cup	125 mL
Baking soda	1 tsp.	5 mL
Salt	½ tsp.	2 mL
Semisweet chocolate chips	1 cup	250 mL
Caramel sundae topping	1½ cups	375 mL
All-purpose flour	¼ cup	60 mL

Melt butter with vanilla in large saucepan.

Add next 5 ingredients. Stir well. Press ⅔ in ungreased 9 x 13 inch (22 x 33 cm) pan.

Sprinkle with chocolate chips.

Stir butterscotch sauce and last amount of flour together. Drizzle over chocolate chips. Sprinkle with remaining ⅓ rolled oat mixture. Bake in 350°F (175°C) oven for about 25 minutes until golden brown. Cool. Cuts into 54 squares.

Pictured below.

Turtle Oat Squares

Main Courses

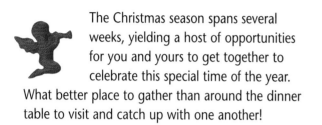

The Christmas season spans several weeks, yielding a host of opportunities for you and yours to get together to celebrate this special time of the year. What better place to gather than around the dinner table to visit and catch up with one another!

And that in turn calls for a special meal—one that is a little out of the ordinary but still suited to the majority, and a change from the traditional turkey fare that dominates the menu at Christmas.

Whether they're old favorites with a different twist or entirely new to you, our main course selections will make your holiday meals noteworthy.

Cajun Spareribs

Hot and tasty. There is lots of extra sauce to serve over rice.

Pork spareribs, cut short	3 lbs.	1.35 kg
Brown sugar, packed	½ cup	125 mL
All-purpose flour	1 tbsp.	15 mL
Dry mustard powder	1 tbsp.	15 mL
Chili powder	1 tsp.	5 mL
Salt	1 tsp.	5 mL
Pepper	1 tsp.	5 mL
Water	1 cup	250 mL
Ketchup	½ cup	125 mL
Worcestershire sauce	2 tsp.	10 mL
Hot pepper sauce	⅛ tsp.	0.5 mL
Large onion, sliced	1	1
Green pepper, seeded and chopped	1	1

Cut ribs into sections of about 3 ribs each. Place in 3 quart (3 L) casserole or small roaster.

Stir next 6 ingredients in medium bowl.

Add next 4 ingredients. Mix. Pour over ribs. Cover. Bake in 325°F (160°C) oven for 1 hour.

Scatter onion and green pepper over top. Cover. Cook in 300°F (150°C) oven for 1½ hours. Serves 4 to 6.

Pictured on page 139.

Stuffed Crown Roast Of Pork

So elegant—and showy! Choose your own combination of colors for the decorative "crowns". Apple in stuffing adds a delicate tartness.

Salt	2 tsp.	10 mL
Pepper	½ tsp.	2 mL
Worcestershire sauce	½ tsp.	2 mL
Garlic powder	¼ tsp.	1 mL
Rib roast, 16 ribs (about 7 lbs., 3.2 kg)	1	1
Stuffing:		
Margarine (butter browns too fast)	6 tbsp.	100 mL
Finely chopped onion	1 cup	250 mL
Finely chopped celery	½ cup	125 mL
Dry bread crumbs	6 cups	1.5 L
Medium cooking apples (McIntosh are good), peeled, cored and diced	2 cups	500 mL
Poultry seasoning	2 tsp.	10 mL
Salt	1 tsp.	5 mL
Pepper	¼ tsp.	1 mL
Parsley flakes	1 tbsp.	15 mL
Apple juice	1½ cups	375 mL

Combine salt, pepper, Worcestershire sauce and garlic powder in small bowl. Rub into sides of meat. Place in roaster, bone ends down. Cover. Roast in 325°F (160°C) oven for 2 hours. Prepare stuffing while roast is cooking.

Stuffing: Melt margarine in frying pan. Add onion and celery. Sauté until soft. Turn into large bowl, including all remaining margarine.

Add next 6 ingredients. Toss together well.

Add 1 cup (250 mL) of the apple juice. Stir well. Add the rest if needed so stuffing will hold together when squeezed lightly. Remove roast from oven. Turn so rib ends are up. Make a sleeve out of foil and push into center of roast. Fill with stuffing. Cover stuffing with foil. Place leftover stuffing in small greased casserole. Return roast and small casserole to oven. Continue roasting until thermometer reaches 170°F (78°C). This will take about 1½ hours more. Make Gravy, page 133, using ½ recipe. Serves 8.

Pictured on page 131.

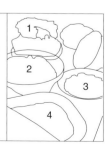

1. Stuffed Crown Roast of Pork, page 130
2. Waldorf Spinach Toss, page 158
3. Carrot Medley, page 171
4. Festive Scalloped Potatoes, page 171

Turkey Au Gratin

A quick and easy casserole for leftover turkey.

Canned asparagus pieces, drained	12 oz.	341 mL
Cooked turkey, cut up	2 cups	500 mL
Cheese Sauce:		
Butter or hard margarine	2 tbsp.	30 mL
All-purpose flour	2 tbsp.	30 mL
Salt	¼ tsp.	1 mL
Milk	¾ cup	175 mL
Grated medium or sharp Cheddar cheese	½ cup	125 mL
Condensed cream of chicken soup	10 oz.	284 mL
Topping:		
Butter or hard margarine	1 tbsp.	15 mL
Dry bread crumbs	⅓ cup	75 mL
Grated medium or sharp Cheddar cheese	2 tbsp.	30 mL

Arrange asparagus in bottom of greased 1½ quart (1.5 L) casserole. Spread turkey over top.

Cheese Sauce: Melt butter in saucepan. Mix in flour and salt. Stir in milk until it boils and thickens.

Add cheese. Stir to melt.

Add soup. Stir until smooth. Pour over turkey.

Topping: Melt butter in saucepan. Stir in bread crumbs and cheese. Sprinkle over top. Bake, uncovered, in 350°F (175°C) oven for about 25 minutes until hot and browned. Serves 4 to 6.

Pictured on page 136.

Golden Glazed Ham

Easy preparation. Glaze glistens.

Fully cooked boneless ham	6 lbs.	2.7 kg
Apricot Glaze:		
Apricot Jam	½ cup	125 mL
Brown sugar, packed	½ cup	125 mL
Cider vinegar	1½ tbsp.	25 mL
Prepared mustard	1 tsp.	5 mL
Ground cloves	⅛ tsp.	0.5 mL

Bake ham in covered roaster in 325°F (150°C) oven for about 2½ hours. Internal temperature should be 130°F (55°C). Drain off juice.

Apricot Glaze: Mix all ingredients in small saucepan. Heat and stir until hot and mixed well. Brush over top and sides of ham. Continue to bake, uncovered, at 350°F (175°C) for about 15 minutes until glaze dries. Serves 12.

Pictured on page 141.

Tourtière

A traditional meat pie.

Lean ground pork	2 lbs.	900 g
Lean ground beef	1 lb.	454 g
Chopped onion	2 cups	500 mL
Salt	1 tbsp.	15 mL
Pepper	½ tsp.	2 mL
Poultry seasoning	¼ tsp.	1 mL
Pickling spice, in tea ball or tied in bag	2 tsp.	10 mL
Water, to almost cover		
Pastry for 2 double crust pies, your own or a mix		

Combine first 7 ingredients in large saucepan. Add water until you can just see it coming up the edge. Heat, stirring often until mixture comes to a boil. Simmer for about 20 minutes. Drain liquid into separate container. Chill liquid and meat overnight. In the morning discard fat from top of liquid. Combine liquid with meat. Stir.

Roll ½ pastry and line 2, 9 inch (22 cm) pie plates. Spread 4 cups (1 L) meat mixture in each crust. Roll top crusts. Moisten edges with water. Put top crusts in place. Trim. Crimp to seal. Cut several slits in top crusts. Bake in 400°F (205°C) oven for about 50 minutes until browned. Makes 2 double crust pies.

Pictured on page 136.

Gravy

This recipe works for any meat gravy.

Pan drippings	¾ cup	175 mL
All-purpose flour	¾ cup	175 mL
Salt	1 tsp.	5 mL
Pepper	¼ tsp.	1 mL
Water, including remaining drippings, fat removed (see Note)	6 cups	1.5 L

Pour first amount of drippings into large saucepan. Mix in flour, salt and pepper. Stir in water until it boils and thickens. A whisk works well for this. If gravy is pale, add a bit of gravy browner. Taste for salt and pepper, adding more if needed. Makes 6½ cups (1.45 L).

Note: Vegetable water, drained from potatoes, Brussels sprouts, carrots or other vegetable may be used.

Spiced Apricots

Serve with Roast Goose, page 140 or Golden Glazed Ham, page 132.

Brown sugar, packed	¼ cup	60 mL
White vinegar	1 tbsp.	15 mL
Ground cinnamon	¼ tsp.	1 mL
Ground nutmeg	⅛ tsp.	0.5 mL
Ground ginger	⅛ tsp.	0.5 mL
Reserved apricot syrup	1 cup	250 mL
Canned apricots, drained, syrup reserved	2 x 14 oz.	2 x 398 mL

Place first 6 ingredients in saucepan. Heat, stirring often, until mixture simmers. Simmer 15 to 20 minutes.

Add apricots. Simmer an additional 5 to 10 minutes. Serve hot or cold. Makes 2½ cups (625 mL).

Pictured on page 141.

Turkey Fajitas

A fun way to use up leftover turkey.

Hard margarine (butter browns too fast)	1 tbsp.	15 mL
Large onion, thinly sliced	1	1
Red pepper, seeded and cut in strips	1	1
Green or yellow pepper, seeded and cut in strips	1	1
Butter or hard margarine	1 tbsp.	15 mL
Leftover cooked turkey, cut in strips	3 cups	750 mL
Salt, sprinkle		
Pepper, sprinkle		
Tomatoes, seeded and diced	1 cup	250 mL
Grated medium Cheddar cheese	1 cup	250 mL
Shredded lettuce, lightly packed	1 cup	250 mL
Sour cream	1 cup	250 mL
Salsa	1 cup	250 mL
Guacamole	1 cup	250 mL
Flour tortillas, 10 inch (25 cm), heated in covered bowl	8-10	8-10

Melt margarine in frying pan. Add onion and peppers. Stir-fry until lightly browned.

Melt butter in saucepan. Add turkey. Sprinkle with salt and pepper. Cover. Heat, stirring as little as possible so turkey doesn't break up.

Put next 6 ingredients in separate bowls.

To prepare for eating, lay 1 tortilla on plate. Place some onion-pepper mixture down center. Add some turkey strips, then whatever you would like of the 6 garnishes. Fold tortilla over mixture. Makes 8 to 10 fajitas.

Pictured below.

Turkey Fajitas, page 133
Veal Birds, page 135

Chicken Provençale

Colorful. Pleasing to the eye.

Cooking oil	1 tbsp.	15 mL
Chicken pieces, skin removed	3 lbs.	1.3 kg
Salt, sprinkle		
Pepper, sprinkle		
Red or green pepper seeded, cut in strips	1	1
Sliced onion	1 cup	250 mL
Garlic clove, minced (or ¼ tsp., 1 mL, garlic powder)	1	1
Sliced fresh mushrooms	2 cups	500 mL
Medium tomatoes, peeled, seeded and diced	2	2
Whole oregano	1 tsp.	5 mL
Salt, sprinkle		
Pepper, sprinkle		
White wine (or alcohol-free wine), optional	½ cup	125 mL
Cornstarch	3 tbsp.	50 mL
Water	¼ cup	60 mL

Heat cooking oil in frying pan. Add chicken. Brown both sides well. Transfer to small roaster. Cover. Bake 15 minutes in 350°F (175°C) oven while preparing vegetables.

Sauté green pepper, onion and garlic in frying pan for 3 minutes, adding more cooking oil if needed.

Add mushrooms, Continue to stir-fry until vegetables are soft.

Dip tomatoes in boiling water for about 2 minutes. Peel under cold running water. Dice and add to vegetables. Add oregano, second amounts of salt and pepper and white wine. Spoon over chicken. Continue to cook, covered, for 35 to 45 minutes until chicken is cooked. Remove chicken and vegetables from roaster.

Stir cornstarch in water. Add to liquid in bottom of roaster. Heat, stirring, until thickened. Return chicken and vegetables to roaster. Stir gently but thoroughly. Serves 4 to 6.

Pictured on this page.

Chicken In Gravy

Serve with rice or potatoes as there is lots of gravy.

All-purpose flour	⅔ cup	150 mL
Salt	2 tsp.	10 mL
Pepper	½ tsp.	2 mL
Seasoned salt	1 tsp.	5 mL
Dry mustard powder	¼ tsp.	1 mL
Paprika	2 tsp.	10 mL
Chicken parts	4 lbs.	1.8 kg
Buttermilk, fresh or reconstituted from powder	1 cup	250 mL
Hard margarine (butter browns too fast)	¼ cup	60 mL
Gravy:		
All-purpose flour	6 tbsp.	100 mL
Salt	1 tsp.	5 mL
Pepper	¼ tsp.	1 mL
Hard margarine (butter browns too fast)	1-5 tbsp.	15-75 mL
Water	5 cups	1.25 L

Mix first 6 ingredients in paper bag.

Dip chicken in buttermilk. Shake in seasoned flour to coat.

Heat margarine in frying pan. Add chicken. Fry quickly to brown both sides. Place in small roaster or large casserole.

Gravy: Add flour, salt and pepper to frying pan. Mix in. Add margarine as needed to mix. Stir in water until it boils and thickens. It will be thin but will thicken as chicken cooks. Taste to see if more salt needs to be added. Pour over chicken. Cover. Bake in 350°F (175°C) oven for 1 to 1½ hours until very tender. Serves 6.

Pictured on page 137.

Tamale Casserole

Great for the buffet table.

Boiling water	3¾ cups	925 mL
Salt	1½ tsp.	7 mL
Cornmeal	1 cup	250 mL
Chopped pitted ripe olives	1 cup	250 mL
Hard margarine (butter browns too fast)	2 tbsp.	30 mL
Chopped onion	1 cup	250 mL
Medium green pepper, seeded and chopped	1	1
Lean ground beef	1 lb.	454 g
Salt	1 tsp.	5 mL
Canned tomatoes, broken up	14 oz.	398 mL
Chili powder	2 tsp.	10 mL
Cayenne pepper	¼ tsp.	1 mL

Pour boiling water and salt into saucepan. Slowly stir cornmeal into boiling liquid. Cook, stirring continually, for 5 minutes.

Add olives. Stir.

Melt margarine in frying pan. Add onion, green pepper, ground beef and salt. Sauté until lightly browned and meat is no longer pink.

Add tomatoes, chili powder and cayenne pepper. Stir. Spread ½ cornmeal mixture in greased 3 quart (3 L) casserole. Spread meat mixture over top. Spread second ½ cornmeal mixture over meat. Bake, uncovered, in 350°F (175°C) oven for about 30 minutes until hot and lightly browned. Serves 6 to 8.

Pictured on page 137.

Beef Roast In Gravy

So easy to prepare. You can visit with guests while it's cooking.

Boneless rolled beef roast, sirloin tip, rump, chuck	4½ lbs.	2 kg
Envelope dry onion soup mix	1 × 1¼ oz.	1 × 38 g
Condensed cream of mushroom soup	10 oz.	284 mL

Place roast beef on foil in small roaster.

Stir onion soup mix into soup in bowl. Spoon over meat. Fold foil over top. Cover with roaster lid. Cook in 300°F (150°C) oven for 4 to 4½ hours depending on the degree of doneness you want. Serves 8 to 10.

Pictured on page 137.

Veal Birds

Make and freeze ahead of time. Freeze pan drippings separately. Make gravy just before serving. Slice birds 1 inch thick.

Veal steak, cut into 6 to 8 pieces, pounded thin	2 lbs.	900 g
Salt	1½ tsp.	7 mL
Pepper	¼ tsp.	1 mL
Ground thyme	¼ tsp.	1 mL
Stuffing:		
Large egg	1	1
Beef bouillon powder	1 tsp.	5 mL
Dry bread crumbs	1½ cups	375 mL
Poultry seasoning	½ tsp.	2 mL
Salt	¼ tsp.	1 mL
Pepper	⅛ tsp.	0.5 mL
Onion powder	¼ tsp.	1 mL
Water, to moisten		
Hard margarine (butter browns too fast)	3 tbsp.	50 mL
Hot water	½ cup	125 mL
Beef bouillon powder	1 tsp.	5 mL
White wine	½ cup	125 mL
Gravy:		
Cornstarch	1 tbsp.	15 mL
Water	3 tbsp.	50 mL

Lay veal pieces on counter.

Mix salt, pepper and thyme together in small bowl. Sprinkle over meat.

Stuffing: Beat egg in small bowl. Stir in next 6 ingredients. Add water to moisten until mixture holds together when squeezed in your hand. Divide among veal pieces. Roll up and tie in bundles with string.

Heat margarine in frying pan on medium. Add veal bundles. Brown well on all sides. Place in 2 quart (2 L) casserole.

Stir hot water, second amount of bouillon powder and white wine together in frying pan that veal was cooked in. Scrape up any brown bits from pan. Pour over veal. Cover. Bake in 325°F (160°C) oven for 1½ hours until tender. Remove to serving platter. Keep warm.

Gravy: Mix cornstarch and water together in small cup. Slowly stir into pan juices left in casserole. Heat and stir until thickened. Makes about 1 cup of gravy. Remove string from veal. Pour gravy over veal birds on platter. Serves 6 to 8.

Pictured on page 133.

Fancy Macaroni

A new twist to macaroni and cheese.

Elbow macaroni	1 cup	250 mL
Boiling water	2 qts.	2 L
Cooking oil	1 tsp.	5 mL
Salt	1 tsp.	5 mL
Large onion, grated	1	1
Grated sharp Cheddar cheese	1 cup	250 mL
Chopped pimiento	2½ tbsp.	37 mL
Egg yolks (large)	3	3
Green pepper, seeded and chopped	1	1
Parsley flakes	1 tsp.	5 mL
Butter or hard margarine, melted	¼ cup	60 mL
Salt	1 tsp.	5 mL
Milk	1½ cups	375 mL
Dry bread crumbs	½ cup	125 mL
Egg whites (large), room temperature	3	3

Cook macaroni in large uncovered saucepan in boiling water, cooking oil and salt for 5 to 7 minutes until tender but firm. Drain. Return macaroni to saucepan.

Stir in next 10 ingredients in order given.

Beat egg whites in bowl until stiff. Fold into mixture. Turn into greased 2 quart (2 L) casserole. Place in larger container and surround casserole with hot water. Bake, uncovered, in 350°F (175°C) oven for about 45 minutes. Serves 6 to 8.

Pictured on page 136 and 137.

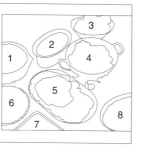

Lazy Ravioli

A little more preparation time needed, but it's worth it! Serves a crowd.

Fusilli twists	12 oz.	375 g
Boiling water	3 qts.	3 L
Cooking oil	1 tbsp.	15 mL
Salt	1 tbsp.	15 mL
Hard margarine (butter browns too fast)	1 tbsp.	15 mL
Lean ground beef	1½ lbs.	680 g
Spaghetti sauce	14 oz.	398 mL
Tomato sauce	7½ oz.	213 mL
Tomato paste	5½ oz.	156 mL
Chopped onion	2 cups	500 mL
Canned sliced mushrooms, drained	10 oz.	284 mL
Frozen chopped spinach, thawed and squeezed dry	10 oz.	300 g
Granulated sugar	2 tsp.	10 mL
Salt	1 tsp.	5 mL
Pepper	¼ tsp.	1 mL
Garlic powder	¼ tsp.	1 mL
Sour cream	1 cup	250 mL
Grated medium or sharp Cheddar cheese	2 cups	500 mL
Grated mozzarella cheese	2 cups	500 mL

Cook fusilli in boiling water, cooking oil and salt in large uncovered pot for 8 to 10 minutes until tender but firm. Drain. Rinse with cold water. Drain.

 Melt margarine in frying pan. Scramble-fry ground beef until no pink remains in meat. Transfer to Dutch oven.

Add next 10 ingredients to Dutch oven. Heat, stirring often, for about 20 minutes until onion is tender. Assemble in small ungreased roaster or 5 quart (5 L) casserole.

Assemble in layers: 1. ½ fusilli in bottom
2. ½ meat sauce
3. all sour cream
4. ½ Cheddar
5. ½ fusilli
6. ½ meat sauce
7. ½ Cheddar
8. all mozzarella

Cover. Bake in 350°F (175°C) oven for 45 minutes. Remove cover. Bake another 15 minutes until cheese is melted and browns slightly. Serves 12.

Pictured on page 136.

Roast Turkey

Always a welcome tradition whether served on Christmas Eve, Christmas Day or New Year's Day.

Young turkey, pan ready	15 lbs.	6.8 kg
Onion chunks or stuffing		

To Roast Unstuffed: Put 2 or 3 onion chunks in cavity. Tie string around body holding wings close to sides. Tie legs to tail. Place on rack in roaster. Cover with lid or foil. (To cook uncovered, rub skin with butter. You will need to baste a few times.) Roast in 400°F (205°C) oven for 30 minutes. Reduce heat to 325°F (160°C). Cook for about 5 hours, basting occasionally, until a thermometer inserted in thigh reads 190°F (95°C). Meat should show signs of pulling away from bone. Drumstick meat should feel soft when pressed. Leg should move and twist easily. To brown, remove cover for 20 to 30 minutes.

To Roast Stuffed: Stuff front and back cavities loosely. Tie string around body to hold wings close to sides. Skewer skin together to hold stuffing in place. Tie legs to tail. Cook as above, allowing an extra half hour to cook. When thermometer is inserted into center of stuffing it should read 165°F (75°C).

Remove bird and rack to platter. Remove stuffing to bowl and keep covered. Cover turkey while you make gravy. It will be easier to carve meat after it stands 30 minutes. Serves 12.

Pictured on front cover.

Left: Seafood Lasagne, page 145   Top Right: Showy Meatloaf, page 139   Bottom Right: Cajun Spareribs, page 130

Showy Meatloaf

The name says it all. So pretty when it's sliced.

Lean ground beef	2 lbs.	900 g
Large eggs	2	2
Fresh bread slices, blended to coarse crumbs	2	2
Ketchup	1/4 cup	60 mL
Milk	1/4 cup	60 mL
Salt	1 1/2 tsp.	7 mL
Pepper	1/4 tsp.	1 mL
Whole oregano	1 tsp.	5 mL
Onion powder	1/2 tsp.	2 mL
Thin slices of cooked ham	6	6
Frozen spinach, thawed and squeezed dry	10 oz.	300 g
Salt	1 tsp.	5 mL
Mozzarella cheese slices, cut in half diagonally	3	3

Place first 9 ingredients in large bowl. Mix well. Pat out on sheet of foil to 10 × 12 inch (25 × 30 cm) size.

Lay ham slices on top, keeping 1 inch (2.5 cm) in from edges. Spread spinach over ham. Sprinkle with second amount of salt. Roll up starting from long end, removing foil as you roll. Carefully transfer to baking sheet with sides. Pat in sides to smooth them. Bake in 350°F (175°C) oven for 1 1/4 hours.

Arrange cheese triangles over top. Return to oven for 1 to 2 minutes until cheese starts to melt. Cut into slices to serve. Serves 6 to 8.

Pictured above.

The secret to making a meatloaf that will slice nicely is threefold: first mix it well with your hands, pack it very well into the pan and let the cooked meatloaf stand at least 10 to 15 minutes before cutting.

Roast Goose

A nice change from turkey.

Potato Stuffing:

Medium potatoes, peeled and quartered	3	3
Boiling water		
Milk	1 cup	250 mL
Hard margarine	¼ cup	60 mL
Chopped onion	1¼ cups	300 mL
Chopped celery	½ cup	125 mL
Croutons (tiny)	5 cups	1.25 L
Parsley flakes	2 tsp.	10 mL
Sage, or poultry seasoning	1½ tsp.	7 mL
Salt	1 tsp.	5 mL
Pepper	¼ tsp.	1 mL
Goose	10 lbs.	4.5 kg

Potato Stuffing: Cook potatoes in boiling water until tender. Drain. Mash well.

Add milk. Mash. Mixture will be runny.

Melt margarine in frying pan. Add onion and celery. Sauté until soft. Turn into large container. Add mashed potato.

Add croutons, parsley, sage, salt and pepper. Toss well. Let stand for about 30 minutes so croutons can absorb moisture. If not moist enough, some water can be added.

Stuff goose. Skewer shut. Tie wings to body and legs to tail. Roast, covered, in 450°F (230°C) oven for 20 minutes. Reduce heat. Continue to roast in 350°F (175°C) oven for 3½ to 4 hours until very tender. Meat thermometer, inserted in breast area, should read 190°F (87°C). To brown, remove cover for about 10 minutes at the end of cooking. Serves 6 to 8.

Gravy:

Fat drippings from pan	½ cup	125 mL
All-purpose flour	½ cup	125 mL
Salt	½ tsp.	2 mL
Pepper	⅛ tsp.	0.5 mL
Pan drippings, without fat, plus water	4 cups	1 L
Gravy browner, if needed		

Stir fat, flour, salt and pepper in large saucepan. Mix in pan drippings and water until mixture boils and thickens. Add a bit of gravy browner if needed to make a rich brown. Taste for salt and pepper, adding more if needed. Makes 4 cups (1 L).

Pictured on this page.

Roast Goose, page 140   Potato Rolls, page 59

Turkey Wizard

Garnish with sliced almonds just before baking.
Uses leftover turkey.

Chopped onion	1½ cups	375 mL
Bacon slices, diced	8	8
All-purpose flour	2 tbsp.	30 mL
Curry powder, or to taste	1 tbsp.	15 mL
Water	1 cup	250 mL
Orange marmalade (or apricot jam)	¼ cup	60 mL
Ketchup	2 tbsp.	30 mL
White vinegar	1½ tbsp.	25 mL
Beef bouillon powder	2 tsp.	10 mL
Salt	½ tsp.	2 mL
Pepper	½ tsp.	2 mL
Leftover cooked turkey chunks	4 cups	1 L

Fry onion and bacon in frying pan until onion is soft and bacon is cooked.

Mix in flour and curry powder. Add water. Stir until it boils and thickens.

Add marmalade, ketchup, vinegar, bouillon powder, salt and pepper. Stir.

Place turkey in ungreased 3 quart (3 L) casserole. Pour onion mixture over top. Bake, uncovered, in 350°F (175°C) oven for 30 to 40 minutes until hot and bubbly. Serves 6.

Pictured on page 143.

Sausage Rice Casserole, page 145   Spiced Apricots, page 133   Golden Glazed Ham, page 132

Sausage Stuffing

*A more substantial filling than the
traditional bread stuffing.*

Pork sausage meat	1 lb.	454 g
Chopped onion	1 cup	250 mL
Chopped celery	1 cup	250 mL
Parsley flakes	1 tbsp.	15 mL
Poultry seasoning	1 tbsp.	15 mL
Salt	1½ tsp.	7 mL
Pepper	½ tsp.	2 mL
Dry bread crumbs and cubes	8 cups	1.8 L

Water, if needed

Scramble-fry sausage meat, onion and celery until meat is
no longer pink, onion is clear and celery is soft.

Measure parsley, poultry seasoning, salt, pepper and bread
crumbs into large bowl. Mix well. Add sausage meat, onion
and celery.

Add water if needed so that when you squeeze a handful
lightly it holds together. Makes enough stuffing for a 12 to
14 pound (5.4 to 6.3 kg) bird.

Pictured on front cover.

Swiss Steak

*Excellent dish for company. Prepare ahead and
leave in fridge ready to bake.*

Round steak	2 lbs.	900 g
All-purpose flour	½ cup	125 mL
Salt	2 tsp.	10 mL
Pepper	½ tsp.	2 mL
Cooking oil	3 tbsp.	50 mL
Chopped onion	2 cups	500 mL
Canned tomatoes, broken up	14 oz.	398 mL

Cut steak into serving size pieces. Place on waxed paper.

Mix flour, salt and pepper in bowl. Sprinkle over steak.
Pound as much as possible into steak on both sides.

Heat cooking oil in frying pan. Brown steak on both
sides. Transfer to small roaster. Add onions to frying
pan. If needed, add a bit more cooking oil. Fry onions until
browned. Spread over meat.

Add tomatoes. Cover. Bake in 350°F (175°C) oven for
about 1½ hours or until tender. Serves 6 to 8.

Pictured on page 143.

Chicken Breasts Florentine

A very attractive dish. Nice for a sit-down dinner party.

Sour cream	½ cup	125 mL
Plain yogurt	½ cup	125 mL
Dry mustard powder	1½ tsp.	7 mL
Dill weed	½ tsp.	2 mL
Dry bread crumbs	1½ cups	375 mL
Boneless chicken breast halves, skin removed	8	8
Florentine Sauce:		
Butter or hard margarine	¼ cup	60 mL
All-purpose flour	¼ cup	60 mL
Salt	1 tsp.	5 mL
Pepper	¼ tsp.	1 mL
Onion powder	¼ tsp.	1 mL
Chicken bouillon powder	1 tsp.	5 mL
Dill weed	2 tsp.	10 mL
Ground nutmeg	¼ tsp.	1 mL
Milk	3 cups	675 mL
Frozen chopped spinach, thawed, squeezed dry	10 oz.	300 g
Grated Havarti or Muenster cheese	1 cup	250 mL

Mix first 4 ingredients in small bowl.

Place bread crumbs in another small bowl.

Dip chicken in sour cream mixture, then in bread crumbs. Arrange on greased baking sheet. Bake in 375°F (190°C) oven for 35 to 45 minutes until tender, turning chicken at half time.

Florentine Sauce: Melt butter in saucepan. Mix in next 7 ingredients. Stir in milk and spinach until mixture boils. Simmer gently, stirring often, for about 3 minutes.

Stir in cheese to melt. Place chicken breasts on platter or individual plates. Spoon sauce over top. Makes 8 servings.

Pictured below.

Chicken Breasts Florentine

Cauliflower Ham Bake

Cauliflower Ham Bake

Sharp cheddar taste complements the ham and cauliflower.

Medium cauliflower, broken in florets	4 cups	1 L
Boiling water, to cover		
Cubed cooked ham	2 cups	500 mL
Canned sliced mushrooms, drained	10 oz.	284 mL
Butter or hard margarine	2 tbsp.	30 mL
All-purpose flour	2 tbsp.	30 mL
Salt	½ tsp.	2 mL
Milk	1 cup	250 mL
Cubed sharp Cheddar cheese	1 cup	250 mL
Sour cream	½ cup	125 mL
Fine dry bread crumbs	1 tbsp.	15 mL

Cook cauliflower in boiling water until tender-crisp. Drain. Put into bowl.

Add ham and mushrooms to cauliflower. Mix well.

Melt butter in saucepan. Mix in flour and salt. Stir in milk until it boils and thickens.

Add cheese. Stir until melted. Add sour cream. Stir until smooth. Put ham and vegetable mixture into ungreased 3 quart (3 L) casserole. Pour sauce over top.

Sprinkle with crumbs. Bake, uncovered, in 350°F (175°C) oven for 30 to 40 minutes until heated through. Serves 6.

Pictured above.

Coquilles St. Jacques Casserole

Serve with a salad and vegetable or use for a buffet.

Boiling water	½ cup	125 mL
Sauterne wine (or alcohol-free white wine)	½ cup	125 mL
Salt	½ tsp.	2 mL
Cayenne pepper, just a pinch		
Scallops, halved or quartered if large	1 lb.	454 g
Butter or hard margarine	2 tbsp.	30 mL
Sliced fresh mushrooms	1 cup	250 mL
Finely chopped onion	½ cup	125 mL
All-purpose flour	¼ cup	60 mL
Finely grated lemon rind	½ tsp.	2 mL
Garlic powder	½ tsp.	2 mL
Reserved liquid from scallops		
Egg yolk (large)	1	1
Whipping cream	½ cup	125 mL
Chopped fresh parsley (or ½ tsp., 2 mL, parsley flakes)	1 tbsp.	15 mL
Pasta:		
Tiny shell pasta	1 cup	250 mL
Boiling water	2 qts.	2 L
Salt	1½ tsp.	7 mL
Cooking oil	1 tbsp.	15 mL
Topping:		
Butter or hard margarine	1 tbsp.	15 mL
Dry bread crumbs	½ cup	125 mL
Grated Parmesan cheese	2 tbsp.	30 mL
Chopped fresh parsley (or ½ tsp., 2 mL, parsley flakes)	1 tbsp.	15 mL

Combine first 5 ingredients in frying pan. Bring to a boil. Cover. Boil slowly for 3 to 5 minutes until scallops are opaque. Use slotted spoon to remove scallops to small bowl. Pour liquid into cup and reserve.

Melt butter in frying pan. Add mushrooms and onion. Sauté until soft.

Mix in flour, lemon rind and garlic. Stir in reserved liquid until mixture boils and thickens.

Mix egg yolk, cream and first amount of parsley in large bowl. Stir well. Stir into mushroom mixture. Cook and stir for 3 minutes. Add scallop mixture. Stir.

Pasta: Combine pasta, boiling water, salt and cooking oil in saucepan. Cook, covered, for about 15 minutes until tender. Drain. Add to scallop mixture. Stir. Put into 2 quart (2 L) ungreased casserole.

Topping: Melt butter in saucepan. Stir in bread crumbs, cheese and second amount of parsley. Sprinkle over top. Bake, uncovered, in 400°F (205°C) oven until browned and heated through, about 15 minutes. Serves 4 to 6.

Pictured below.

Top Left: Turkey Wizard, page 140
Top Right: Coquilles St. Jacques Casserole, page 143
Bottom Left: Seafood Deluxe, page 144
Bottom Right: Swiss Steak, page 141

Seafood Deluxe

Mustard adds a nice zip.

Sauce:
Butter or hard margarine	¼ cup	60 mL
All-purpose flour	¼ cup	60 mL
Salt	1 tsp.	5 mL
Pepper	¼ tsp.	1 mL
Evaporated skim milk	13½ oz.	385 mL
Milk	¼ cup	60 mL
Worcestershire sauce	1 tsp.	5 mL
Prepared mustard	1 tsp.	5 mL
Onion powder	¼ tsp.	1 mL
Grated medium or sharp Cheddar cheese	½ cup	125 mL
Scallops, halved if large	1 lb.	454 g
Boiling water	2 cups	500 mL
Canned crabmeat, drained, membrane removed	4 oz.	113 g

Topping:
Butter or hard margarine	2 tsp.	10 mL
Dry bread crumbs	¼ cup	60 mL
Dried parsley flakes	1 tsp.	5 mL
Grated medium or sharp Cheddar cheese	2 tbsp.	30 mL

Sauce: Melt butter in saucepan. Mix in flour, salt and pepper. Stir in both milks, Worcestershire sauce, mustard and onion powder. Heat and stir until mixture boils and thickens.

Stir in cheese until melted. Set aside.

Combine scallops and boiling water in saucepan. Cook, covered, for about 5 minutes until opaque. Drain. Add to sauce.

Add crabmeat. Stir. Turn into ungreased 2 quart (2 L) casserole.

Topping: Melt butter in saucepan. Stir in crumbs and parsley flakes. Sprinkle over top.

Scatter cheese over bread crumbs. Bake, uncovered, in 350°F (175°C) oven for about 25 minutes until hot. Serves 4.

Pictured on page 143.

Triple Seafood Noodles

Great combination of seafood, wine and basil.

Medium egg noodles	¾ lb.	375 g
Boiling water	4 qts.	4 L
Cooking oil	1 tbsp.	15 mL
Salt	1 tbsp.	15 mL
Hard margarine (butter browns too fast)	3 tbsp.	50 mL
Sliced fresh mushrooms	4 cups	1 L
Sliced green onion	¼ cup	60 mL
Canned tomatoes, broken up, drained, reserve juice	14 oz.	398 mL
Sweet basil	2 tsp.	10 mL
Chicken bouillon powder	2 tsp.	10 mL
Beef bouillon powder	1 tsp.	5 mL
Parsley flakes	1 tsp.	5 mL
Garlic powder	½ tsp.	2 mL
White wine (or alcohol-free wine)	¼ cup	60 mL
Butter or hard margarine	3 tbsp.	50 mL
Canned lobster, drained, cut up	5 oz.	142 g
Canned shrimp, rinsed and drained	4 oz.	113 g
Canned crabmeat, drained, membrane removed	4.2 oz.	120 g

Cook noodles in boiling water, cooking oil and salt in large uncovered pot about 5 to 7 minutes until tender but firm. Drain.

Melt margarine in frying pan. Add mushrooms and green onion. Sauté until soft. This is easier to do in 2 batches.

Put next 7 ingredients into Dutch oven. Heat, stirring often, until mixture boils. Simmer for 2 to 3 minutes.

Melt butter in frying pan. Add lobster, shrimp and crabmeat. Sauté until hot. Add to tomato mixture. Add noodles. Toss. Serves 8 to 10.

Pictured below.

Triple Seafood Noodles

Sausage Rice Casserole

Have this ready to serve when the gang gets back
from skiing, skating or tobogganing.

Long grain rice	1 cup	250 mL
Chopped onion	1 cup	250 mL
Salt	½ tsp.	2 mL
Boiling water	2 cups	500 mL
Sausage meat	1 lb.	454 g
Condensed cream of tomato soup	10 oz.	284 mL
Milk or water (use can to measure)	10 oz.	284 mL
Grated medium or sharp Cheddar cheese	1 cup	250 mL

Cook rice and onion in salt and boiling water for about 20 minutes until tender and water is absorbed.

Shape sausage meat into 1 inch (2.5 cm) balls. Flatten each ball into a tiny patty. Fry, browning both sides, until no pink remains in meat.

Whisk soup and milk together in bowl until smooth. Layer ½ the rice in bottom of 2 quart (2 L) ungreased casserole. Pour ½ soup mixture over rice. Add second ½ rice. Cover in single layer, with sausage patties. Pour remaining ½ soup mixture over patties.

Sprinkle with cheese. Bake in 350°F (175°C) oven for 35 to 45 minutes until bubbly hot. Serves 4 to 6.

Pictured on page 141.

Seafood Lasagne

Fussy but fabulous. Assemble the day before, cover and
refrigerate. Bake just before serving.

Lasagne noodles	8	8
Boiling water	4 qts.	4 L
Cooking oil	1 tbsp.	15 mL
Salt	1 tbsp.	15 mL
Butter or hard margarine	2 tbsp.	30 mL
Chopped onion	1 cup	250 mL
Chopped celery	¼ cup	60 mL
Cream cheese, softened, cut up	8 oz.	250 g
Creamed cottage cheese	1½ cups	375 mL
Large egg	1	1
Grated Parmesan cheese	2 tbsp.	30 mL
Dried basil	2 tsp.	10 mL
Salt	½ tsp.	2 mL
Pepper	⅛ tsp.	0.5 mL
Butter or hard margarine	¼ cup	60 mL
All-purpose flour	¼ cup	60 mL
Salt	½-1 tsp.	2-5 mL
Pepper	⅛-¼ tsp.	0.5-1 mL
Milk	2 cups	500 mL
Cooked shrimp, shelled and deveined (or 2 x 4 oz., 2 x 113 g cans)	2 cups	250 g
Canned crabmeat, drained, membrane removed	2 x 4 oz.	2 x 113 g
White wine (or alcohol-free wine)	⅓ cup	75 mL
Grated Parmesan cheese	¼ cup	60 mL
Grated medium or sharp Cheddar cheese	1 cup	250 mL

Cook lasagne noodles in boiling water, cooking oil and first amount of salt in large uncovered pot for 14 to 16 minutes until tender but firm. Drain.

Melt first amount of butter in frying pan. Add onion and celery. Sauté until soft.

Stir in cream cheese until it melts.

Mix in cottage cheese, egg, first amount of Parmesan cheese, basil, second amount of salt and first amount of pepper.

Melt second amount of butter in saucepan. Mix in flour, third amount of salt and second amount of pepper. Stir in milk until it boils and thickens.

Add shrimp, crabmeat and wine to milk sauce. Stir.

To assemble, layer as follows in greased 9 x 13 inch (22 x 33 cm) pan: 1. Layer of 4 noodles
2. All cottage cheese mixture (see Note)
3. Layer of 4 noodles
4. All seafood mixture (see Note)
5. Parmesan cheese

Bake, uncovered, in 375°F (190°C) oven for about 45 minutes. Sprinkle with Cheddar cheese. Return to oven for 3 to 4 minutes until it melts. Let stand 10 minutes before cutting into 12 pieces. Serves 8.

Note: Layers 2 and 4 may each be made up of ½ cottage cheese mixture and ½ seafood mixture rather than using all of each mixture for each layer.

Pictured on page 139.

Pies & Tarts

Fragrant Mince Pie, page 152, and chewy
Butter Tarts, page 149, are longtime Christmas favorites
and so of course they are included here.

But there are many more kinds of dessert pies that would do
justice to your holiday meals. Bi-Layer Pumpkin Pie, page 150,
Black Russian Pie, page 151, Cranberry Pear Pie, page 148,
and Frozen Peanut Butter Pie, page 148 are among the
intriguing selections for you to choose from.

Tips for making pastry are included, along with recipes
for crusts and fillings that let you go the traditional route
or take a new direction. Try one or the other or
both—your guests will love it!

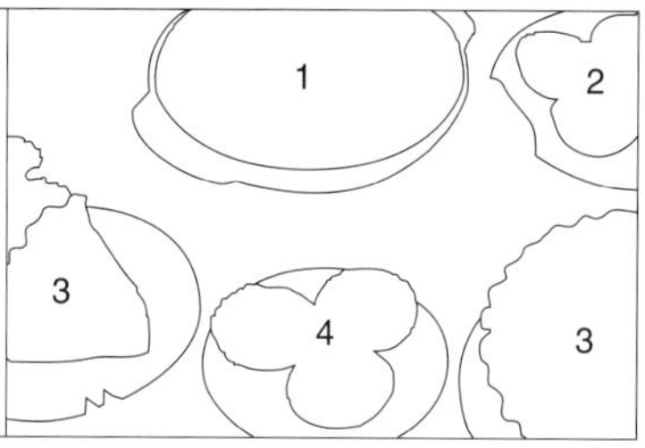

Cranberry Pear Pie

Try this with either the pastry topping or crumb topping. Both are excellent.

Canned pears, drained and sliced, (see Note)	4 × 14 oz.	4 × 398 mL
Cranberries, halved	1 cup	250 mL
Granulated sugar	¾ cup	175 mL
All-purpose flour	3 tbsp.	50 mL
Pastry for 2 crust pie, your own or a mix	1	1
Granulated sugar, sprinkle	¼-½ tsp.	1-2 mL
Crumb Topping:		
All-purpose flour	⅔ cup	150 mL
Brown sugar, packed	6 tbsp.	100 mL
Butter or hard margarine	6 tbsp.	100 mL
Ground cinnamon	½ tsp.	2 mL
Salt	¼ tsp.	1 mL

Stir first 4 ingredients in bowl.

Roll out pastry and line 9 inch (22 cm) pie plate. Fill with fruit mixture.

Pastry Topping: Roll out top crust. Dampen edges of crust in pie plate. Cover with second crust. Trim and crimp to seal. Cut slits in top crust or make decorative cutouts.

Sprinkle with sugar.

Crumb Topping: Mix all ingredients together until crumbly. Sprinkle over fruit.

To cook either pastry-topped or crumb-topped pie, bake in 400°F (205°C) oven on bottom shelf for 15 minutes. Lower heat to 350°F (175°C). Continue to bake for about 30 to 40 minutes. Cool. Makes 1 pie.

Pictured on page 146 and on page 147.

Note: To use fresh pears, peel and slice 5 pears to make 4 cups (1 L). Use ⅓ cup (75 mL) flour instead of ¼ cup (60 mL).

Frozen Peanut Butter Pie

For the peanut butter lover. This freezes well, so you can make ahead.

Crust:		
Butter or hard margarine	⅓ cup	75 mL
Chocolate wafer crumbs	1¼ cups	300 mL
Ground or finely chopped peanuts	⅓ cup	75 mL
Granulated sugar	¼ cup	60 mL
Filling:		
Egg whites (large), room temperature	2	2
Granulated sugar	½ cup	125 mL
Cream cheese, softened	8 oz.	250 g
Granulated sugar	¼ cup	60 mL
Egg yolks (large)	2	2
Creamy peanut butter	1 cup	250 mL
Vanilla	1 tsp.	5 mL
Whipping cream (or 1 envelope topping)	1 cup	250 mL
Granulated sugar	2 tsp.	10 mL
Vanilla	½ tsp.	2 mL
Ground or finely chopped peanuts	2 tbsp.	30 mL
Chocolate, grated or curls, for garnish	2 tbsp.	30 mL

Crust: Melt butter in saucepan. Stir in chocolate crumbs, peanuts and sugar. Press into bottom and sides of 9 inch (22 cm) pie plate. Bake in 350°F (175°C) oven for 10 minutes. Cool.

Filling: Beat egg whites in small bowl until soft peaks form. Gradually beat in first amount of sugar until stiff.

Using same beaters, beat cream cheese, second amount of sugar and egg yolks in separate bowl until smooth. Add peanut butter and vanilla. Beat until mixed. Dough will be quite stiff. Fold in egg whites.

Beat whipping cream, sugar and vanilla until stiff. Fold into peanut butter mixture. Turn into prepared crust. Freeze.

To serve, let pie stand at room temperature for about 35 minutes. Sprinkle with peanuts and chocolate. Makes 1 pie.

Pictured on page 149.

Cranberry Cheese Pie

Cranberry tartness with a sweet cream cheese filling. Crunchy topping.

Crust:

Pastry for 10 inch (25 cm) pie shell, your own or a mix	1	1

First Filling Layer:

Cream cheese, softened	8 oz.	250 g
Large egg	1	1
Icing (confectioner's) sugar	½ cup	125 mL
Sweetened condensed milk	11 oz.	300 mL
Lemon juice, fresh or bottled	¼ cup	60 mL

Second Filling Layer:

Cornstarch	2 tbsp.	30 mL
Canned whole cranberry sauce	14 oz.	398 mL

Topping:

All-purpose flour	⅔ cup	150 mL
Brown sugar, packed	⅓ cup	75 mL
Cinnamon	¼ tsp.	1 mL
Salt	¼ tsp.	1 mL
Butter or hard margarine	¼ cup	60 mL
Chopped pecans or walnuts, optional)	½ cup	125 mL

Crust: Roll out pie shell and line 10 inch (25 cm) pie plate. If you don't have a 10 inch (25 cm) pie plate, use a 9 inch (22 cm) and a 4 or 5 inch (10 or 13 cm) size. If you choose to put all the filling in a 9 inch (22 cm) pie plate, place it on a baking sheet to catch any boil-overs.

First Filling Layer: Beat cream cheese, egg and icing sugar in medium bowl until smooth. Add condensed milk and lemon juice. Beat. Spread in bottom of pie shell.

Second Filling Layer: Stir cornstarch into cranberry sauce in small bowl. Spoon over first filling.

Topping: Mix flour, sugar, cinnamon and salt in bowl. Cut in butter until mixture is crumbly.

Stir in pecans. Sprinkle over second filling layer. Bake in 375°F (190°C) oven for 45 to 55 minutes until set and lightly browned. Lay a piece of foil over pie if topping is getting too brown. Makes 1 pie.

Pictured on page 151.

Butter Tarts

Gooey but not runny. Great and always lots of takers. Freezes well.

Brown sugar, packed	½ cup	125 mL
Corn syrup	½ cup	125 mL
Butter or hard margarine, softened	3 tbsp.	50 mL
Large egg	1	1
Raisins or currants	½ cup	125 mL
Medium or fine coconut	2 tbsp.	30 mL
Finely chopped pecans	2 tbsp.	30 mL
Vinegar	1½ tsp.	7 mL
Salt, just a pinch		
Unbaked pastry tart shells, your own or store bought, (or 24 miniature shells)	12	12

Cream brown sugar, syrup and butter well in medium bowl.

Add next 6 ingredients. Stir well.

Divide among pastry shells. Bake in 375°F (190°C) oven for about 20 minutes for regular size and 10 to 15 minutes for miniature size. Makes 12 large or 24 tiny tarts.

Pictured on page 147.

Top: Frozen Peanut Butter Pie, page 148   Bottom: Bi-Layer Pumpkin Pie, page 150

Bi-Layer Pumpkin Pie

A delicious change from the ordinary.

Graham Crust:

Butter or hard margarine	⅓ cup	75 mL
Graham cracker crumbs	1¼ cups	300 mL
Granulated sugar	2 tbsp.	30 mL

First Filling Layer:

Cream cheese, softened	4 oz.	125 g
Milk	1 tbsp.	15 mL
Granulated sugar	1 tbsp.	15 mL
Frozen whipped topping, thawed	1½ cups	325 mL

Second Filling Layer:

Instant vanilla pudding powders, 4 serving size each	2	2
Milk	1 cup	250 mL
Canned pumpkin, without spice	14 oz.	398 mL
Ground cinnamon	1 tsp.	5 mL
Ground ginger	½ tsp.	2 mL
Ground cloves	¼ tsp.	1 mL

Topping:

Frozen whipped topping, thawed	2 cups	1 L

Graham Crust: Melt butter in saucepan. Stir in graham crumbs and sugar. Press firmly into bottom and sides of 9 inch (22 cm) pie plate.

First Filling Layer: Beat cream cheese, milk and sugar in bowl until smooth.

Fold in whipped topping. Spread in pie shell.

Second Filling Layer: Beat pudding powders and milk together in bowl until smooth.

Add pumpkin and spices. Stir well. Pour over second layer. Chill.

Topping: Spread whipped topping over all. Chill. Makes 1 pie.

Pictured on page 149.

Date Pie

Sweet date flavor. Cut meringue with hot wet knife.

Chopped dates	2 cups	450 mL
Water	1 cup	225 mL
Granulated sugar	¼ cup	60 mL
Milk	1 cup	225 mL
Cornstarch	2 tbsp.	30 mL
Egg yolks (large)	3	3
Vanilla	1 tsp.	5 mL
Baked 9 inch (22 cm) deep dish pie shell, your own pastry or frozen	1	1

Meringue:

Egg whites (large)	3	3
Cream of tartar	¼ tsp.	1 mL
Granulated sugar	6 tbsp.	100 mL

Cook dates, water and sugar slowly in saucepan about 10 minutes until dates are mushy and water has almost disappeared.

Mix milk and cornstarch. Stir into date mixture until it boils and thickens.

Beat egg yolks and vanilla with fork in small bowl. Stir in a few spoonfuls of hot mixture then stir it back into saucepan.

Pour into pie shell. Cool slightly.

Meringue: Beat egg whites and cream of tartar on medium speed until soft peaks form. Continue to beat while adding sugar gradually. Beat until stiff peaks form. Spoon over filling, sealing to crust all around edge. Bake in 375°F (190°C) oven for about 10 minutes until nicely browned. Makes 1 pie.

Pictured on page 151.

Pastry, whether for a filled or unfilled pie shell, should be chilled before rolling. This helps to minimize shrinking. Always wrap dough in plastic wrap if not using immediately.

Top Center: Peachy Prune Pie, page 151   Bottom Center: Date Pie, page 150   Right: Cranberry Cheese Pie, page 149

Peachy Prune Pie

Lovely color combination.

Granulated sugar	1 cup	250 mL
All-purpose flour	3 tbsp.	50 mL
Reserved syrup from peaches	1/2 cup	125 mL
Lemon juice, fresh or bottled	1/4 cup	60 mL
Large egg, beaten	1	1
Pitted quartered prunes	1 cup	250 mL
Canned peach slices, drained syrup reserved	2 x 14 oz.	2 x 398 mL
Pastry for a 2 crust pie, your own or a mix	1	1
Granulated sugar	1/4 tsp.	1 mL

Stir first amount of sugar and flour together well in saucepan. Mix in syrup, lemon juice, beaten egg and prunes. Heat and stir until mixture boils and thickens. Cool. Set saucepan in cold water, stirring frequently to hasten cooling.

Add peaches. Stir.

Roll out pastry and line 9 inch (22 cm) pie plate. Pour filling into pie shell. Roll out second layer. Dampen edge of bottom crust. Top with second crust. Trim. Crimp to seal. Cut slits in top or make decorative cutouts.

Sprinkle with sugar. Bake in 400°F (205°C) oven for about 35 minutes until browned. Makes 1 pie.

Pictured above.

Black Russian Pie

Totally decadent. Oh so smooth.

Chocolate Graham Crust:		
Butter or hard margarine	1/3 cup	75 mL
Graham cracker crumbs	1 1/4 cups	300 mL
Granulated sugar	3 tbsp.	50 mL
Cocoa	2 tbsp.	30 mL
Filling:		
Large marshmallows	24	24
Milk	1/2 cup	125 mL
Salt	1/4 tsp.	1 mL
Kahlua liqueur	1/3 cup	75 mL
Whipping cream (or 1 envelope topping)	1 cup	250 mL
Reserved crumb mixture		
Chocolate-covered coffee beans, for garnish		

Chocolate Graham Crust: Melt butter in saucepan. Stir in graham crumbs, sugar and cocoa. Reserve 1/3 cup (75 mL). Press remainder in bottom and sides of 9 inch (22 cm) pie plate. Bake in 350°F (175°C) oven for 10 minutes. Cool.

Filling: Put marshmallows, milk and salt in large saucepan. Heat, stirring often, until melted and smooth. Chill until it mounds. Stir in Kahlua.

Beat cream in small bowl until stiff. Fold into marshmallow mixture. Turn into cooled pie shell.

Garnish with reserved crumb mixture and coffee beans. Makes 1 pie.

Pictured on page 146 and 147.

Mock Black Bottom Pie

Add red or green food coloring to cream cheese filling for more layered effect.

Graham Cracker Crust:

Butter or hard margarine	⅓ cup	75 mL
Graham cracker crumbs	1¼ cups	300 mL
Granulated sugar	2 tbsp.	30 mL

Black Bottom:

Instant chocolate pudding, 6 serving size	1	1
Milk	1½ cups	350 mL

Filling:

Cream cheese	8 oz.	250 g
Icing (confectioner's) sugar	1 cup	250 mL
Frozen whipped topping, thawed	2 cups	500 mL

Topping:

Frozen whipped topping, thawed	2 cups	500 mL
Chocolate curls or trimettes		

Graham Cracker Crust: Melt butter in saucepan. Stir in graham crumbs and sugar. Press in bottom and sides of 9 inch (22 cm) pie plate. Bake in 350°F (175°C) oven for 10 minutes. Cool.

Black Bottom: Beat pudding powder and milk together in bowl for about 1½ minutes until smooth. Pour into cooled crust.

Filling: Beat cream cheese and icing sugar in bowl until smooth. Chill to firm.

Fold in first amount of frozen topping. Spread over firmed black bottom.

Topping: Spread second amount of frozen topping over filling. Garnish with chocolate curls. Makes 1 pie.

Pictured below.

Mock Black Bottom Pie

Mincemeat

Use to make pies or tarts. Enough to make 4 pies.

Ground beef or pork suet	1 cup	250 mL
Peeled and cored chopped apples	6 cups	1.5 L
Apple juice	1 cup	250 mL
Raisins	2 cups	500 mL
Currants	2 cups	500 mL
Cut candied citron	2 cups	500 mL
Lemons, juice and grated rind	3	3
Brown sugar, packed	4 cups	1 L
Granulated sugar	1 cup	250 mL
Ground cinnamon	4 tsp.	20 mL
Ground allspice	2 tsp.	10 mL
Ground nutmeg	1 tsp.	5 mL
Ground cloves	½ tsp.	2 mL
Brandy or rum flavoring, optional	1 tbsp.	15 mL

Combine first 13 ingredients in large saucepan. Heat, stirring often until mixture comes to a simmer. Simmer, stirring often, for 30 minutes.

Stir in brandy if desired. Cool. Freeze in cartons or store in refrigerator for several months. Makes 8 cups (2 L).

Mince Pie

Always a Christmas favorite.

Filling:

Mincemeat, see recipe above	2 cups	450 mL
Applesauce	¾ cup	175 mL
Minute tapioca	1½ tbsp.	25 mL

Crust:

Pastry for 2 crust pie, your own or a mix	1	1
Granulated sugar	¼-½ tsp.	1-2 mL

Filling: Stir first 3 ingredients together in bowl.

Crust: Roll out pie crust on lightly floured surface. Line 9 inch (22 cm) pie plate. Turn filling into pie shell. Roll out second curst. Dampen edge of first crust. Top with second crust. Trim. Crimp to seal. Cut slits in top.

Sprinkle with sugar. Bake in 400°F (205°C) oven for 30 to 35 minutes until browned. Makes 1 pie.

Mince Tarts

Spoon filling from Mince Pie, above, into 36 tart shells. Filling is especially nice in tarts if run through blender first. Bake at 400°F (205°C) for 20 minutes. Makes 36 tarts.

Pictured on page 146 and 147.

Chocolate Chiffon Pie

This is so velvety. Great flavor.

Unflavored gelatin	1 × ¼ oz.	1 × 7 g
Water	½ cup	125 mL
Milk	1 cup	250 mL
Granulated sugar	⅓ cup	75 mL
Cocoa	½ cup	125 mL
All-purpose flour	2 tbsp.	30 mL
Salt	¼ tsp.	1 mL
Egg yolks (large)	4	4
Vanilla	1 tsp.	5 mL
Egg whites (large), room temperature	4	4
Cream of tartar	½ tsp.	2 mL
Granulated sugar	⅔ cup	150 mL
Baked 9 inch (22 cm) pie shell	1	1
Grated chocolate, for garnish		

Sprinkle gelatin over water in medium saucepan. Let stand 1 minute.

Add milk. Heat, stirring often, on medium until gelatin is dissolved and mixture starts to boil.

Mix next 6 ingredients together in small bowl. Add a little hot mixture and stir until smooth. Pour into mixture in saucepan. Stir until it boils and thickens. Cool.

Beat egg whites and cream of tartar in mixing bowl until soft peaks form. Add sugar gradually as you continue beating until stiff.

Make sure filling will pile nicely before adding egg white mixture. Fold egg whites into chilled filling. Turn into baked pie shell. Chill at least 4 hours before cutting. Makes 1 pie.

Pictured below.

Nutty Mousse Pie

Creamy rich flavor. May be prepared the day before.

Chocolate Crust:		
Butter or hard margarine	⅓ cup	75 mL
Chocolate wafer crumbs	1¼ cups	275 mL
Filling:		
Large marshmallows	30	30
Milk	½ cup	125 mL
Semisweet chocolate chips	1 cup	250 mL
Brown sugar, packed	⅓ cup	75 mL
Whipping cream (or 1 envelope topping)	1 cup	250 mL
Topping:		
Chopped pecans	⅓ cup	75 mL

Chocolate Crust: Melt butter in saucepan. Stir in wafer crumbs. Press into 9 inch (22 cm) pie plate. Bake in 350°F (175°C) oven for 10 minutes. Cool.

Filling: Combine all 4 ingredients in large saucepan. Heat on medium-low, stirring often until melted and smooth. Chill, stirring and scraping down sides of bowl often, until mixture resembles a thick paste. It should pile and hold its shape a while before becoming smooth.

Beat cream in small bowl until stiff. Fold into thickened mixture. Turn into pie shell.

Topping: Sprinkle pecans over pie filling. Chill. Makes 1 pie.

Pictured below.

Chocolate Chiffon Pie

Nutty Mousse Pie

Cranberry Mold

Fruit Salad Mold

Salads

 Salads are such a tasty way to add color and variety to the table at Christmas. This selection of molded and tossed salads (with accompanying dressings) offers you several ways to accomplish this.

Presentation means so much, so take the time to arrange your salad attractively and add a little festive touch wherever possible—maybe a poinsettia decoration on top, or a few nuts or candies.

Consider the color and texture of the salad you choose. The appropriate choice laid out attractively in a holiday dimension will have everyone coming back for more!

Fruit Salad Mold

The color is outstanding! This velvety-smooth salad can work as a main course accompaniment or as a refreshing dessert.

Raspberry flavored gelatin (jelly powder)	2 × 3 oz.	2 × 85 g
Boiling water	2 cups	500 mL
Raspberry sherbet	2 cups	500 mL
Filling:		
Canned pineapple chunks, well drained	14 oz.	398 mL
Canned mandarin oranges, well drained	10 oz.	284 mL
Flaked coconut	1 cup	250 mL
Miniature marshmallows	1 cup	250 mL
Sour cream	1 cup	250 mL

Stir gelatin into boiling water in medium bowl until dissolved. Cool 5 minutes. Add sherbet. Mix in until no streaks appear. Pour into 6 cup (1.5 L) ring mold. Chill for several hours.

Filling: Combine all 5 ingredients in bowl. Stir well. Unmold salad ring onto plate. Spoon fruit mixture into center. Serves 10 to 12.

Pictured on this page.

Variation: Lime-flavored gelatin and sherbet may be used instead of raspberry to have a green colored salad.

Cranberry Mold

Soft mauve-pink color with flecks of red. This will receive a round of applause.

Unflavored gelatin	2 × ¼ oz.	2 × 7 g
Water	½ cup	125 mL
Water	½ cup	125 mL
Canned whole cranberry sauce	14 oz.	398 mL
Crushed pineapple, drained	14 oz.	398 mL
Sour cream	1 cup	250 mL
Icing (confectioner's) sugar	⅓ cup	75 mL

Sprinkle gelatin over first amount of water in small saucepan. Let stand 1 minute. Heat and stir until dissolved.

Add second amount of water. Pour into medium bowl.

Stir in remaining ingredients. Chill, stirring and scraping down sides often, until it shows signs of thickening. Pour into 6 cup (1.5 L) mold. Chill. Serves 8.

Pictured above and on front cover.

Tomato Shrimp Aspic

Glossy red with celery and shrimp peeking through.

Tomato juice	2½ cups	575 mL
Bay leaf	½	½
Onion powder	½ tsp.	2 mL
Unflavored gelatin	2 × ¼ oz.	2 × 7 g
Cold water	½ cup	125 mL
Granulated sugar	3 tbsp.	50 mL
Salt	¾ tsp.	4 mL
Paprika, generous measure	¼ tsp.	1 mL
Chopped celery	¾ cup	175 mL
Canned small shrimp, rinsed and drained	4 oz.	113 g

Put tomato juice, ½ bay leaf and onion powder in saucepan. Heat. Simmer 5 minutes. Discard bay leaf.

Sprinkle gelatin over water in small saucepan. Let stand 1 minute. Heat and stir to dissolve. Add to tomato juice.

Stir in sugar, salt and paprika until sugar dissolves. Chill, stirring and scraping down sides often until mixture shows signs of thickening.

Fold in celery and shrimp. Turn into 3 cup (750 mL) mold. Chill until firm. Serves 6 to 8.

Pictured below.

> Molded salads can be made the day before. Spray the pan with non-stick cooking spray for easier removal. Rub plate with wet hand before unmolding salad so that you can center it. When removing, hold plate against mold, lift both together on end and shake gently. This allows air to enter at edge and loosen salad.

Green Pepper Salad

Green Pepper Salad

This two-tone salad is so festive! Its refreshing flavor works well with turkey, beef or in a buffet.

Lime-flavored gelatin (jelly powder)	3 oz.	85 g
Boiling water	1 cup	250 mL
Lime-flavored gelatin (jelly powder)	3 oz.	85 g
Boiling water	1 cup	250 mL
Cold water	¾ cup	175 mL
Salad dressing (or mayonnaise)	½ cup	125 mL
White vinegar	1 tsp.	5 mL
Finely chopped green pepper	1 cup	250 mL
Finely chopped celery	½ cup	125 mL
Creamed cottage cheese	1 cup	250 mL

Stir first gelatin into first amount of boiling water in medium bowl until dissolved. Chill, stirring and scraping down sides often, until it shows signs of thickening.

As soon as first gelatin goes in the refrigerator, stir second gelatin into second amount of boiling water in another medium bowl until dissolved. Add cold water. Stir. Chill, stirring and scraping down sides often, until it shows signs of thickening.

To first gelatin, whisk in salad dressing and vinegar. Add green pepper, celery and cottage cheese. Stir. Turn into 6 cup (1.5 L) mold. Chill. When second gelatin, is beginning to thicken, pour over top of first gelatin in mold. Chill. Serves 8 to 10.

Pictured above.

Tomato Shrimp Aspic

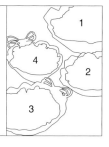

Special Coleslaw

This is a nice brunch or buffet salad. Bright, colorful and great taste.

Grated cabbage, packed	2 cups	500 mL
Crushed pineapple, drained, juice reserved	½ cup	125 mL
Miniature marshmallows	50	50
Slivered or sliced almonds	½ cup	125 mL
Medium coconut	½ cup	125 mL
Salad dressing (or mayonnaise)	½ cup	125 mL
Reserved juice, enough to thin		
Cayenne pepper, just a pinch		

Combine first 5 ingredients in bowl.

Mix salad dressing, reserved juice if needed and cayenne pepper in separate bowl. Pour as much over salad as needed. Toss well to mix. Serves 6.

Pictured on page 157.

Fruity Coleslaw

A nice variation of traditional coleslaw. The dressing is excellent.

Grated cabbage, packed	3 cups	750 mL
Red apples, unpeeled, cored and finely diced	2	2
Chopped walnuts	½ cup	125 mL
Salad dressing (or mayonnaise)	½ cup	125 mL
Milk	1 tbsp.	15 mL
Onion powder	¼ tsp.	1 mL
Paprika	¼ tsp.	1 mL
Granulated sugar	1 tsp.	5 mL

Put cabbage, apple and walnuts into large bowl.

Mix in remaining ingredients in small bowl. Add to cabbage mixture. Stir. Makes 4 cups (1 L).

Pictured on page 159.

Citrus Salad

A very attractive individual salad. The dressing is a pretty pink color.

Lettuce cups	4	4
Pineapple slices	4	4
Oranges, peeled and sectioned	2	2
Grapefruit, peeled and sectioned	1	1
Maraschino cherries for garnish		
Cranberry Dressing:		
Cranberry jelly	½ cup	125 mL
Salad dressing (or mayonnaise)	½ cup	125 mL

Place 1 lettuce cup on each salad plate. Lay pineapple slice on each cup. Arrange, starting from one side on top of pineapple, 1 orange section, 1 grapefruit section, 1 orange section, 1 grapefruit section and 1 orange section.

Place cherry slices here and there to decorate.

Cranberry Dressing: Whisk both ingredients together. Serve on the side or spoon over top just before serving. Serves 4.

Pictured on page 158.

Cottage Salad

This colorful salad will go nicely with a casserole supper or a quiche brunch.

Head of lettuce, cut or torn	1	1
Medium carrots, grated	2	2
Medium tomatoes, cut, seeded and diced, drained well	2	2
Thinly sliced celery	1 cup	250 mL
Continental Dressing:		
White vinegar	2 tbsp.	30 mL
Cooking oil	1 tbsp.	15 mL
Water	1 tbsp.	15 mL
Prepared mustard	½ tsp.	2 mL
Salt	½ tsp.	2mL
Pepper, just a pinch		
Granulated sugar	½-1 tsp.	2-5 mL
Paprika	¼ tsp.	1 mL
Creamed cottage cheese	1 cup	250 mL

Combine first 4 ingredients in large bowl.

Continental Dressing: Whisk first 8 ingredients together in small bowl. Cover and keep chilled until ready to serve salad.

Just before serving salad, add cottage cheese to greens. Toss. Add dressing. Toss lightly. Serves 6 to 8.

Pictured on page 159.

Sauerkraut Salad

Flavor is excellent and color is showy. Best when served the next day.

Canned sauerkraut, drained	28 oz.	796 mL
Chopped celery	1 cup	250 mL
Chopped onion	½ cup	125 mL
Grated carrot	½ cup	125 mL
Chopped red or green pepper	½ cup	125 mL
Pimiento slivers	2 tbsp.	30 mL
Granulated sugar	1 cup	250 mL
White vinegar	½ cup	125 mL

Combine first 6 ingredients in bowl.

Heat and stir sugar and vinegar in saucepan until it comes to a boil. Remove from heat. Cool to lukewarm. Pour over vegetables. Cover. Chill overnight. Makes 5 cups (1.25 L) salad.

Pictured on page 159.

Waldorf Spinach Toss

Take two old favorites and combine for a new holiday salad.

Pecan pieces, lightly toasted	¾ cup	175 mL
Red apple, with peel, cored and sliced in thin wedges	1	1
Orange, peeled (white pith removed), halved and thinly sliced	1	1
Red onion, thinly sliced and separated	½ cup	125 mL
Spinach bunches, torn bite size	2 x 10 oz.	2 x 285 g
Dressing:		
Reserved toasted pecan pieces	¼ cup	75 mL
Granulated sugar	½ cup	125 mL
Dry mustard	1 tsp.	5 mL
Hot pepper sauce	⅛ tsp.	0.5 mL
White vinegar	½ cup	125 mL
Cooking oil	½ cup	125 mL

Toast pecans in 350°F (175 °C) oven for 5 to 8 minutes until lightly browned. Reserve ¼ cup (75 mL) for dressing. Place pecans, apple, orange, onion and spinach in large salad bowl.

Dressing: Combine reserved pecans, sugar, mustard, hot pepper sauce, vinegar and cooking oil in blender. Blend for 2 minutes until smooth. Pour over spinach mixture and toss to coat salad. Serves 6 to 8.

Pictured on page 131.

Colorful Tossed Salad

As the name says, lots of color. Dressing is very tasty.

Parmesan Dressing:		
Salad dressing (or mayonnaise)	½ cup	125 mL
Grated Parmesan cheese	¼ cup	60 mL
Milk	3 tbsp.	50 mL
Granulated sugar	1 tsp.	5 mL
Dill weed	1 tsp.	5 mL
Lemon pepper	1 tsp.	5 mL
Onion powder	¼ tsp.	1 mL
Salad:		
Medium head of lettuce, cut up	1	1
Radishes, thinly sliced	6-8	6-8
Green onions, thinly sliced	3-5	3-5
Diced medium or sharp Cheddar cheese	½ cup	125 mL
Medium tomatoes, halved, seeded and diced	2	2

Parmesan Dressing: Stir all ingredients well in jar. Chill until needed. Makes ⅔ cup (150 mL) dressing.

Salad: Combine first 4 ingredients in large bowl. Chill until needed.

Put tomato into small separate bowl. When ready to serve, drain tomato and add to lettuce mixture. Add dressing as needed. Toss to coat. Serves 8 to 10.

Pictured on page 157.

Citrus Salad, page 156

Sauerkraut Salad, page 158   Cottage Salad, page 156   Fruity Coleslaw, page 156

Turkey Salad

Great for Boxing Day.

Cooked turkey	4 cups	1 L
Seedless grapes, halved	1 cup	250 mL
Sliced celery	1 cup	250 mL
Canned mandarin oranges, drained	10 oz.	284 mL
Toasted slivered almonds	½ cup	125 mL
Diced apple, with peel	1 cup	250 mL
Chopped peeled cucumber	1 cup	250 mL
Bean sprouts, large handful		
Dressing:		
Salad dressing (or mayonnaise)	½ cup	125 mL
White vinegar	2 tbsp.	30 mL
Frozen concentrated orange juice	1 tbsp.	15 mL
Granulated sugar	1 tbsp.	15 mL
Salt	½ tsp.	2 mL
Onion powder	¼ tsp.	1 mL

Put first 8 ingredients into large bowl.

Dressing: Stir all ingredients together well. Add as much as needed to salad. Toss well. Makes ¾ cup (175 mL) dressing. Salad serves 6 to 8.

Pictured on page 157.

Fruit And Cheese Salad

Blue cheese sneaks into this salad for a nice sharp flavor. Dressing is a malty-creamy color.

Medium head of iceberg lettuce, cut or torn	1	1
Small zucchini with peel, sliced thinly	2	2
Oranges, peeled, sectioned and cut into 3 pieces each	2	2
Grapefruit, peeled, sectioned and cut into 4 pieces each	1	1
Tiny cauliflower florets	2 cups	500 mL
Crumbled blue cheese	½ cup	125 mL
Sour Cream Dressing:		
Sour cream	1 cup	250 mL
Balsamic vinegar	2 tbsp.	30 mL

Combine all 6 ingredients in large bowl. Cover and chill until needed.

Sour Cream Dressing: Mix sour cream with balsamic vinegar. Pour over salad and toss or serve on the side. Salad serves 8 to 10.

Pictured on page 157.

Soups

If there's a forgotten item on the holiday menu it's likely soup, and that shouldn't be. Soups have a presence of their own, from the clear broths that accompany the higher-profile dishes at dinner to the chunky chowders, cream soups and bisques full-bodied enough to be a meal by themselves.

Discover the possibilities of this underestimated component and give soups their due. Appreciate their potential and they will return the favor in their own way.

Top: Smooth Bean Soup, page 164   Left Center: Broccoli Soup, page 160
Bottom: Corn Chowder, page 160   Right Center: Tomato Consommé, page 161

Corn Chowder

Creamy, rich and thick.

Diced potatoes	3 cups	750 mL
Chopped celery	1 cup	250 mL
Grated carrots	1 cup	250 mL
Chopped onion	1 cup	250 mL
Water	2 cups	500 mL
Bacon slices, diced	4	4
All-purpose flour	¼ cup	60 mL
Milk	2¼ cups	500 mL
Evaporated skim milk (or light cream)	13½ oz.	385 mL
Cream-style corn	14 oz.	398 mL
Salt	1 tsp.	5 mL
Pepper	½ tsp.	2 mL
Cayenne pepper, optional	½ tsp.	2 mL

Cover and cook potato, celery, carrot and onion in water in large saucepan until tender. Do not drain.

Fry bacon in frying pan.

Mix flour in with bacon. Stir in both milks until mixture boils and thickens. Add to potato mixture.

Add corn, salt, pepper and cayenne pepper. Stir and heat through. Makes 10 cups (2.5 L) chowder.

Pictured on this page.

Broccoli Soup

Perfect after an outdoor winter activity.

Head of broccoli, finely cut	1	1
Medium onion, finely chopped	1	1
Butter or hard margarine	1 tbsp.	15 mL
Salt	¾ tsp.	4 mL
Pepper	⅛ tsp.	0.5 mL
Water, to just cover		
Canned evaporated milk	13½ oz.	385 mL
Parsley flakes	1 tsp.	5 mL

Put broccoli, onion, butter, salt and pepper in saucepan. Add water. Bring to a boil. Boil until vegetables are tender.

Add milk and parsley. Return to a boil. Boil, slowly for 15 minutes. Taste for salt and pepper, adding more if needed. Makes 3½ cups (800 mL) soup.

Pictured above.

Note: if your want a smooth soup, run through blender before adding milk and parsley flakes.

Variation: Add 3 to 4 strips of cooked, crumbled bacon or add 4 oz. (125 g) Velveeta cheese. Try adding both bacon and cheese for a pleasant change.

Onion Soup

This always hits the spot! Nice beefy broth.

Thin sirloin steak, diced	1 lb.	454 g
Water	9 cups	2.25 L
Chopped celery	1 cup	250 mL
Thinly sliced narrow carrots	2 cups	500 mL
Diced potato	2 cups	500 mL
Bay leaf	1	1
Whole garlic cloves	2	2
Salt	2 tsp.	10 mL
Pepper	½ tsp.	2 mL
Beef bouillon powder	3 tbsp.	50 mL
Sliced onion	4 cups	1 L
French bread slices, toasted	10	10
Grated mozzarella cheese	1 cup	250 mL

Combine steak and water in large saucepan. Bring to a boil. Boil slowly for 15 minutes.

Add next 9 ingredients. Return to a boil. Simmer for about 1 hour until vegetables are tender. Discard bay leaf. Ladle into oven-proof soup bowls.

Lay a slice of toast on top of each bowl, cutting to fit if necessary. Sprinkle heavily with cheese. Bake in 450°F (230°C) oven to melt and brown cheese. If bowls aren't oven-proof, melt and brown cheese on toast slices placed on a baking sheet then transfer to bowls. Makes 10 cups (2.5 L) soup.

Pictured on page 165.

Tomato Consommé

A smooth beginning to a holiday meal.

Beef bouillon cubes	3	3
Boiling water	3 cups	675 mL
Tomato juice	6 cups	1.35 L
Lemon juice, fresh or bottled	1 tbsp.	15 mL
Soy sauce	1 tbsp.	15 mL
Worcestershire sauce	2 tsp.	10 mL
Onion powder	2 tsp.	10 mL
Granulated sugar	1½ tsp.	7 mL

Chopped chives, for garnish

Dissolve bouillon cubes in boiling water in saucepan.

Add next 6 ingredients. Bring to a boil.

Ladle into 8 soup bowls. Garnish with chives. Makes 9 cups (2.25 L) consommé.

Pictured on page 160.

Carrot Cauliflower Soup

Lovely orange color. Very thick. Freezes well.

Medium potato, diced	1	1
Medium carrots, diced	4	4
Chopped onion	1 cup	250 mL
Small head of cauliflower, cut up	1	1
Water	2 cups	500 mL
Water	2 cups	500 mL
Chicken bouillon powder	4 tsp.	20 mL
Beef bouillon powder	1 tsp.	5 mL
Prepared mustard	1 tsp.	5 mL
Ground nutmeg	½ tsp.	2 mL
Salt	1 tsp.	5 mL
Pepper	¼ tsp.	1 mL
Grated medium Cheddar cheese	1 cup	250 mL
Sherry (or alcohol-free sherry)	3 tbsp.	50 mL

Combine first 5 ingredients in saucepan. Cook until vegetables are done. Do not drain. Remove from heat.

Stir in next 8 ingredients. Pour into large bowl. In 3 or 4 batches, purée in food processor or blender. Return to saucepan.

Add sherry. Heat until very hot. Makes generous 7 cups (1.75 L) soup.

Pictured below.

Carrot Cauliflower Soup

Hearty Scallop Chowder

Nice chunky chowder. Easily doubled.

Water	2 cups	500 mL
Chicken bouillon cubes	2	2
Diced potatoes	3 cups	750 mL
Chopped onion	1 cup	250 mL
Diced carrot	½ cup	125 mL
Diced celery	1 cup	250 mL
Small bay leaf	1	1
Salt	½ tsp.	2 mL
Pepper	¼ tsp.	1 mL
Ground thyme	¼ tsp.	1 mL
Butter or hard margarine	4 tsp.	25 mL
Fresh mushrooms, sliced	½ lb.	225 g
Scallops, fresh or frozen, cut in half or smaller	½ lb.	225 g
Dry white wine (or apple juice)	2 tbsp.	30 mL
Cream (the heavier the better)	1 cup	250 mL

Put first 10 ingredients into large saucepan. Simmer, stirring often, to dissolve bouillon cubes and cook vegetables. Remove bay leaf. Cool a bit and run mixture through blender. Set aside in saucepan.

Combine butter and mushrooms in frying pan. Sauté until mushrooms are beginning to brown.

Add scallops and wine. Cover and steam fry about 1 minute, stirring 2 or 3 times. Add to puréed vegetables.

Stir in cream. Heat but don't boil. Garnish with parsley or chives. Makes about 6 cups (1.5 L) chowder.

Pictured on page 163.

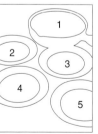

Scallop Bisque

Thick creamy soup. Serve with crackers.

Butter or hard margarine	6 tbsp.	100 mL
Leeks, chopped (white part)	2	2
All-purpose flour	¼ cup	60 mL
Salt	¼ tsp.	1 mL
Pepper	⅛ tsp.	0.5 mL
Chicken bouillon powder	2 tsp.	10 mL
Boiling water	2 cups	500 mL
Milk	2 cups	500 mL
Tomato sauce	7½ oz.	213 mL
Scallops, fresh or frozen, cut up	1 lb.	454 g
Whipping cream	1 cup	250 mL

Put butter into frying pan. Add leeks and sauté about 5 minutes.

Mix in flour, salt, pepper and bouillon powder. Stir in water until mixture boils and thickens.

Add milk, tomato sauce and scallops. Return to boil. Simmer for 5 minutes to cook scallops.

Add cream. Process in blender until smooth. Heat and serve. Makes about 8 cups (2 L) bisque.

Pictured on page 163.

Shrimp Chowder

Chunky, rich and thick. Nice combination of shrimp and cheese. Light orange in color.

Chopped onion	2 cups	500 mL
Butter or hard margarine	3 tbsp.	50 mL
Diced potato	3 cups	750 mL
Water	1¼ cups	300 mL
Salt	½ tsp.	2 mL
Pepper	⅛ tsp.	0.5 mL
Milk	1 cup	250 mL
Velveeta cheese, cut up	8 oz.	250 g
Canned broken shrimp, drained	2 x 4 oz.	2 x 113 g

Sauté onion in butter in large saucepan until soft.

Add potato, water, salt and pepper. Cover and cook until potato is tender. Do not drain. Mash about half the potatoes.

Add milk and cheese. Heat slowly, stirring often to melt cheese.

Add shrimp. Keep just below boiling to blend flavors. Makes 6 cups (1.5 L) chowder.

Pictured on page 163.

Tomato Cream Soup

Quick and easy.

Hard margarine (butter browns too fast)	2 tbsp.	30 mL
Chopped onion	1 cup	250 mL
Canned condensed tomato soup	2 × 10 oz.	2 × 284 mL
Soup cans of milk	2 × 10 oz.	2 × 284 mL
Cream cheese, diced	4 oz.	125 g

Melt margarine in large saucepan. Add onion. Sauté until soft.

Add soup, milk and cheese. Heat and stir to blend flavors and melt cheese. Makes 6 cups (1.5 L) soup.

Pictured on page 163.

Smooth Bean Soup

Looks can be deceiving. Wonderful flavor!

Dried navy beans	2 cups	500 mL
Water, to cover		
Meaty ham bone	1	1
Water	4 cups	1 L
Chopped carrot	3/4 cup	175 mL
Chopped celery	1/2 cup	125 mL
Chopped onion	1 cup	250 mL
Medium potatoes, cut up	3	3
Salt	1 tsp.	5 mL
Pepper	1/8 tsp.	0.5 mL
Lettuce, cut up, packed	3 cups	750 mL
Whipping cream	1 cup	250 mL

Put beans into bowl. Pour first amount of water over top to come 2 to 3 inches (5 to 8 cm) above beans. Let soak overnight.

Drain beans. Put beans into large saucepan or Dutch oven. Add next 8 ingredients. Cook slowly, stirring often for 2 hours.

Run bean mixture, along with lettuce, through blender. Return to saucepan.

Add cream. Heat through, without boiling. Makes 9 cups (2.25 L) soup.

Pictured on page 160.

Lobster Chowder Feed

Start a Christmas Eve tradition. Serves a large group—but be prepared for seconds. Good with Drop Cheese Biscuits, page 61.

Butter or hard margarine	1/2 cup	125 mL
Chopped onion	3 cups	750 mL
Diced celery	2 cups	500 mL
Small green peppers, seeded and diced	2	2
All-purpose flour	1/2 cup	125 mL
Boiling water	4 cups	1 L
Diced potato	5 cups	1.25 L
Salt	3 1/2 tsp.	17 mL
Pepper	1/2 tsp.	2 mL
Butter or hard margarine	1/4 cup	60 mL
Frozen cans of lobster, thawed	2 × 11 1/2 oz.	2 × 320 g
Boiling water	1 cup	250 mL
Scallops, halved if large	1 lb.	454 g
Haddock fillets, cut bite size	2 lbs.	900 g
Canned evaporated milk	2 × 13 1/2 oz.	2 × 385 mL
Homogenized milk	3 cups	750 mL

Melt first amount of butter in frying pan. Add onion, celery and green pepper. Sauté until tender.

Sprinkle flour over vegetables. Mix in well.

Put first amount of boiling water, diced potato, salt and pepper in large heavy Dutch oven. Stir. Cover. Cook until potatoes are tender-crisp. Add flour mixture.

Melt second amount of butter in frying pan. Add lobster. Sauté just long enough for the red color from the lobster to go into the butter. Add to potato mixture.

In separate small saucepan, put second amount of boiling water and scallops. Cook for 3 to 5 minutes until opaque. Do not drain. Set aside. Add to potato mixture.

Add haddock to potato mixture. Cook until fish turns white and flakes or falls apart.

Add both milks. Heat, stirring occasionally, until hot. Watch closely so it does not boil. Makes 6 quarts (6 L) chowder.

Pictured on page 163.

Minestrone, page 165   Tomato Cabbage Soup, page 165   Onion Soup, page 161

Tomato Cabbage Soup

This will be a big hit with cabbage or soup lovers! Serve before a main course entrée or for lunch.

Margarine (butter browns too fast)	2 tbsp.	30 mL
Chopped onion	1½ cups	375 mL
Chopped celery	⅔ cup	150 mL
Canned tomatoes, broken up	2 × 14 oz.	2 × 398 mL
Coarsely grated cabbage, packed	6 cups	1.5 L
Thinly sliced carrots	1½ cups	375 mL
Chili sauce	¼ cup	60 mL
Granulated sugar	2 tsp.	10 mL
Salt	2 tsp.	10 mL
Pepper	½ tsp.	2 mL
Water	8 cups	2 L
Beef bouillon powder	2 tbsp.	30 mL
Whole oregano	¼ tsp.	1 mL
Sweet basil	¼ tsp.	1 mL

Melt margarine in Dutch oven. Add onion and celery. Sauté until soft.

Add remaining ingredients. Bring to a boil, stirring often. Cover. Boil slowly until vegetables are tender. Makes 13 cups (3.25 L) soup.

Pictured above.

Minestrone

Perfect for a cold winter evening. Serve with salad and buns.

Cooking oil	2 tbsp.	30 mL
Lean ground beef	1 lb.	454 g
Chopped onion	1½ cups	375 mL
Chopped celery	1 cup	250 mL
Boiling water	6 cups	1.5 L
Beef bouillon powder	3 tbsp.	50 mL
Canned tomatoes, broken up	3 × 14 oz.	3 × 398 mL
Grated cabbage, packed	2 cups	500 mL
Thinly sliced narrow carrot	¾ cup	175 mL
Parsley flakes	1 tbsp.	15 mL
Salt	1 tsp.	5 mL
Pepper	¼ tsp.	1 mL
Garlic powder	¼ tsp.	1 mL
Elbow macaroni	1 cup	250 mL
Canned red kidney beans, with juice	14 oz.	398 mL

Grated Parmesan cheese

Heat cooking oil in frying pan. Scramble-fry ground beef, onion and celery until no pink remains in beef and vegetables are soft. Put into large saucepan or Dutch oven.

Mix boiling water and bouillon powder. Add to pot.

Add next 7 ingredients to pot. Bring to a boil, stirring occasionally. Boil slowly for 15 minutes.

Stir in macaroni. Boil for 10 minutes more.

Add kidney beans. Stir. Boil until macaroni is tender, about 5 minutes.

Sprinkle each serving with Parmesan cheese. Makes 12 cups (3 L) soup.

Pictured above.

Vegetables

Holiday dinners need vegetables to accompany the main dishes. Familiar is fine but how about giving those basic veggies a slightly new shape?

These recipes incorporate that little something—a dressing, a topping, an extra ingredient or two—that turns the expected into a memorable taste experience.

Many of these vegetable recipes are for casserole-type dishes which can be prepared ahead of time—another plus on the big day.

Make the ordinary extraordinary when it comes to vegetables this holiday season.

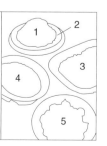

Stewed Tomato Casserole

Christmas colors—red and green. Extra easy, extra good!

Small zucchini with peel, sliced	2	2
Boiling water, to cover		
Canned stewed tomatoes	2 × 14 oz.	2 × 398 mL
Onion flakes	1 tbsp.	15 mL
Granulated sugar	½ tsp.	2 mL
Salt	⅛ tsp.	0.5 mL
Pepper, light sprinkle		
Hot pepper sauce drops	4	4
Dry bread crumbs	½ cup	125 mL
Butter or hard margarine	½ cup	125 mL
Fresh bread crumbs	1¼ cups	300 mL

Combine zucchini and boiling water in large saucepan. Bring to a boil. Boil 1 minute. Drain.

Combine next 7 ingredients in bowl.

Melt butter in saucepan. Stir in bread crumbs. Cover bottom of 2 quart (2 L) greased casserole with ½ crumb mixture. Add layer of ½ zucchini, layer of ½ tomato mixture then the remaining ½ zucchini and ½ tomato mixture. Top with second ½ crumbs. Bake, uncovered, in 350°F (175°C) oven until hot and browned. Serves 6 to 8.

Pictured on page 167.

Honey Glazed Onions

A quick addition to the dinner table.

Small white pearl onions, peeled	2 lbs.	900 g
Boiling salted water		
Butter or hard margarine	3 tbsp.	50 mL
Honey	3 tbsp.	50 mL
Salt, sprinkle		
Pepper, sprinkle		
Cornstarch	2 tsp.	10 mL
Water	1 tbsp.	15 mL

Cook onions in about 2 inches (5 cm) boiling water until tender. Drain.

Stir butter and honey together in small bowl to mix well. Add to onions. Heat and stir slowly until glazed. Sprinkle with salt and pepper. Stir. Remove onions.

Mix cornstarch in water. Stir into remaining liquid to thicken. Return onions to saucepan. Stir. Serves 6 to 8.

Pictured on page 167.

Cauliflower Au Gratin

The cheese sauce has a nice nip to it. Cut in wedges to serve.

Large head of cauliflower, left whole, leaves removed	2 lbs.	900 g
Boiling salted water		
Cheese Sauce:		
Butter or hard margarine	3 tbsp.	50 mL
All-purpose flour	3 tbsp.	50 mL
Salt	½ tsp.	2 mL
Paprika	¼ tsp.	1 mL
Cayenne pepper, just a pinch		
Milk	2 cups	500 mL
Grated sharp Cheddar cheese	1 cup	250 mL

Cook cauliflower in large saucepan in about 2 inches (5 cm) boiling salted water until tender. Drain.

Cheese Sauce: Melt butter in saucepan. Mix in flour, salt, paprika and cayenne. Stir in milk until it boils and thickens.

Add cheese. Stir until it melts. Place whole cauliflower in serving bowl. Pour cheese sauce over top. Serves 6 to 8.

Pictured on page 167.

Dressed Peas

Serve this as a hot or cold vegetable. Either way the basil and mustard flavors are just right with the peas.

Dressing:		
Water	¼ cup	60 mL
Cornstarch	1 tsp.	5 mL
Red wine vinegar	2 tbsp.	30 mL
Granulated sugar	1 tsp.	5 mL
Sweet basil	1 tsp.	5 mL
Prepared mustard	1 tsp.	5 mL
Salt	¼ tsp.	1 mL
Pepper, just a pinch		
Nutmeg, just a pinch		
Frozen peas	2¼ lbs.	1 kg

Dressing: Measure first 9 ingredients in saucepan. Heat and stir until it boils and thickens slightly.

Cook peas according to directions on package. Drain. Add dressing to warm peas just before serving. Stir. Serves 12.

Pictured on page 167.

Sauced Broccoli

Nice contrast in color between sauce and broccoli.

Broccoli heads, cut up	2-3	2-3
Boiling water		
Poppy Seed Sauce:		
Sour cream	1½ cups	375 mL
Granulated sugar	2 tsp.	10 mL
Chopped chives	1 tsp.	5 mL
Poppy seed	1 tsp.	5 mL
Salt	¼ tsp.	1 mL
Pepper	⅛ tsp.	0.5 mL

Cook broccoli in boiling water until tender-crisp. Drain.

Poppy Seed Sauce: Mix all ingredients. Heat and stir until very warm. Pour over broccoli. Serves 6 to 8.

Pictured on front cover.

Hasselback Potatoes

Hasselback Potatoes

A new look to baked potatoes. Serve with sour cream and chives.

Smooth oval medium baking potatoes, peeled	8	8
Butter or hard margarine, softened	2 tbsp.	30 mL
Salt, generous sprinkle (see Note)		
Pepper, light sprinkle		

Place 1 potato on tablespoon. Set on counter. Make cuts ¼ inch (6 mm) apart from top almost to bottom. Tablespoon should keep knife from reaching bottom of potato. Set potatoes cut side up in greased 9 x 13 inch (22 x 33 cm) pan. Pat tops dry with paper towel.

Brush potatoes with butter. Sprinkle with salt and pepper. Bake, uncovered, in 450°F (230°C) oven for about 40 minutes until tender when pierced with tip of sharp knife. Brush again with butter at half time. Serves 8.

Pictured above.

Note: Sprinkle with seasoned salt for a zippier flavor.

Squash Casserole

Tomato Bean Dish

The red and green colors make this particularly festive.
Best made the day of serving.

Frozen green beans, cooked and drained	6 cups	1.5 L
Medium tomatoes, chopped	6	6
Grated medium or sharp Cheddar cheese	2 cups	500 mL
Topping:		
Large eggs	4	4
Milk	1 cup	250 mL
Biscuit mix	1 cup	250 mL
Salt	1 tsp.	5 mL
Cayenne pepper	½ tsp.	2 mL
Sweet basil	1 tsp.	5 mL

Spread green beans in layer in ungreased 9 × 13 inch (22 × 33 cm) pan. Layer tomatoes over top. Sprinkle with cheese.

Beat eggs in mixing bowl. Add milk, biscuit mix, salt, cayenne and basil. Beat. Pour over cheese. Bake, uncovered, in 350°F (175°C) oven for about 50 minutes until browned and heated through. Serves 10 to 12.

Pictured below.

Squash Casserole

Beautiful golden yellow color. Pecan Topping is attractive for festive occasions or use the Butter Topping.

Acorn squash	4	4
Squash pulp, approximately	8 cups	2 L
Butter or hard margarine	¼ cup	60 mL
Large eggs	2	2
Salt	1½ tsp.	7 mL
Pecan Topping:		
Butter or hard margarine	¼ cup	60 mL
Brown sugar, packed	½ cup	125 mL
All-purpose flour	¼ cup	60 mL
Chopped pecans	½ cup	125 mL
Butter Topping:		
Butter or hard margarine	2 tbsp.	30 mL
Salt, sprinkle		
Pepper, sprinkle		

Cut squash in half lengthwise. Discard seeds. Place cut side down on greased baking sheet with sides. Bake, uncovered, in 350°F (175°C) oven for about 50 minutes until tender. Cool until you can handle. Scoop out pulp into saucepan.

Mash pulp with butter, eggs, and salt using fork for coarser texture or food processor for smoother texture. Turn into 3 quart (3 L) ungreased casserole.

Pecan Topping: For a special topping melt butter in saucepan. Stir in sugar, flour and pecans. Sprinkle over top. Bake, uncovered, in 350°F (175°C) oven for about 30 minutes. Serves 16.

Pictured above.

Butter Topping: Simple but good. Make indentations with back of tablespoon all over surface. Put dab of butter in each one. Sprinkle whole surface with salt and pepper. Bake as in Pecan Topping. Serves 16.

Tomato Bean Dish

Broccoli Casserole

Sweet Potato Bake

Assemble the night before but do not bake. Marshmallow topping is added during last few minutes of baking.

Quick cooking rolled oats	½ cup	125 mL
All-purpose flour	½ cup	125 mL
Brown sugar, packed	½ cup	125 mL
Ground cinnamon	1 tsp.	5 mL
Butter or hard margarine	6 tbsp.	100 mL
Sweet potatoes drained and cubed (see Note)	2 × 19 oz.	2 × 540 mL
Cranberries, fresh or frozen, coarsely chopped	2 cups	500 mL
Reserved crumb mixture	1 cup	250 mL
Miniature marshmallows	2 cups	500 mL

Place first 5 ingredients in bowl. Stir to mix well. Measure out 1 cup (250 mL) and reserve for cranberry mixture.

In large bowl, combine sweet potato, cranberries and crumb mix. Toss well. Turn into ungreased 1½ quart (1.5 L) casserole. Sprinkle with remaining crumbs. Bake, uncovered, in 350°F (175°C) oven for 30 minutes.

Cover with single layer of marshmallows. Bake for 10 to 12 minutes until lightly browned. Serves 8 to 10.

Pictured below.

Note: Two large fresh sweet potatoes may be substituted for canned. Cook in boiling water until just tender.

Broccoli Casserole

The green broccoli and red pimiento make this a showy Christmas casserole.

Frozen chopped broccoli	3 × 10 oz.	3 × 300 g
Salt	½ tsp.	2 mL
Boiling water		
Condensed cream of mushroom soup	10 oz.	284 mL
Grated sharp Cheddar cheese	1 cup	250 mL
Salad dressing (or mayonnaise)	¼ cup	60 mL
Chopped pimiento	2 tbsp.	30 mL
Topping:		
Butter or hard margarine	2 tbsp.	30 mL
Cracker crumbs	½ cup	125 mL

Cook broccoli in salted boiling water until tender-crisp. Drain well. Transfer to 2 quart (2 L) ungreased casserole.

In separate bowl stir soup, cheese, salad dressing and pimiento. Pour over broccoli.

Topping: Melt butter in small saucepan. Stir in cracker crumbs. Sprinkle over top. Bake, uncovered, in 350°F (175°C) oven for 30 to 40 minutes until browned and bubbly hot. Serves 8 to 10.

Pictured above.

Sweet Potato Bake

Festive Scalloped Potatoes

Red onion makes a colorful contrast.

Medium potatoes, thinly sliced	8	8
Medium red or white onion, thinly sliced in rings	1	1
Sauce:		
Butter or hard margarine	½ cup	125 mL
All-purpose flour	½ cup	125 mL
Salt	2 tsp.	10 mL
Pepper	½ tsp.	2 mL
Paprika	½ tsp.	2 mL
Milk	4½ cups	1.1 L
Paprika, generous sprinkle		

Place potato slices in 1 container and onion slices in another.

Sauce: Melt butter in saucepan. Mix in flour, salt, pepper and paprika. Stir in milk until it boils and thickens. To assemble, layer ½ potatoes, then ½ onion in greased 3 quart (3 L) casserole. Pour ½ sauce over top. Layer second ½ potatoes and onion followed by second ½ sauce.

Sprinkle with paprika. Bake, covered, in 350°F (175°C) oven for about 1 hour until tender. Remove cover for last 10 minutes. Serves 8 to 10.

Pictured on page 131.

Carrot Medley

Slightly dressier carrots. Use for sit-down dinner or buffet.

Margarine (butter browns too fast)	2 tbsp.	30 mL
Coarsely chopped onion	2 cups	500 mL
Sliced fresh mushrooms, (1 lb., 454 g)	4 cups	1 L
Carrots, cut in thick slices	2 lbs.	900 g
Chicken bouillon powder	2 tsp.	10 mL
Water	1 cup	250 mL

Melt margarine in frying pan. Add onion. Sauté until soft. Remove to bowl.

Add mushrooms to frying pan along with more margarine if needed. Sauté until soft. Add to onions.

Put carrot, bouillon powder and water in large saucepan. Bring to a simmer. Simmer, covered, until tender-crisp. Add onion and mushroom mixture. Simmer until tender. Serves 8.

Pictured on page 131.

Zucchini Casserole

Delicious casserole for formal or informal entertaining.

Medium zucchini with peel, sliced	4	4
Boiling salted water		
Hard margarine (butter browns too fast)	6 tbsp.	100 mL
Chopped onion	1 cup	250 mL
Grated carrot	½ cup	125 mL
Top of stove stuffing mix and envelope seasoning	1½ cups	375 mL
Condensed cream of mushroom soup	10 oz.	284 mL
Sour cream (or plain yogurt)	½ cup	125 mL
Hard margarine (butter browns too fast)	2 tbsp.	30 mL
Remaining stuffing mix		

Boil zucchini in boiling salted water for 8 to 10 minutes until tender. Drain.

Melt first amount of margarine in frying pan. Add onion and carrot. Sauté until soft. Transfer to large bowl.

Mix stuffing and seasoning in separate bowl. Measure out 1½ cups (375 mL). Reserve remainder for topping.

Add mushroom soup, sour cream and stuffing mix to onion mixture. Stir well. Add zucchini. Stir lightly. Turn into ungreased 2 quart (2 L) casserole.

Keep onions in cold storage or in the refrigerator. A cold onion produces few, if any tears! For a milder flavor, soak Spanish and purple onions in cold water for ½ hour before serving.

Melt second amount of margarine in frying pan. Add remaining stuffing mix. Sauté until browned. Sprinkle over casserole. Bake in 350°F (175°C) oven for 30 to 40 minutes. Serves 6 to 8.

Pictured on page 167.

Table Centerpieces, Decorations & Settings

A brightly-lit tree in the living room and outside the front door. Pine boughs along the staircase and around the doorways. A Christmas village on a table in the corner. Christmas is a time for decorating the house inside and out.

The dinner table is no exception. While the menu is important, so is the atmosphere, and that's where candles, wreaths, sprigs of holly, silver garlands and other Yuletide decorations add so much.

A well-appointed table is a delight at any time of year, but especially at Christmas. Polish the silver and get out the best china and linen. Decorate with a flourish. It's worth the extra effort because you're creating memories.

Centerpieces

"Wrap-Up" Your Table Centerpiece

You will need:

1	Piece of styrofoam or board 10″ x 30″ x ½″ (25 cm x 75 cm x 1.5 cm)
1	Piece of plain broadcloth material 18″ x 36″ (45 cm x 90 cm) <small>This can either complement the tablecloth or blend in with it.</small>
9 to 14	Small empty boxes of varying shapes and sizes <small>We used 13.</small>
4 to 5	Rolls of coordinated Christmas wrapping paper <small>We used 4 different wraps—2 solid foil and 2 patterned foil.</small>
4 to 5	Rolls of coordinated Christmas ribbon <small>We used 2 wired and 2 non-wired.</small>
4 to 5	Christmas picks <small>Picks are available at craft stores in a variety of colors and styles; choose a color that accents, blends or matches a secondary color.</small>
4 to 5	Pieces of short garland or fir boughs
	Hot glue gun

Base:

1. Center styrofoam on material.
2. Starting on one long side, pull edge of material over base. Put dabs of glue on styrofoam about ¼″ (1 cm) in under material. Press material down over glue spots.
3. Repeat on second long side, pulling taut.
4. For ends, fold material in at sides then pull up and over end. Repeat gluing process.
5. Repeat on other end to form smooth and tightly-wrapped finish.

Presents:

1. Wrap half the boxes with at least one of each of the papers, gluing rather than taping. (Do not choose the ribbons yet.)
2. Begin arranging the boxes on the base, keeping in mind that your highest point should be near the center. (Do not begin to glue yet.)
3. Once the central boxes have been established, choose additional boxes that will create a pleasing extension to both ends. Wrap these boxes in the papers that work best to balance the color and design.
4. Choose your ribbons for each box to create additional color effect and balance of color. (Do not do bows yet.) Glue ribbons to paper, rather than tying or taping.
5. Beginning with the boxes that are touching the base, put dabs of glue just in from each corner on the underside of the box and press it into its "spot" on the base. When those boxes are in place, continue gluing the other boxes into place on top of the other ones. Where one box leans against another, put just one dab of glue where they touch.
6. Make bows from the various ribbons and glue into place on each box. Use narrower ribbon to gather loops of wider ribbon together to form bow. The wired ribbon forms wonderful bows.

Finishing Touches:

Glue pieces of garland or boughs at various spots around the base of the boxes making sure they overhang slightly.

Stand back and take a look at the centerpiece from both sides. Determine the locations for the Christmas picks. Tuck and glue them into the little "caves" that show, as well as glue them under the ends of one or two boxes.

Your table is now ready to greet family and friends this festive season.

Create a special effect for your holiday table with the Wrap-Up Centerpiece. Its size, shape, color and theme possibilities are endless — limited only by your imagination.

Here are a few suggestions to get you started.

For Family/Young Children
Choose red and green wrappings that have a Santa Claus/reindeer theme. Finish with candy canes and holly.

For A Country Christmas Buffet Or Brunch
Cover the boxes with gingham material in various colors. Decorate with burlap, wool strands, cinnamon sticks, dried flower and eucalyptus.

For An Elegant Dinner
Go formal with gold, lace, netted ribbons and balls, or try a combination of silver and winter white.

Festive Ribbon Centerpiece

You will need:

1 Piece of gold, red or green metallic mesh ribbon 72" (2 m) length, 6" (15 cm) wide

1 Piece of thin, pliable wire, 12" (31 cm) length

1 Piece of red or green felt, ½" × 3" (12 mm × 7.5 cm) length

1 Pine cone, large
Leave natural, or spray lightly with gold, or glue glitter to some of the edges.

2 Sprigs of plastic greenery

2 Picks (berries and/or small poinsettias)

1 Christmas pick (small gift package or ball and ribbon)
Picks are available at craft stores in a variety of colors and styles; choose a color that accents, blends or matches a secondary color.

Hot glue gun

To Assemble:

1. Fold ribbon back and forth, starting in middle, under itself two times increasing length of each fold, to form bow shape. Leave enough on one side to form tail and to cut off 10" (25 cm) as tail for other side (see Figure 1).

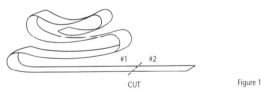

Figure 1

2. Take the 10" (25 cm) piece and place underneath the other side so both sides have a tail (see Figure 2).

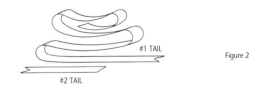

Figure 2

3. Thread wire up and down through the center of all layers and pull loosely to form bow shape. Bring ends of wire around bow and twist together underneath. Thread wire ends through ribbon so they don't show (see Figure 3).

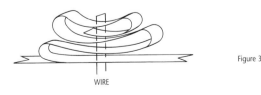

Figure 3

4. Glue felt piece to bottom center of ribbon, covering the wire.

5. Arrange pine cone and greenery on the top side in the middle of the ribbon. Pine cone should be in center with enough greenery around to offset it. Don't glue yet.

6. Arrange the berries, holly, poinsettias, etc. on top of the greenery, so that the centerpiece looks pleasing from all sides.

7. Once everything is placed as you like it, carefully remove the layers and start gluing. Start with the greenery, then the pine cone, then the picks.

8. Cut the ribbon tails in a "V" shape and fluff up the ribbon.

Variation:

Make this centerpiece on a smaller scale, using narrower ribbon, smaller pine cones, etc.

Decorations

Large Wreath Candleholder

You will need:

1	Circle of corrugated cardboard, 10″ (25.5 cm) diameter
1	Circle of red or green felt, 5″ (12.5 cm) diameter.
1	Straight pin
50-60	Pine cones, various sizes Leave natural or create a glittery look by spray painting a few gold or glue glitter on the tips of some cones.
1	Candle, 6″ (15 cm) tall; 3″ (7.5 cm) diameter
10-12	Unshelled walnuts, pecans, hazelnuts, almonds, or Brazil nuts, All of one kind or a combination
	Plastic greenery or silk poinsettias (optional)
	Spray varnish, gloss or matte
1	Red, green or gold ribbon, 42″ (107 cm) length. Should be wide enough to cover the thickness of the cardboard.
	Hot glue gun

To Assemble:

1. Mark the center of the cardboard circle by drawing 5 intersecting lines across the diameter of the circle. Where they meet will be the center.

2. Glue the felt circle onto the center of the cardboard. To help keep felt centered on the cardboard, first push a pin up from the bottom, through the cardboard and then push felt down over pin. Glue down in spots.

3. The pattern created on your wreath will depend on the size of your pine cones. Glue one row of pine cones around the outside of the circle with bottoms facing out. Make sure they come to the edge of the cardboard or just slightly over.

4. Glue another row of cones to the inside of the first layer—this time with the tops facing out.

5. Push the candle onto pin to hold in center.

6. Using more pine cones, fill in the area left free between the candle and the two rows of glued pine cones. These cones should be snug against the candle but still allow the candle to be removed and inserted easily. (Be careful not to glue the cones to the candle.)

7. Fill in any holes or spaces with small pine cones and nuts.

8. Remove candle and pin. Spray wreath with a thin coat of varnish, gloss or matte, depending on what look you want. Make sure to spray from the inside of the circle out, so all surfaces are covered. Let dry and spray once more if needed.

9. Tie the ribbon around the circle of cardboard, ending with a bow. Put a small dot of glue on the knot to hold in place.

10. Stand back and take a good look at your wreath. If there are any spaces that look empty, fill with a few pieces of greenery or silk poinsettias.

Small Wreath Candleholder

You will need:

1	Circle of corrugated cardboard, 3½″ (9 cm) diameter
1	Circle of red or green felt, approximately 1.5″ (4 cm) diameter
1	Straight pin
1	Taper candle, 4½″ (11.5 cm) tall
3	Pine cones, medium Leave natural, or spray lightly with gold, or glue glitter to some of the edges.
12-14	Pine cones, small
	Spray varnish, gloss or matte
1	Red, green or gold ribbon, 20″ (50 cm) length Wide enough to cover the thickness of the cardboard
	Hot glue gun

To Assemble:

1. Mark the center of the cardboard circle by drawing 5 intersecting lines across the diameter of circle. Where the lines meet will be the center.

2. Glue the felt circle onto the center of the cardboard. To help keep felt centered on the cardboard, first push a pin up from bottom, through the cardboard and then push felt down over pin. Glue down in spots.

3. Push the candle onto pin to hold in center.

4. Before gluing any cones, arrange a pattern of cones around the candle to see which looks best. Place the 3 medium cones against the candle to create a holder. (It is important to use cones that can hold the candle upright.) Place a row of small cones around the outside of circle, being careful to come to edge of cardboard or just slightly over. When you are satisfied with the arrangement, remove cones and glue to cardboard circle, being careful not to glue cones to candle.

5. Check for spaces. Glue small cones in place to cover any spaces. (If you can't find cones small enough, cut the tips off less-than-perfect larger cones.)6.   Remove the candle. The pin may be left in to help hold the candle firmly, or remove if you like. Spray the wreath with varnish. Make sure all surfaces are covered with a thin coat. Let dry. Spray again if needed.

7. Tie the ribbon around the cardboard circle, ending with a bow. Put a small dot of glue on knot to hold in place.

Large Wreath Candleholder

Small Wreath Candleholder

Yuletide Log Candleholder

You will need:

1   Birch log, 10" to 12" (25 cm to 31 cm) length, split in half lengthwise

6   Felt circles, 1" (2.5 cm) diameter

1   Small bag of moss
If you gather your own, dry in 140°, (65°C) oven for 1 hour to kill bacteria.

1   Taper candle, 12" (31 cm) length

2   Christmas picks (with small presents, balls or cones) to match candle
Picks are available at craft stores.

3   Sprigs of plastic greenery

10-12   Pine cones, small

2-4   Picks (berries and/or small poinsettias)

   Hot glue gun

To Assemble:

1. Drill a hole in the center of birch log, the diameter of the candle.

2. Glue the felt circles to bottom of the log to prevent scratching table surface.

3. Glue the moss to the log, starting from the top, outside of log down to middle, bottom. Continue around log. When you look down onto top of log, the moss should be in a diamond shape. (see Figure 1)

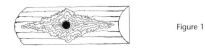

Figure 1

TOP VIEW

4. Put the candle in the hole; if loose, put dab of glue at bottom of hole to hold the candle upright.

5. Pull apart the greenery sprigs. Glue pieces on top of the moss, keeping to diamond shape.

6. Cut long stems from the two Christmas picks. Place just off center on each side of the candle on the long part of log. Glue in place close to the candle, but do not glue to candle.

7. Fill in spaces with small cones, balls, berries or poinsettias. The overall shape, when looking from the side, should form a triangle, with the two Christmas picks and candle forming the tip. (see Figure 2)

Figure 2

"Wrap-Up" Napkin Holder

You will need (for 1 napkin holder):

1   Wired ribbon, 2" (5 cm) wide, 30" (75 cm) length
Ribbon should be the same pattern (or be solid) on both sides

1   Piece gold cord, 8" (20 cm) length

1   Christmas pick
Picks are availble at craft stores in a variety of colors and styles.

    Hot glue gun

To Assemble:

1. Fold ribbon in half crosswise. Form loop 2½" (6.25 cm) in diameter from folded end. Tie tightly with gold cord. (See Figure 1).

Figure 1

2. To make bow, form loop at knot 6½" (16 cm), using ribbon 1. Hold ribbon in place between fingers, and repeat with ribbon 2. Tie ends of gold cord around bow. Make a knot.

3. Glue Christmas pick to knot in center of bow.

4. Open out loop that will hold napkin. Open out 2 loops to form bow.

5. Repeat steps 1 through 4 for as many napkin holders as you need.

"Wrap-Up" Place Cards

You will need (for 1 place card):

1   Tiny box, rectangular
Use a matchbox, raisin box or jewelry box.

1   Piece of wrapping paper, approximately 2½ times the size of the box.

1   Ribbon, solid-colored, 2 inch (5 cm) wide, circumference of box crosswise plus ½" (6 mm).

    Hot glue gun

    Gold ink pen

To Assemble:

1. Wrap box, having seam of paper meet on underside of box, horizontally. Glue sparingly. Fold side flaps down, to make points. Fold points down on underside of box.

2. Place center point of ribbon on center point of top side of box, keeping ribbon horizontal. Fold ends of ribbon around sides of box to underside and glue sparingly. (Note: Ribbon will hold flaps of wrapping paper in place.)

3. On top side of box, write or print the guest's name on the solid portion of ribbon. Let dry 2 minutes before using.

4. Repeat steps 1 through 3 for as many place cards as you need.

Variation:

Use a different size and shape of tiny box for each guest or a different pattern or color of wrapping paper for each guest.

Buffet "Mitten"

You will need (for 1 mitten):

1   Piece of brown paper (or other heavier paper), approximately 6" x 8"(15 cm x 20 cm)

     Pencil

     Ruler

     Scissors

1   Piece of black felt (or other color), approximately 9" x 12" (23 cm x 30 cm)

     Tailor's chalk or colored pencil
     Use contrasting color to felt.

     Pinking shears

     Sewing machine

1   Piece silver cord, 8" (20 cm) length

     Hot glue gun

1   Tiny pine cone, sprayed silver, or silver jingle bell

To Assemble:

1. To enlarge pattern, draw a rectangle 4" x 5" (10 x 12.5 cm) on brown paper. Mark into 1 inch (2.5 cm) squares. Using Figure 1, transfer pattern to brown paper grid, matching lines within each square. Cut out pattern.

2. Using tailor's chalk, trace pattern twice onto felt. Cut out with pinking shears.

3. Place mitts together, matching edges. Sew together, using $^1/_8$" (3 mm) seam allowance, along outer edge from Point A to Point B.

4. Tie cord into a bow.

5. Glue bow onto mitten at Point C. (Be sure and glue bow on same side of each mitten.)

6. Glue pine cone or bell to middle of bow.

7. Fray ends of corded ribbon.

8. Repeat steps 2 through 7 for as many "mittens" as you need.

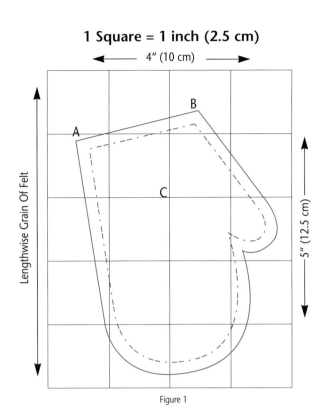

1 Square = 1 inch (2.5 cm)

4" (10 cm)

5" (12.5 cm)

Lengthwise Grain Of Felt

A   B   C

Figure 1

Santa Napkin Holder

You will need (for 1 napkin holder):

1   Piece of brown paper (or other heavier paper), approximately 10" x 10" (25 cm x 25 cm)

    Pencil

    Ruler

    Pair of scissors

1   Piece of felt in each of red, flesh-tone or light pink, black, and white

    Tailor's chalk or colored pencil
    Use contrasting color to felt.

    Hot glue gun

Figure 1

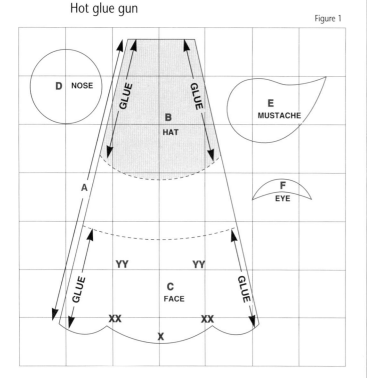

To Assemble:

1. To enlarge pattern: Draw a rectangle 7" x 7" (18 cm x 18 cm) on brown paper. Mark into 1 inch (2.5 cm) squares. Using Figure 1, transfer patterns to brown paper grid, matching lines within each square. Cut out patterns.

2. Using tailor's chalk, trace pattern A, B and D onto red felt, pattern C onto flesh-toned felt, pattern E onto white felt and pattern F onto black felt. Cut out.

3. Glue hat (pattern B) onto background (pattern A) matching top and sides as shown. Note: Glue only side edges together.

5. Glue nose (pattern D) onto face (pattern C) at X. Note: Glue only top half of nose; rest will hang below face.

6. Glue both mustaches (pattern E) onto face (pattern C) at XX, slightly overlapping onto nose (pattern D).

7. Glue both eyes (pattern F) onto face (pattern C) at YY.

8. To use: fold white paper napkin in thirds forming a triangle/diamond shape. Starting at the bottom, push the long point of the napkin up behind face and continue up behind hat to form the point of the hat and Santa's "beard".

9. Repeat steps 2 through 8 for as many napkin holders as you need.

Settings

Buffet Dinner

Guests should be able to move easily around the buffet table and to serve themselves in a logical order. Traffic should flow toward the seating area. The buffet table can be positioned in several places in the dining room depending on your space and number of guests. The most common arrangement is in the center of the room, allowing traffic to flow comfortably around the table using either the one-line or two-line layout. If more space is needed, the table can be placed against a wall with the food line moving in one direction.

Against-The-Wall Buffet

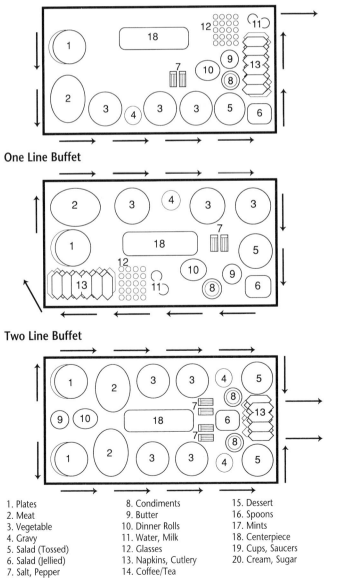

One Line Buffet

Two Line Buffet

1. Plates	8. Condiments	15. Dessert
2. Meat	9. Butter	16. Spoons
3. Vegetable	10. Dinner Rolls	17. Mints
4. Gravy	11. Water, Milk	18. Centerpiece
5. Salad (Tossed)	12. Glasses	19. Cups, Saucers
6. Salad (Jellied)	13. Napkins, Cutlery	20. Cream, Sugar
7. Salt, Pepper	14. Coffee/Tea	

Sit-Down Dinner

Make your table the center of attraction. Put extra thought into colors by coordinating your centerpiece, dishes and linens. Neat and orderly settings will make any table look inviting. Plates and cutlery should be 1 inch (2.5 cm) in from the edge of the table. Too much cutlery on a table can be overwhelming and look cluttered. Set only the cutlery needed.

Basic setting.

Setting for main course and dessert. This works if salad is served along with the main course.

Setting for salad course and main course. Teaspoon can be used for a spoon-eaten dessert or dessert forks can be brought in on dessert plates.

Setting for soup, salad, main course and dessert. To serve salad after the main course, move salad fork to the right of dinner fork.

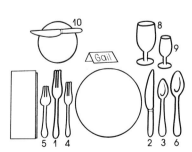

1. Dinner Fork	5. Salad Fork	9. Wine Glass
2. Dinner Knife	6. Soup Spoon	10. Butter Knife
3. Teaspoon	7. Juice Glass	
4. Dessert Fork	8. Water Glass	

Measurement Tables

Throughout this book measurements are

given in Conventional and Metric measure.

To compensate for differences between

the two measurements due to rounding,

a full metric measure is not always used.

The cup used is the standard 8 fluid ounce.

Temperature is given in degrees Fahrenheit and Celsius.

Baking pan measurements are in inches

and centimetres as well as quarts and litres.

An exact metric conversion is given below

as well as the working equivalent (Standard Measure).

Oven temperatures

Fahrenheit (°F)	Celsius (°C)
175°	80°
200°	95°
225°	110°
250°	120°
275°	140°
300°	150°
325°	160°
350°	175°
375°	190°
400°	205°
425°	220°
450°	230°
475°	240°
500°	260°

Pans

Conventional Inches	Metric Centimetres
8x8 inch	20x20 cm
9x9 inch	22x22 cm
9x13 inch	22x33 cm
10x15 inch	25x38 cm
11x17 inch	28x43 cm
8x2 inch round	20x5 cm
9x2 inch round	22x5 cm
10x4$^1/_2$ inch tube	25x11 cm
8x4x3 inch loaf	20x10x7 cm
9x5x3 inch loaf	22x12x7 cm

Spoons

Conventional Measure	Metric Exact Conversion Millilitre (mL)	Metric Standard Measure Millilitre (mL)
$^1/_8$ teaspoon (tsp.)	0.6 mL	0.5 mL
$^1/_4$ teaspoon (tsp.)	1.2 mL	1 mL
$^1/_2$ teaspoon (tsp.)	2.4 mL	2 mL
1 teaspoon (tsp.)	4.7 mL	5 mL
2 teaspoons (tsp.)	9.4 mL	10 mL
1 tablespoon (tbsp.)	14.2 mL	15 mL

Cups

$^1/_4$ cup (4 tbsp.)	56.8 mL	50 mL
$^1/_3$ cup (5$^1/_3$ tbsp.)	75.6 mL	75 mL
$^1/_2$ cup (8 tbsp.)	113.7 mL	125 mL
$^2/_3$ cup (10$^2/_3$ tbsp.)	151.2 mL	150 mL
$^3/_4$ cup (12 tbsp.)	170.5 mL	175 mL
1 cup (16 tbsp.)	227.3 mL	250 mL
4$^1/_2$ cups	1022.9 mL	1000 mL (1 L)

Dry measurements

Conventional Measure Ounces (oz.)	Metric Exact Conversion Grams (g)	Metric Standard Measure Grams (g)
1 oz.	28.3 g	30 g
2 oz.	56.7 g	55 g
3 oz.	85.0 g	85 g
4 oz.	113.4 g	125 g
5 oz.	141.7 g	140 g
6 oz.	170.1 g	170 g
7 oz.	198.4 g	200 g
8 oz.	226.8 g	250 g
16 oz.	453.6 g	500 g
32 oz.	907.2 g	1000 g (1 kg)

Casseroles (Canada & Britain)

Standard Size Casserole	Exact Metric Measure
1 qt. (5 cups)	1.13 L
1$^1/_2$ qts. (7$^1/_2$ cups)	1.69 L
2 qts. (10 cups)	2.25 L
2$^1/_2$ qts. (12$^1/_2$ cups)	2.81 L
3 qts. (15 cups)	3.38 L
4 qts. (20 cups)	4.5 L
5 qts. (25 cups)	5.63 L

Casseroles (United States)

Standard Size Casserole	Exact Metric Measure
1 qt. (4 cups)	900 mL
1$^1/_2$ qts. (6 cups)	1.35 L
2 qts. (8 cups)	1.8 L
2$^1/_2$ qts. (10 cups)	2.25 L
3 qts. (12 cups)	2.7 L
4 qts. (16 cups)	3.6 L
5 qts. (20 cups)	4.5 L

Index

C

D